# Reeves: An Autobiography

Dan Reeves with Dick Connor

92    91    90    89    88              5    4    3    2    1

Library of Congress Catalog Card Number: 88-70929

International Standard Book Number: 0-933893-64-7

**Bonus Books, Inc.**
160 East Illinois Street, Chicago, Illinois 60611

*Printed in the United States of America*

*To Mom and Dad. I can't thank you enough for all the love you've given me through the years.*

*To Pam, who has been a great wife and mother and also a tremendous friend. Thanks for putting up with me.*

# Contents

# Foreword

ONE OF the best things that ever happened to me in pro football was getting to room with Dan Reeves my first four years in the league. Veteran players get to choose their roommate. I thought it was really quite an honor that Dan came up to me and wanted to know about me rooming with him. And I thought, man, now that's good. Me just a common rookie, you know, getting to room with the veteran, even though Dan had only played one more year than I had. I found out later that the only reason he picked me was that he didn't like the guy he was rooming with and I really was the only guy on the team that could understand his southern accent and drawl. So he finally found somebody to communicate with.

Rooming with Dan was damn near like rooming with one of the coaches, because he probably helped me learn more about football than the coaches did, cuz he had been there. He taught me that there was more to football than just getting hold of the football and running with it. And then he taught me how to really study the games together. How he'd study. He'd help me with the audibles. What audibles to listen for in what situations. Ah hell, I never knew anything about looking at the defenses, but he taught me to study the defenses in certain situations and know what the defenses were expected to do. Dan always knew as much as a quarterback did about what was happening in a game. Now quarterbacks, they've got to know everything. Dan even corrected Don Meredith, who was our quarterback at that time. I know we were on the goal line and Dan was in the back field with Meredith. Meredith had called some particular audible, but it was the wrong audible. It wouldn't work against the defense they ran and Dan corrected even Meredith. I took that to heart

1

and you know Don changed the audible at the line again and the play worked. And that was just because Dan knew what was happening.

You know when you think about Dan Reeves you smile. I've never seen a guy that was as fierce a competitor as Dan. Around the goal line he was probably the best back I've ever seen with a nose for the goal line. He knew what it took to get to the end zone or to make a big play, but anything else, he wanted to win, whether he was shooting pool, playing golf, throwing darts, or playing dominos out there at camp, or cards, or whatever. I mean he had to win and to figure out a way to win.

Dan gave me my first set of golf clubs. He was working for some sporting goods company. I don't remember the name of it, but anyway he got me a set of golf clubs. He gave them to me and I'd never played before. I think the best thing he did was give me some good advice with the clubs. He said Walt there's more business deals cut on a golf course than in any office, and, he said, you're going to meet a lot of good, influential people on the golf course, so learn to play. He said you don't have to shoot par, but learn to play respectable so you won't slow the game down and make 'em mad. So I did. And playing with Reeves, I'll tell you, I picked up a lot of extra clubs. When Dan first played golf, anytime he'd make a bad shot he'd likely throw a golf club out there in the woods and just say the hell with it. But my pride would let me go pick it up and put it in my bag.

Dan's the kind of guy that could hardly ever say no to kids or to charitable organizations. I mean if somebody wanted him to come and make a talk for some kids, he'd do it. If somebody called him and wanted him to come to the hospital to visit a kid you know he would do it and he's still that way. I mean whatever needs to be done Dan will do. He'd be the guy that stopped to help an old lady or an old man change a flat tire on a highway while probably the rest of us would drive on by. Dan means well in everything he does.

He and Pam have been super friends for years. She's been with him through the good, through the bad, through failures and successes and I must say she deserves a lot of the credit for what Dan has become—a very successful head coach in the NFL.

After Dan became somewhat of a household word around the Dallas area, he was always conscious about his image. He was always the one that was in style. He was the first guy I knew that went to a hair stylist instead of a barber. In fact, he got me to go to one before my first wedding. I come back from the Army and my hair was standing up. Looked like a horse's mane had been roached. It was sticking up about four inches and wouldn't lay down or nothing and he took me to his hair stylist and that's where they tease it all around and cut it off and then they lay it over and put hairspray on it. And Dan he was always a big clothes nut. If there was a new style out then Dan would go buy a suit, or a sport coat, or whatever—shoes, belts—to be in style and he always was. Hell, I'm glad blue jeans come back in style about once every 10 or 15 years. I wish they'd make another movie like *Urban Cowboy,* so I'd be back in style again.

Dan and I roomed together for four years. Coach Landry, of course, saw that he was going to be a good football coach and so he turned him into a player coach. Well when he's a player coach he can't room with a common player, because they don't want any of that insider trading going on. Dan was a special team coach a year and then the next year he came back and he was the offensive back field coach. I think that was real difficult on both Dan and myself, although we never talked about it, because I think I probably worked harder when Dan was my coach than I did before, because I didn't want anybody saying well, yeah, you and Reeves room together. That's the only reason you're playing. I think maybe Reeves subconsciously was a little tougher on me in the meetings and stuff. You know, he always asked me tough questions. I think he wanted everybody to know there's a reason Walt's playing and it ain't because we're friends. It's because he knows the game and he can play every week.

Dan has always been a player's coach. I think what makes him such a great coach is the fact that he's been there. He knows what a player goes through in training camp and during the season if you get beat or whatever. He's been there and I think the players formed some kind of camaraderie with Dan. He can get more out of a player than a coach that just tells them what to do. They know Dan's speaking from experience.

As you'll read, Dan got out of coaching for awhile and went into real estate. In fact, he got me into a real estate deal and we all lost some money on that, but Dan wasn't happy when he was in real estate. I mean he was always thinking sports. He was always thinking football and if he'd have put his mind to real estate he would have been a super real estate salesman, but that just wasn't what he wanted, I don't think. So he stayed in that a year and then he has an opportunity to come back and, of course, everybody in Denver along with the Cowboys is glad he did.

3

Dan's always been a friend of mine. He was one of the groomsmen at my wedding. He even came to the hospital when my oldest son, Marty, was born. I think the greatest thing that he did, for me, I called him one night and had some bad news as far as I was concerned. My father had passed away. Dan was in Georgia and he says well when's the funeral and I said tomorrow. I said I wasn't really calling to ask you to come or nothing and he said, shoot, I'll be on the next plane, and he was.

Dan Reeves. Now he's a guy I respect, admire and appreciate very much. He'd been my roommate for awhile. He was my teacher while he was my roommate. He's my coach. He's also been my biggest rival in any kind of game. Ah, but I think the thing I'll always be grateful for is that he was and still is my best friend.

*Walt Garrison*
*Lewisville, Texas*

# SUPER LOSSES, SUPER LESSONS

Part I

# 1

# Good Enough to Get There

IT HAPPENED so fast. I don't remember a lot. One moment, we led 10–0. The next, we trailed 35–10.

You know you are in trouble, know what kind of day it has been, when you walk up to the other coach at the end of the game and he apologizes.

That's what happened to me at the end of Super Bowl XXII. When it was over, Joe Gibbs and I walked toward each other on the field. All those camera people followed us, and players walked out to shake hands.

Joe shook hands, and he leaned in close and he said, "I'm sorry." Things can't be too good when that happens.

Going into the game, I really and truly thought we had a good chance to win. I personally didn't think we should be favored, as we were, but I did think we had a good chance to win it. The year before, we had played the New York Giants earlier in the season, and felt like we could compete with them in the Super Bowl. Then they beat us 39–20 in Pasadena.

This time, we had beaten Washington 31–30 the previous season. We felt we could compete with them, too. There were some changes, of course. They had Doug Williams starting at quarterback instead of Jay Schroeder, who had played against us before. Doug had more poise, more experience, but normally he was going to stay in the pocket. He would be a better target than Jay. I thought one would offset the other.

Another difference was that Washington had started playing very good defense, excellent defense at the right time, toward the end of the season and through the playoffs.

Then, to start the way we did, scoring on our opening play and moving the ball the next two times we got it, I felt good. We were moving, and we were stopping them.

That's when it all turned around. And for the second straight year, we not only wound up losing a Super Bowl, we got embarrassed doing it. It turned so quickly, so fast you really didn't have time to react.

As the guy calling plays, I remember trying to come up with something that was going to sustain each possession and put some points up. The second quarter was totally unexpected. I had no idea that anybody could score on us like that. Thirty-five points in a game was unusual, but 35 in a quarter was unbelievable.

I did something I normally never do. I went over to Joe Collier at one point, after they had scored their third touchdown and led 21–10.

"You need to get the defense together, Joe," I said. "We're struggling right now. They've got a lack of confidence and we need to turn it around."

Joe Gibbs and I are good friends, and at the end, all he could say was, "I'm sorry." I don't even remember what I said to him. Probably just "Congratulations." There really wasn't anything either of us could say to the other.

They had played a much better football game than us, and you could just sit there and wonder.

Why? Why is this happening? Why does it have to happen to us two years in a row?

I've thought about it since. A lot. The only conclusion I have come to is we were not ready for it yet. We're not a good enough football team to be world champions.

Now, when that is going to be or if it is going to be, I don't know. You just have to go about your job as coach of this football team— whether you had won it or lost it—trying to improve, trying to get better.

Hopefully, one of these days when we make it back, we'll win. The two losses hurt. They hurt deeper than any other losses. It is the last game. You are so close to the goal that everybody else is chasing. And to be that close, and yet not close, really hurts.

I know, as a coach, you try to come up with something when the ball game is over. The year before, up in Pasadena, I wanted everybody to remember how bad that loss hurt. That was what I told them in the dressing room before we let the press in. "Remember this. Remember how much it hurts."

I thought if we did that, certainly it would help us to get back there and win the thing. I think it did. But I don't think anybody on our football team expected what happened in San Diego in the second quarter.

The night before, I had really felt good about our chances. Joe Gibbs and I and some players had gone to a joint devotional service, and I had gotten up and talked about how much trouble we have, sometimes, understanding the plan God has in mind for us.

I talked about tearing up my knee, and wondering "Why me, Lord?" I didn't realize that was the first step toward me becoming a coach, even toward standing there that night on the eve of the Super Bowl.

Then I went back to the hotel. The lobby was a zoo. Fans were everywhere. We had tried to find a different hotel to move the team to that Saturday night, but we couldn't find any within an hour's drive. So we stayed. It's one of the things I would change next time.

Anyway, Pam and I stayed in, and ordered up some food, and I watched some more film. Some friends of ours, the Dave Manders and the Lee Roy Jordans, had gone out to see the Frank Sinatra show, and I just watched film.

That was when I decided we would throw deep on the first play the next day if we got the ball in decent field position. We needed to make them conscious of it, and relieve bump and run pressure on the corners. We wanted to throw deep at least five or six times in the game.

I was comfortable with our game plan. I felt good about it, but then I had been happy with it the year before, in Pasadena, against the Giants. We thought we could run against Washington easier than we had against the Giants. Washington liked to bring Dexter Manley and Charles Mann, their ends, straight up field, to keep Elway in. Knowing this, we felt we could start to run wide, then cut up inside.

And we also had a draw play in, knowing they would be very conscious of John.

I felt we could move the ball, and I was happy with our defensive scheme, too. I knew we'd have to pressure Williams, and we were going to bring our nickel package in on second down more than we had and go after him.

The Manders and Jordans came back from the Sinatra show, and we sat around and talked, and then they left and we went to bed. I have never had trouble sleeping, no tossing or turning and things like that.

The phone woke me. It must have been about 7:30 Sunday morning. It was a friend. I had gotten him some tickets and he had just gotten into town and wanted to know where to get them.

Super Sunday had started.

We had scheduled our pregame meal for 11 A.M., but we had also set up an earlier breakfast if some of our people wanted it. I went down and had some juice and fruit, and visited around a little. Then I went to our devotional, and to the pregame meal.

We had had trouble with sending buses at various times, and had decided to keep them together. We would all go to the stadium at the same time instead of some earlier, the rest later. We allowed extra time, thinking there would be heavy traffic.

We didn't hit any. We went right through, and got there almost three hours before the game. That's a lot of time to kill on a day like that.

I didn't want to watch any football. We watched golf: the Seniors Skin game. I also sat down with Mike Shanahan, who would be upstairs in the booth, and he checked me on the plays, who would have to be in for this one or that one, that sort of thing.

We didn't have as many running plays as we normally carry. In the regular season, we have maybe 14 running plays. For the Super Bowl, we only had eight or ten, but as I said, we felt good about them, felt they would work if we could keep the game in range.

"First out, ten minutes," I told them. We send the team out in three groups for warmups.

I had decided to throw deep on the first play, but I hadn't told John. He doesn't want to know. He told me one time he'd rather just get it on the sideline, so I waited to see where we'd get the ball.

When it was our ball, first and 10 at our own 46, I figured, "Okay. Here we go."

I told him we'd go for it.

"Good," he said. "Does it matter which side?"

It really didn't. We could throw it to either side, but we had the best speed matchup on the right, where Barry Wilburn was lined up against Ricky Nattiel. That's where John went—Ron 69, and it went 56 yards for a touchdown the first time we touched the ball.

You don't really expect to score on it. You just want to make them conscious of it, relieve pressure on the receivers. But Ricky got away from the bump, and John made a great throw, and one play into the game, we led 7-0.

It bothered me at the time, even when we were sending out the extra point team. When you score like that, too easy, you tend to think you can do it any time you want. I have seen it too many times. It worried me. We were all happy, of course, but I had to get the Amigos aside and tell them it was a little early to be celebrating. They had done a little of it in the end zone. "We don't need a penalty on the kickoff," I told them.

Nobody, nobody, could have imagined a 35-point second quarter. It's the most devastating thing I've been through on a football field.

We had scored on our first play, we had led 10-0, and then it just collapsed on us.

We might even have accepted it better if it had been a close loss. But to have such a one-sided victory with all those records set against us, hurt even more. It's just so hard to explain. I don't know that anybody can put their finger on it.

Standing on the field, it would not have been as bad if I just had myself to worry about. The pain wouldn't have been as great. But what is going through your mind is all the people who are feeling close to the same way because of you.

That's even more of a burden.

I know this is not the classic way to start a book about yourself, talking about something as painful as what happened to us in two straight Super Bowls. But it is how we are remembered as I write this, and so it is something that needs to be addressed.

I had worked all my coaching life for those two chances, and we had lost both of them. We were good enough to get there. We were not good enough to win. And all people will remember is the second part, not the first.

The Super Bowl is special, different from any other final game in any other sport. One of the biggest differences is the stigma that is put on the loser. I remember, a couple of weeks after San Diego, we had our annual Colorado Sports Hall of Fame banquet in Denver.

I got up to receive an award, and I told about 1,200 people that night that "There were 26 other coaches just wishing they could have been in that game, and in the middle of the third quarter, I would have been willing to let any one of them take my place."

The Super Bowl does that to you.

I felt I had let down coaches, players, our owner, the organization and all those fans who have supported us so much. But most of all, standing on the sideline in Jack Murphy Stadium, I kept thinking about my immediate family.

I knew exactly how Pam and Dana and Lee and Laura were feeling. They had suffered it the year before, and they were hurting because they didn't think it was fair that this was happening again to her husband, their daddy.

The disappointment is so great, but the pain is even greater. If you've ever been extremely hungry, had pains in your stomach so bad that you couldn't believe how hungry you really were, that is similar. Except it keeps going deeper. It almost feels like somebody has gone inside and taken your intestines out and they haven't put them back in yet. You are functioning without intestines.

As I said, it wouldn't be as bad if you were just worrying about that for yourself. But so many people are involved, including those around you down there on the sideline—the ones you've worked with all year from July on.

It's not the questions you have to answer as you try to put rhyme or reason to it. It's not the fact you came up short. That happens to a lot of people. It's just the hurt that you caused so many people.

That's the most difficult part of the whole thing—to get there, and to come up short, and to be embarrassed.

Is it too big a price? I don't know that anybody can put a price on it. Nobody made me feel the way that I did. I think you cause that pain yourself. You are close to the pinnacle of your profession, and still you aren't there yet.

You think you are close. Three years before, we were 11-5 and didn't go to the playoffs. We lost twice to the Raiders in overtime. I pulled for the Raiders to go on and win the world championship because it would show how close we were. They got beat the first playoff game.

So how far down are you?

Then, over the last two years, we've been there, and gotten beat 39-20 and 42-10. We have beaten Cleveland twice in two of the greatest games I've been part of to reach the Super Bowl, then been beaten handily once we got there.

Again, how far are you from being the team you want to be? So, regardless of whether there is too much or too little significance put on that game, that's not the question. The question is you are disappointed because you aren't there, aren't good enough to win, and it affects so many people. It goes on and on.

The reason the Super Bowl is different is the fact it is a one-game finale. There is no seven game World Series, no best of seven NBA. In basketball, in baseball, they can have a bad game and come back the next day and redeem themselves, remove the blot, show the kind of performance that put them there in the first place. Not in football. It's a one-game, one-shot deal with all that tremendous hype and buildup. And if you aren't performing up to your best it is completely over.

For Denver now, twice in a row, it has been that way. That's how good seasons have ended, in front of the world, being embarrassed. And as I said, nobody remembers the good seasons that led up to those games. They just remember 39–20 and 42–10.

Somehow, we have not been ready in all phases to handle the Super Bowl. We haven't been ready mentally, physically or spiritually. You think on any given day you can compete with anybody, but for whatever the reason, it hasn't happened to you.

During all the times that I thought I was ready to be a head coach, it didn't happen. Maybe that's because I wasn't ready.

We are just not there yet. We are not the football team that is ready to be world champions. Heck, I worried about that all year, all through the 1987 season. But we kept getting closer and kept getting closer, and when it got down to the final game, you think, "Hey. We're as good as anybody. We can play with them."

Had we played as well as we were capable, that would have been true. But, for whatever reason, we weren't ready.

How many times do you have to be there before you are ready? A lot of teams have done it the first time. Minnesota has been there four times and has lost four times. Were they a bad football team? No.

Are we a bad football team? No, we are not.

We had a devotional speaker that morning, prior to the game. I thought he made a great statement. He said, "There's a difference between success and excellence. You can experience success without experiencing excellence."

That pretty much sums us up as a football team. We are a successful football team. But we haven't experienced that excellence yet.

Why, I don't know. We have to keep striving. I think we are a good team, one that has experienced as much success over the past four or five years as anybody in the National Football League. We have gone 9–7, 13–3, 11–5, 11–5 and 10–4–1 and gone to two Super Bowls the past three years. Nobody else has done that well.

But we have not won that last game, experienced the excellence that comes from being great.

That's what gnaws at you. I held up good after the Redskins game. I did well at the party. We had a big circus tent across the street from the hotel, and I felt like I had to be the guy that put everything in perspective. You have to be the one that puts things in place, shows you can handle it.

Nobody wants to go to a party after something like that. It's like having a parade afterward. Nobody wants one at that stage.

But I felt like it was up to me to set the tempo. I was truly proud of what they had accomplished. Not many teams ever do as many things as they had in view of what they had to overcome.

It took a lot of character, a lot of guts. To get to where they did, it hurt to come up and play a poor game, get beat like that.

I did great. I went to the party, met players' relatives and friends, tried to be as cordial as I could.

I did great until Pam and I got back to the hotel, just the two of us.

That's when we both had a great cry. We hugged each other and cried for a half hour. I needed it. I deserved it. I had answered all the questions, and taken all the criticism.

Then we cried in each other's arms.

I have a sign on my office wall, right across from my desk. It says, "Difficulties in life are intended to make us better, not bitter."

Believe me, I have thought about that a thousand times since that ball game.

# 2

# John Elway

HE HAS been to two Super Bowls now, helped us to win two American Football Conference championships, and probably is one of the better known athletes in the nation today.

It may sound odd, considering who he is and what he has done since, what he has gone through, but the first time I met John Elway, I could tell that he was a person who is embarrassed by the limelight.

It's still true.

He doesn't feel comfortable in it. He is not a person who is going to seek out the excitement around him. He would just as soon be alone with his family. All the success he has brought us and enjoyed himself has attracted incredible attention, and I think he has gotten very good at handling it. But I don't imagine he will ever actually go and seek it out, as some might. That's just not him.

The spring after our Super Bowl in Pasadena, for instance, he didn't even do all the endorsement and personal appearance things that are open to Super Bowl quarterbacks. It's the way he is. I remember going to training camp the summer we obtained him from Baltimore in 1983.

There had been all the publicity about his being the No. 1 choice in the whole draft, and then his refusing to sign with Baltimore, and the trade to our team.

We got to camp that summer, and we had what the papers called "The Elway Watch."

I had been at Dallas when we got Roger Staubach. If I go back even more, I had been at Dallas with Don Meredith and there was an awful lot of publicity surrounding Meredith wherever he went. Craig Morton came in the same year I did, 1965, and he was a highly publicized quarterback. Bob Hayes was an Olympic gold medal winner. We had a lot of very high visibility people at Dallas. Tony Dorsett was another.

But nothing compared to what Elway had to endure that first summer. I had absolutely no idea anybody could draw that much attention. Everything he did. Everything he wore. How he stood. What he ate. Any little thing he said. They followed him everywhere but to the bathroom. It was unbelievable.

Yet John had great patience. He had very little time, and yet he would make time to deal with the press. I think he has always handled that aspect well. He talked to the press through the hard times, too. He has never dodged. Basically, he has always been able to stand up and face them, and I think some of that strength goes back to that first summer.

It was like steel being hardened in fire. NBC, for example, wanted to do a little piece with him about not starting when I named Steve DeBerg to take over for John during that season. John didn't want to do the piece. We sat down and we talked about it.

"You are in the entertainment business," I told him. "We all are. I think not talking will eventually hurt you. I think it's a bad way to go."

I advised him to talk, and he has done that ever since, and I think he has handled it extremely well.

You could see, right from day one, that he was special. I could sense the electricity in camp even when he threw his first pass. The spectators were excited. I had never heard a guy cheered for throwing passes in training camp. John was. There was just an awful lot of interest in everything John did.

Expectations were that every pass he threw was going to be a touchdown.

That became part of the problem. It still is, even today. They see a big salary, and all that publicity, and MVP of the league, and they don't allow him any room to be human, to have bad games or even just average ones.

In the 1983 preseason, you could see the tremendous talent that

John had. He played well during the preseason, and in almost every statistic, he and Steve DeBerg were pretty even. When we talked about it as a staff, not a single coach on our staff didn't believe we should start John.

Everyone felt like, down the road, halfway through the season, with the experience he would gain, John would give us a much better football team at the end.

That's when we announced John would be our starter. I remember calling him into my office, and I think he was shocked when I told him. But he was pleased, too. He didn't say anything that made me think, "Well, maybe this is the wrong decision."

He has been a competitor all his life. He wanted to start. But I think John had figured that a veteran like Steve would get the assignment, and John was surprised.

It probably was a mistake. No. It was a mistake. He was not ready.

The best way to explain it is that John, from a physical standpoint, could see the field all right. He could do the physical side of it. What really snowballed and hurt him was the language.

It was almost like a person could take a Spanish class—take the tests, do well in class, make an A. Yet, if you sent him to Mexico City and he had to talk to the people there, he couldn't do that. They would talk too fast.

That happened to John. He would feel very uncomfortable talking the language, the terminology we used. He would get into the huddle. We would signal in a play, and that took some time. Then he had to call the formation, call the play.

Now, after that year, until recently, we tried to simplify things a little. But they were even more difficult then, his first summer, than they are now that he is a veteran.

Let me try to explain what I'm talking about. Take a play like "Ace right slot stretch, wing sam, bootleg right, fake 38, wing spurt."

Ace right slot stretch is the formation. We are in a slot. We are in a stretch, which means the H back is split out wide. Then we are going to bring the wing—Wing Sam—on a short motion.

That's just the formation. John then has to call that formation when we signal in the play. Then we are going to go bootleg right, we are going to fake 38, wing spurt. That's the play.

So bootleg tells everybody this is going to be a bootleg. John has some protection on. We are going to fake a sweep to the left, and the wing is going to come across on the spurt route. Now, under that same situation, John has also got to know that, if they are in a certain defense, we are going to audible 36 or 37. We'll come off the original play if they are not in the defense we expect. Or he is going to audible to 885 or 985, which is a scramble route that will get him out of the pocket.

He has all that to remember. All we do is send in the bootleg, with the fake 38. He then has to put the rest of it together.

It was too much for him as a rookie at that point. He had to get the signal, the play, set the formation, and the snap count. By the time he got to the line of scrimmage, the 30 second clock would be down to seven...six...five...four...three.

John had no time to look across the line of scrimmage and anticipate anything. Anticipation is so important. So everything happened to him after the snap. He would get away with it because he had such tremendous physical talent, but everything was almost like watching the Keystone Cops. Everything was too fast.

We opened the season in Pittsburgh. The Steelers are a fine defensive team. John struggled. He completed only one of eight passes, threw an interception, had some delay of game penalties. They blitzed John with almost everything you could think of. He was battered and beat.

Yet he kept coming back until I felt like, for us to win the game, we had to make a change. I put DeBerg in.

Poor John. I don't know the last time he had been yanked. He is so competitive that this was something he didn't understand. It wasn't in his experience. Maybe it had never happened before.

That probably started the doubts he had, doubts about himself, and doubts about me as a coach.

We decided to stick with him the next week when we went to Baltimore, and that was an even bigger mistake on my part.

In all the years I have been in football, that decision subjected a person to the worst abuse I have ever seen. Remember, John had refused to sign with the Colts. It had nothing to do with the city, but Baltimore fans thought it did, and John was the focus of all their anger and frustration.

Here, they had almost signed a player who a lot of people said would be the next Unitas and things like that. Then he had refused. Now he was with a team coming back into their city.

From the moment John walked out from the dugout for warmups, the crowd was just absolutely unmerciful. I never felt so sorry for someone. It was like John was my son and I was almost in tears for him. I wanted him to do well, but he had very little chance, less even than in Pittsburgh.

To magnify all the problems we talked about, setting the formations, remembering options and all that, now in the huddle, the players couldn't hear him. The guy next to him couldn't hear. The crowd booed so loudly when we were on offense you couldn't hear. I mean, you absolutely could not hear what was going on.

We had several plays set up in that game that would have been perfect against certain defenses, and we couldn't get them off. The 30 second clock would run down, and we'd get a delay of game penalty.

We'd get the right play and they'd come with the blitz we expected and the clock would run out. It was very frustrating. I had to make a change again to get the win. Steve went back in, it quieted down, and for the second week, he got a win for us on the road.

But we decided to stay with John in our home opener against Philadelphia. After Baltimore, we had to let him hear some cheers, as well. And actually, he didn't play too bad. He threw his first touchdown pass to Rick Parros, and I can remember the excitement.

It tied the game in the fourth quarter. But in the two minute period, Ron Jaworski hit Mike Quick to set up a field goal and we lost, 13–10.

The following week, we played the Raiders—another great defensive team. They smothered us and they made John look bad in particular. They beat us 22–7.

That's when I felt we had to make a real choice. It was getting worse, not better. The pressure was growing on John. Everybody felt that every time he threw a pass it should go either for a touchdown or a first down. I just decided he wasn't ready and that I had made a mistake by putting him in there in the first place.

I called him into my office that week. John understood. If anything, I think it was kind of a relief to him by that point. I felt bad. I told him, "I was the one who made the decision to start you, John. And it was a mistake on my part, not yours."

Still, starting him was probably one of the best things that ever happened to him for several reasons. I didn't feel that way at the time, of course, and if I had it to do over, I wouldn't start him.

But it helped long range. If he had been successful right at the start, he might have thought it was too easy. As it was, nobody has had a rockier start, and now he knew how much work it was going to take, how much concentration and dedication.

And with DeBerg starting, now John had time to study and draw a deep breath. He was going to prove people wrong, too. Because by that point, they were saying he had been a bad choice, wasn't worth being picked first in the whole draft.

We were in the heat of it. Steve DeBerg was doing a great job and John could watch and study and listen, and our team was in contention. Then, the 10th week, we went up to Seattle and Steve got hurt.

John Elway was our quarterback again. He has been ever since.

The week after Seattle, we went to the coast to play the Raiders. John played well, but we lost 22-20. Still, it helped his confidence to do well against them in the Los Angeles Coliseum.

He just got better after that, but we still had some run-ins—the biggest one two weeks later in San Diego. John had another rough day. He had thrown some interceptions, and once, concentrating on the play, he had come out of the huddle and lined up behind our left guard, Tom Glassic, instead of center Billy Bryan.

It's hard to imagine who was more startled, Glassic or John. That happened to me when I played quarterback at South Carolina. You are thinking so hard, trying to look at the defense, remember audibles, all that. You don't realize it until you see there isn't a towel draped from his belt.

But when John Elway does it, it's coast to coast news. Anyway, it was that kind of day, and when he came off after an interception, I grabbed him by the arm. I wanted to talk to him.

He yanked his arm away. "I know! I know!" he shouted.

So I grabbed him again, and we had a real shouting match, right there on the sideline in front of the team and everybody. His pride was hurt. He is saying he knows what he did wrong, and I am trying to get to him, settle him down. I have a low boiling point at times, too.

I don't know how long it lasted, yelling back and forth. Maybe 30 seconds, maybe longer. It's the only time we've done it quite like that.

I have learned since then to give him some time before I approach him in that kind of situation. You'll see him walk off by himself. The players don't bother him, either. Then, when we both cool down, we'll get back together and talk about it.

We met and talked about the incident the week after the San Diego game. I tried to explain to him it was my job to talk to him and get him to realize what he did wrong. He had to understand that to get any better.

He said he felt like he was wrong for what he did on the sideline.

His dad, Jack, was a coach, and I am sure that helped John realize what he had done and that it was wrong. And he tried to explain to me why he was that way. He is very competitive, and it was very difficult for him, right after doing something wrong, to talk about it.

He has gotten better, and I have learned better timing.

The first year set the groundwork for a lot of things, and helped John mature a lot. We got to the playoffs, and John helped get us there. He won some games for us. One especially tough one was the next to last game, at home against Baltimore. He could still remember the second game of the season, of course.

We were down like 19-7 in the fourth quarter, and it didn't seem like there was any way we could win. But all of a sudden, John gets hot. He carries us down for a touchdown, the defense holds, we get the ball back, and John took us in again with very little time left. He hit Gerald Willhite for the score, and we clinched a playoff spot.

It was a preview of what he would do for us over the years to come.

We got killed in Kansas City that next week, but we had finished 9-7 and made the playoffs. And now I had another decision to make.

Steve DeBerg was healthy again. The coaches and I felt that Steve's experience would help, especially in Seattle where the noise level is such a factor in that indoor stadium. Well, nothing helped. We got beat 31-7. I probably stayed with Steve too long.

John had earned the right to play, and I had waited too long. It really made John mad. I think he was really hurt after that game. He didn't say anything, but I did.

"John, listen. If you ever get in that situation, I want you to know I treated Steve the same way I will treat you. I am not going to pull you early. So I think you have got to understand why I left Steve DeBerg in there the way I did."

I don't think John understood. At least not then. He was hurt. Unlike most of the players, he didn't stay in Denver in the offseason. He went back to California. There was a lot of criticism. A lot of people criticized him for not being here in the offseason.

I felt that if he was to become the quarterback he wanted to be, he needed to be in Denver. But I also understood his feelings. Then he got married, and I traded Steve DeBerg to Tampa Bay. I think John saw from that that we were committed to him as our future.

In 1984, we went 13-3, but John got hurt several times. I had Roger Staubach talk to him that offseason about John's offseason program. Roger was very much like John. He ran the ball and scrambled a lot.

And Roger going into pro ball did not think that weights were that important. As he continued to play, though, he realized that to take the constant pounding, the quarterback has to be strong.

The end of his second year, that 13-3 season, we were going to play Pittsburgh in Denver in the first round—and I ended up making another coaching mistake.

We had two weeks to get ready for the Steelers, and we wanted to put in some things that took advantage of things they did. We changed our protection a little and changed our "hot" routes, things like that.

John was just finishing his second year. He was starting his first playoff game. We missed big plays several times during that game because John wasn't ready for the changes we had made. Now, John didn't have a bad game. The bad game was basically brought on by us changing. So I learned from that experience, and, again, it was at John's expense.

You can't make those kinds of changes with a young quarterback. We would have been better off doing the same things we did all year, the things that helped us get to 13-3 and one of the best records in football. John got hurt in that game, too. He hurt his knee, and it was operated on after the season.

But it wasn't going to get any worse by playing, and I told him, "Don't stay in there at the expense of the team. But as long as you feel you can execute, stay in."

Late in the game, Pittsburgh made a good play, intercepted a pass and ran it down to the one and scored and beat us. But we had missed early scoring chances. So that was a tough experience, too, to have one of the best records and then end up losing a playoff game at home in the first round.

We had improved, and with John's ability, anything was possible. We came back 11-5 the next season and didn't even make the playoffs. More adversity. But there was progress, too.

Late that season, we were in Pittsburgh, and John threw an interception, and the Steelers ran it back for a score.

All John could think of was the one he had thrown in the playoffs. He was really down. He came to the sideline, and he was as low as I'd seen him in a long time.

"John," I said. "You gotta have fun. This game, if you don't have some fun out of it, if you don't relax, forget about things, go out and have some fun, this game is miserable.

"Just relax. Let's have some fun."

Boy, he went back out there, relaxed a little. He really did. He took us down, hit Clarence Kay and then Steve Sewell took it in, and we ended up pulling the game out 31–23.

I think it was a turning point for John. He relaxed. He learned that, "Hey, all the pressure's not on me. The others are responsible, too. I'm going to throw interceptions. I have to learn to move on to the next play."

It was another stage. For both of us.

I used to kid Roger Staubach about pulling games out in the final two minutes. I'd tell him, "That's great, but if you had played better the first 58 we wouldn't be in that predicament at the end."

But that ability—very few have it. Everybody in the stadium knows you are going to throw, they have set the defense to stop it. You gotta have a tremendous arm and tremendous ability and tremendous poise and tremendous confidence.

Staubach had all that. So does John.

He is amazing. He has the greatest arm strength and physical strength I have ever seen for a quarterback. You just can't get better arm strength than John has. I've never been around anything like it. Roger Staubach came the closest, but it wasn't as good as John.

John completed a pass to Steve Watson in Seattle one year that had to have traveled 73 yards in the air. The Seahawks' defensive backs kind of gave up on it because they didn't think it would travel that far. Our receivers never stop running because they know he can get it to them from anywhere.

You saw it in Cleveland in 1987 in the AFC championship game. That was another growing stage for John with that much on the line. He took our team 98 yards. He made some great plays. It was a tremendous achievement. But that is going to be typical of his career. I think it's no more than halftime for him, in that sense. He still has a lot ahead of him, and there are still going to be some bad times.

I have worked with some great quarterbacks at Dallas and now here, and John is right there. I see an awful lot of their qualities in him.

Don Meredith had tremendous talent, but he played the game more for the fun of it than he did the seriousness of it. If he had been as dedicated as John, no telling what he might have accomplished.

He was very competitive once the game began, but he didn't want to pay the price to be that great. He was a very good quarterback who could have been one of the all time great quarterbacks.

And of course that always led to friction with Coach Landry, who couldn't understand that type of thinking.

Craig Morton came in with me in 1965, and he was as talented a guy as I have ever seen. Staubach was drafted that year, too, but he went to the Navy. Craig had all the tools—intelligence, great size, and as strong an arm as I have seen. He could run in those days, too.

He didn't have great touch as a rookie. Whether you were 5 yards or 55, the ball came with the same velocity. John had that problem at the start, too.

Craig had as good a football mind as I have been around, and he had great mechanics. He worked hard. Maybe not as hard as Staubach, but he did work. He probably had a bad reputation because he was single, and a good looking guy. He never got the credit he should have from Coach Landry for being a guy who did work to prepare himself.

He paid the price, and I really thought he would be one of the greats. Maybe, had it not been for an injury...

I remember when he finally got the starting job, he was hitting like 70 percent of his passes. Then we went to play the Falcons in Atlanta.

We had a play called Roll 19 EGO, screen back to the fullback. We would roll out one way or the other and throw the ball back across on a screen. Most of the time we did it rolling to the right.

This particular time we called it and Craig rolled to his left. The guard didn't sustain his block quite long enough, and Craig was knocked down and really tore up his shoulder, his left shoulder. It was bad.

The ball went to Walt Garrison on the other side, and Garrison ran it down deep. And down there, John Wilbur, the guard who had let the guy in to hit Craig, blocked the Falcons linebacker, Tommy Nobis. It tore up Nobis' knee.

On one play, Wilbur got two No. 1 draft choices in the league. Craig was tough. He came back and played, and we went to the Super Bowl against Baltimore. But he was not the same, his motion wasn't the same. Baltimore beat us, but they did it on a field goal set up on an interception off my hands.

A lot of people blamed Craig for the game, but the courage the guy showed was incredible.

Roger was the most dedicated person I have ever seen. He was going to work twice as hard, no matter how hard you worked. That appealed to Coach Landry.

There was talent there, too. We played both of them, but you knew it would not continue. Most of our coaches thought Craig should be the quarterback. But Coach Landry had a feeling that Roger was the guy we should go with. And of course we went on to win the Super Bowl from Miami with Roger at quarterback.

It put Craig in a situation where he wanted out. In 1973, when I got out of coaching for a year, Craig called me for advice.

"You are never going to be happy in Dallas," I told him. "As long as Roger is here, he is going to be the starting quarterback no matter how hard you work or how successful you are in preseason."

So he ended up demanding he be traded, and he went to the New York Giants and then here to Denver, where our paths crossed again.

When I came back into coaching in 1974, I coached Roger. I never enjoyed coaching anybody as much as I did Roger. Regardless of what you asked, he was going to do it. If he felt like that was the best thing for our football team, he was going to do it.

He wasn't going to do it half speed or three quarter speed. He was going to do whatever you asked of him at full speed. It was easy, when you had that kind of leadership, to get others to work hard.

We used to run a mile and a half after working on weights each Monday. I don't care. Somebody could start two minutes ahead of Roger. We had kind of a cross-country route that we ran across this big field. He was always the first one back. He was not going to let somebody beat him running.

He was so competitive. He was so conscious of interceptions that he wouldn't throw the ball early in the game because he didn't want to make a mistake. He was always low on interceptions.

But when it came down to the fourth period, the two minute drill, he would make some great passes into little ol' tiny holes he would never have chanced early in the game.

And he brought us back game after game after game, and took us to a bunch of Super Bowls.

I see an awful lot of those things in John. John has more speed than Roger. Roger had more moves. But they are both very similar because of the tremendous competitive nature and their arms and ability.

John can throw the ball a little bit better on the move than Roger could. Roger was a better scrambler because he could make people miss him more. John's ability to scramble is because of his tremendous speed. If Roger had John's speed, he would have been one of the great running backs. Ever. You couldn't hem him up in the open field. He used to make people look completely silly.

John and I are alike in a lot of ways—competitiveness, fiery temper, the desire to win. We've grown a lot closer over the years, understand each other's moods and so forth. You have to as coach and quarterback. It has to become almost like a father-son relationship. We are going to clash at times, but it's because we are both trying so hard to win.

I'll never forget something Edgar Kaiser told me about the hours he spent talking to Robert Irsay before we were able to get John.

Irsay had been dealing with San Diego and with the Raiders, and he had gotten mad at them.

"You want John Elway?" Edgar said Irsay told one of them.

"Okay. You're going to get John Elway—twice a year on another team."

I'm just thankful we get him 16 times a year—on our side.

# 3

## The Hiring:
## Ship to Shore to Denver

I KNEW we were gonna crash.

We had taken off in the dawn, and we were out over all this water, with just an occasional little island down there, and I was thinking to myself:

"Here we are. We're gonna crash. I have been going through this all these years, all these interviews at New York and Los Angeles, and Atlanta and New England, all this waiting and hoping, wanting to be a head coach.

"And now I have finally made it. And now, we're gonna crash, and except for Pam, ain't nobody gonna know about it. We'll crash down there in the ocean without a trace, and they'll never know, and they'll never find us."

It was March of 1981, and maybe I had been flying too much that weekend, gone without sleep. Maybe it was fatigue and jet lag that made me think like that. Or maybe it was just the reaction to finally getting what I had wanted so long.

I was the new head coach of the Denver Broncos.

A lot of head coaches have been hired in the National Football League. I'm not sure, though, that any of them ever went through what I did, the way I did.

Parts of it read like one of those spy novels.

It was mid-March, and basically, all the coaching changes had been made in the league by then. Down in Dallas, we had worked through January and February planning for the next year. We had had a staff meeting that morning, in fact, and then broke at noon, and Mike Ditka and I had rushed for a golf course.

We went over to Bent Tree Country Club where I had reserved a 12:30 tee time. But when I got there, the clubhouse attendant said I had a call from Coach Landry.

I thought, "Oh, my goodness. We've got a staff meetin' this afternoon and we left without checking with him." So I called, and Coach Landry said the new owner of the Denver Broncos, Edgar Kaiser, wanted to talk to me about the head coaching position. "I think this is a good opportunity for you," Coach Landry said. "You ought to talk to him. He said he'd call you tonight at home at seven o'clock."

I said fine, and went back out and we played 18 holes. I wasn't too excited at that point. I had been through so many of these things I didn't think anything would come of it. It seemed like every time there was an opening, my name came up and then somebody else got the job.

I had really made up my mind I would be back in Dallas that year. But it was a little surprising, because I hadn't heard that Red Miller had been fired. I didn't know until later, in fact, that at that point, nobody had talked to Red. He didn't know.

I finished playing, and went home, and at seven o'clock on the nose, the phone rang. It was a ship to shore call from Edgar Kaiser's yacht.

"I'm Edgar Kaiser," he said. "I'd like to talk to you about being head coach of the Denver Broncos. Are you interested?"

"Sure. I'd love to talk to you."

"My secretary will be back in touch with you with the details."

"Uh, well, thank you."

He hung up. The whole thing took maybe 30 to 40 seconds. Then a few minutes later his secretary rang back and said there'd be a plane ticket waiting for me at the airport on Sunday, was that all right?

I said sure. She said they'd route me from Dallas to Denver to Seattle, and then there'd be a private plane in Seattle to fly me up to Canada to Mr. Kaiser's house.

When I got to Seattle, they had said to go to this area for private planes, but when I got there, they told me, "Mr. Reeves, the plane just took off. It will be back to pick you up." When I had walked over to this area, I had seen these little float planes taxiing out to take off, but I hadn't thought much about it. I was just curious because I had never seen a float plane before.

I sat there and read the Broncos press guide. I wanted to learn everything I could so I'd be familiar with them when he asked me a question.

About an hour later, this float plane came back, and it was the one. It was a little scary. I sat in the front seat and we took off and headed toward Canada, and we were out over all that water. Every once in a while you'd see a little island, or some logs floating in the water.

Then we started losing altitude.

"Better fasten your shoulder straps," the pilot told me.

"I got my seat belt on," I said.

"Sometimes we hit the water pretty hard," he said. "Better fasten your shoulder straps, too."

"Oh, my God!" I thought. But it was the smoothest landing I've ever been through. Then he turned toward the land. I looked up. There was one huge, white house, sitting about halfway up the side of this mountain, with big, beautiful green trees. It was gorgeous, with other houses all around it, maybe four or five other ones.

The flowers were beautiful, the colors, it looked like every blade of grass had been clipped the same height. A big, huge yacht was sitting down on the water.

I thought, "It's like Fantasy Island." We floated up to the dock, and here come two men along the dock. One is dressed like a butler, and the other gentleman is dressed casual.

Of course, I don't know then how old Edgar Kaiser is or anything. I don't even know what he looks like. I got out. I have an attache case in my hand, and I've been traveling all day, from Dallas to Denver to Seattle, then the wait, then the float plane. I've been traveling a bunch of hours.

Mr. Kaiser reached for my attache case and gave it to the butler and said, "Take this to Australia."

I thought, "Oh, my God! I been traveling all day, and now we're goin' on to Australia? What is this?"

Well, come to find out, Australia is the name of one of those houses, guest houses, up by the big house, by his house. Australia was one of those, and it was bigger than my house in Dallas. It was huge. It had three bedrooms, a big dining room, big kitchen, big living area. It was just beautiful. When I walk into the meeting, three men are already there—Edgar Kaiser, Hein Poulus and Grady Alderman.

Hein eventually became Denver's vice president and general manager. He was Edgar's right hand man, and very, very bright. He was born in Indonesia and raised there and in Holland. He took a law degree in Canada and studied as a Commonwealth Scholar at the London School of Economics. He had been Edgar's top aide in all his various businesses before Edgar bought the team, and Edgar installed him as his personal representative here.

I sat down. Mr. Kaiser said, "I just hired Grady Alderman as our general manager, and Grady and I have decided we want you to be our head coach. What will it take for you to be our head coach?"

Just like that. It stunned me. All the conversations I had ever had, all the other interviews I had ever gone through, there's a formula, almost a script, that you follow.

You meet, you sit, you talk. They ask you what your philosophy is, what you believe in, what kind of powers you want, blah, blah, blah.

I had been rehearsing all weekend. And here was this guy I have just met, and he's offering me the job. No questions, no nothing. We shake hands, sit down and then it's just, "I want you to be my head coach. What's it going to take?"

"Well, I would really like to be head coach of the Denver Broncos," I said.

"What about size of the contract?"

"Well, really, the contract doesn't make any difference to me, but I really don't think you have a chance unless you have a three year or more contract."

He nodded. "You got it. Three years."

I said fine.

He said, "Okay, what about salary?" The other two are sitting there, watching, listening. "What about $100,000? $110,000?"

I said, "What's to say $100,000 is right? What's to say $125,000 isn't right?"

"You got it. $125,000," he said.

I thought to myself, "That was really dumb. Why didn't you say something like $150,000 or $175,000 or somethin'?"

So, the contract itself was settled quickly, as quickly as it takes to read about it. We talked about a television show and a radio show, and I said I wouldn't have time, starting so late. But he said they were important for other reasons. They would negotiate them, he said, and we'd split.

"Fine."

Now, I knew Denver was one of the places I'd like to live, and I knew they had a good football team. It wouldn't be like starting at the bottom as you'd have to do with a lot of jobs.

"What kind of authority will I have?" I asked him. "Those are the kinds of things that are important to me. As a coach, I wouldn't take the job if I didn't have control over the draft, control over cuts and trades."

Grady said, "Well, I think the general manager needs those things."

"You two need to get together and work that out," Edgar said. Grady and I walked up to Australia, just the two of us. It must have been about eight or nine o'clock by then. I assumed at that point that Grady had been a general manager or assistant general manager at Minnesota. I didn't realize all he had worked on was helping build the stadium or the practice complex there. He had no experience whatsoever as a general manager. He didn't know a lot about it.

The guy that gets fired is the coach, not the general manager. I wouldn't budge on what I felt I needed, and neither would Grady. We spent a long time up there, maybe two hours, before the phone rang. It was Edgar.

"What's the problem? Are you ready to eat?"

"We're having a problem as to who is going to have control over what," I told him.

"Well, dinner's ready. Why don't you come down for dinner." So we went to the main house, the mansion. They have got probably six or seven maids and butlers waiting on us—just the four of us sitting there.

They brought out the meal, one course at a time. We had some beef that was flown in from Japan. They massage the cattle and all that stuff, and I mean it was tender. You could cut it with a fork. Edgar went through the history of what it was and where it came from.

But, over the meal, we started talking about draft choices and trades and all those things.

Edgar said, "We'll give it to you, but you gotta check with me. I don't want you trading our football team away so you and I will have to work that out. But you will have the final say."

That was all I wanted to hear. We would take everybody into consideration, and I would talk with scouts and coaches and all, but I would have the last say if it came down to a final choice. We have never had that situation arise, where it was really an argument who we would take. It hasn't been a factor, but I felt it was important.

So we had agreed, but we really didn't have a contract in writing. That became important later, because in a couple of weeks, all of a sudden, Edgar wanted to trade Randy Gradishar because Randy had such a big salary. Joe Collier and I went over to Edgar's office and spent hours over there telling him it just didn't work that way.

He argued, "This is just like any other company I have ever run. We've got to cut the costs. Basically, the way to cut costs is if you have high salaried people you can replace you get rid of those people."

"Randy's not willing to take a cut."

We knew that was unprecedented. We finally convinced him Randy was different, football was different. We convinced him the people in Denver would raise the roof. Here was the most popular player and you are talking about trading him or getting rid of him because of his salary.

He was pretty well set that was what he wanted to do. That's where it hurt, too, with Grady not having experience. He knew what we were saying was true, but he couldn't explain that to Edgar.

Grady was really capable of getting the job done, but Edgar never gave him the authority to get the job done. I'm glad that incident happened, though, because it eventually led to an important clause in the contract when I did sign one:

I couldn't trade a first, second or third round draft choice, or a starter without consulting him. But it also had in there that the owner couldn't do the same without my consent. So it really worked out for the best. It wasn't like I wanted to be a dictator. It worked out well between us. We talked.

The point is, although we had filed a salary and length of contract document with the league, we really didn't have the rest of those things in writing. I didn't sign a real contract that whole first season, in fact, just the one stipulating salary and a three year deal.

I said I wanted to talk to Pam. I went back up to Australia, called her, and she was willing to go wherever I thought the opportunity was best. I said I liked Denver, and thought Edgar and I were the same age (I was 37, he was 38 at the time).

Then I went back down to the big house and we shook hands. He wanted to announce it on Tuesday morning. He wanted me to fly back to Texas the next morning, Monday, and then he'd send his private plane to fly me back to Denver that night, and we'd announce it the next day.

That was the first time I realized that Red Miller had not been fired yet. Edgar had made up his mind, but he had not actually fired him. I felt uncomfortable with that situation. I thought when he started talking to me that Red had already been told. "When I go in there tomorrow morning, I'll talk to him so when you come in tomorrow night that will already be done," Edgar said.

We made some plans. "You'll have to leave early," he said. "My driver will pick you up outside Australia and drive you to the airstrip on the island. We'll fly you to Seattle to get started toward Texas."

I probably didn't get an hour's sleep. It must have been two, three by the time I got to bed, and I had to get up at 5:30. And I was sitting there, thinking. After all these years, it was happening so fast and it wasn't anything like what I thought it would be.

All of a sudden, almost like snapping your fingers, you go from assistant coach to head coach, from $69,000 to $125,000, from being an advisor or somebody that just listens and watches to being the one who makes the decisions.

All this is going through my mind as I try to go to sleep, and you start having some doubts.

Is this really the job you want? Should you stay in Dallas? Everyone says you'll be the next head coach there. Should you stay around and wait until Coach Landry retires? But you also know this is the right move. There are no guarantees, and this is a good job, with a good team, in a good organization.

But for almost the first time in professional football, I have to really start thinking about all this, about leaving a town we've lived in and been happy in for 16 years.

I don't know how much I slept. When I got up and went outside, it was pitch dark. I had no idea where this driver was supposed to be, where I was supposed to go.

But when I walked out, the lights came on in this vehicle 50 or 75 yards away. It starts easing up toward the house. It's eerie, like you see in movies, this dark car sliding up through the dark.

He took me to the airport. The plane was tiny, and you could see every rivet on the side. It was all silver, and the pilot was wearing one of those caps with the ear flaps on it.

The plane looked like a crop duster, an Orville Wright type deal.

There's just room for the two of us and my hangup bag and attache case. He's got one of those wind type things on a pole, so you know which way the wind is blowing.

There are no lights on the runway, no tower, no nothing. Just this little airstrip in the dark, and we take off.

I had some time in Seattle before my flight, so I called my mom and dad and brother in Georgia. I wanted them to know.

Back in Dallas, we talked it over, and then I had to get dressed. I was supposed to meet Edgar's plane about six o'clock, seven o'clock. I packed my coats and ties and everything and went into the little terminal out at Love Field.

The pilot and co-pilot walked up. "Coach Reeves?"

"Yes."

"Follow us, please," they said.

I'm looking for a little bitty plane, and there's this passenger size thing out there, like a 16 passenger G2 jet. This plane takes off almost straight up. I've got an altimeter on the bulkhead, right in front of me, and there was a telephone.

Did I need to make any calls? No thank you. There were three different choices of food for dinner. I am met by a limousine, and the driver comes over and gets my bag. We drive to the Fairmont Hotel in downtown Denver, and when we pulled up, there is a crowd of people.

Nobody is supposed to know I'm coming in, but they have announced Red's firing that day.

Hein jumped in the car. "We've got to go around to the side," he said.

There are cameras all around the elevator. "Are you the coach?" I can't say anything. I just got on the elevator, and upstairs, we sat around and talked about what would go on the next day.

Edgar always wanted to plan carefully. I remember, a good example is something that happened a year later or so. He was looking for a partner, a minority partner.

I had gone on a trip up into Wyoming, and a guy picked me up in a plane. It was Bob Adams. I really liked him. He had mentioned on that trip that he had tried to buy the Broncos, and really was upset that Gerald Phipps didn't let him know he was interested in selling.

So, when Edgar was looking, I mentioned it to Bob Adams and he said yeah, he would definitely be interested. I told Edgar.

I was amazed at the planning that went into that. We would meet, and we would simulate a meeting with Adams.

Hein, ooh, that Hein was sharp. They would sit there, and Edgar would say, "Okay, Hein. I'm going to say to Adams, 'If I give you the opportunity now to buy 40 percent but you have no vote in this,' what is he going to say?"

And they'd speculate. And they'd say, "Dan, what do you think he is going to say?"

"Okay. If he says this, this is what we'll do. If he says this, this is what we'll do."

We met like two hours one day to plan the meeting we were going to have. I mean, Edgar didn't go into anything that he and Hein didn't have planned.

I'm sure when I went up there to be hired he said, "He's gonna come through the door and we're gonna offer him the job and he's gonna say 'I want a three year deal,' and we're gonna say, 'Okay, you got it.' And he's gonna say, 'I want $125,000, and we're gonna say, 'Okay, you got it.' "

I'm sure of that. Edgar never went into anything not ready.

Up in the suite that night before the press conference, I said I wanted a chance to talk to the coaches the next morning before the announcement. After March 1, I couldn't even talk to other coaches. I couldn't even ask permission. If I had wanted to hire Mike Ditka, I couldn't even call Coach Landry and ask to talk to Mike. It would have been illegal under league rules.

So I really was tied as far as assistants were concerned. I wanted to know if the assistants were interested in staying, because I knew some of them might have a loyalty to Coach Miller and might not want to stay.

I came in the next morning, and talked to them, and all of them were interested in staying.

One of the funniest was Richie McCabe, the defensive backs coach who died of stomach cancer a few years later.

We sat down. "Richie," I started, "I am interested in you staying."

He looked at me. "Coach, I can coach," he said. "And I am a damn good coach. And whether you keep me or not, I can coach in this league so it's really up to you."

I was scared to death. I had never interviewed a coach, and I didn't know these guys from Adam, and I was trying to be nice and say I'd like to talk to you, and there's this guy saying, "I'm a damn good coach."

It was really impressive. And he really was a damn good coach.

35

Of course, Joe Collier was Joe Collier. Exactly like he is now. I said I had a lot of respect for the defense and if he was interested I would like to have him stay. Joe was real calm.

"Yeah, I'd like to," he said. "We've got a pretty good football team. I think injuries are the reason we were 8-8 last year. We've got a good nucleus."

It was a tough time. I had butterflies like crazy during that whole time. I knew I was going into a bad situation. It didn't take me long to figure out people didn't like anybody from Texas, particularly ones from the Cowboys.

They had won the Super Bowl in 1977 and I was succeeding a man who was very popular—who had won here. I knew it wasn't going to be a popular move.

But the press conference seemed to go okay. "Are you going to use the Dallas offense?" My whole philosophy was based on what I knew from Dallas. I could see friction there. But I knew things would turn out all right when we began winning.

I tried to talk to Red. When I finally did reach him, I guess it was a couple weeks later. He handled it with class. He didn't make any comments, which I appreciated. He could have made it very tough, but he didn't.

It was a tough conversation for me. Basically, I told him that, because of the job he did, the league was looking at assistant coaches again. They had been going after college coaches, but because of Red, they were going back to hiring assistants like me.

I told him that. I also said I certainly had nothing to do with him not keeping the job. It was an opportunity for me, but I didn't want it at his expense.

"I know that doesn't help your feelings at all, but I wanted you to know that," I told him. "I'm sorry you had to lose your job for me to get one."

He said thank you and that was basically it.

I don't know the details of what went on between Red and Edgar. Edgar never told me, and I never asked.

I was extremely nervous that day. You think you are ready for all those things. Ever since I got back in coaching in 1974, I had been chasing this. But there is no way—no way—you can actually train somebody to be a head coach.

One of the men I tried to hire right then was Coach Marvin Bass, my coach at South Carolina. He had been like a father to me, and I always said if I ever got a head coaching job, he would be the first I hired. I felt his experience would be invaluable, and I felt he would be an outstanding special assistant.

He was at an age where I wanted to get him off the field, so I called him. He was coaching in Canada. He came on when their season ended. Joe of course stayed as defensive coordinator, and that was a brilliant move. He's like a rock. You can always count on him.

I never did call Mike Ditka. His opportunity was going to be there, in Dallas, to succeed me, take over the passing game. Had it been before March 1, we would certainly have talked.

I remembered the ride in Edgar's plane, the one from Dallas to Denver. The altimeter had gone from 10,000 to 20,000 to 30,000 to 40,000. I was the only passenger.

I was sitting there, on this airplane, thinking about that island, the big white house, Australia, the car lights in the dark, all those years wanting this job, and now I've got it.

"You're a long way from Americus, Georgia," I thought.

# GEORGIA
# KID

Part II

# 4

## Fee-lay Mee-non
## and other Prep Hazards

THE FIRST thing I can remember was when I was about three or four years old. I was in the hospital, laying in the bed.

I didn't know what was wrong with me. They were bringing my brothers and sister in outside my window. I was on the first floor of the little hospital there in Americus, the Sumter County Hospital. I can remember looking and seeing my older brother and sister outside with my dad and some of my cousins and so forth.

And that was the way they would come by. They wouldn't allow anybody in my room.

I had an infection between my gall bladder and kidney and it was supposedly inoperable, I learned later. Supposedly I would eventually die from it.

But then they came out with one of the mycins. I don't know which one it was. I would get a shot every four hours. It was twice the adult dose. My mother said the fever I was running was so high that it gave me a touch of rheumatic fever. I felt like a pin cushion. The nurse I had I remember was great. Every day she would bring me a boxcar to a train. I had a really long train before I got out of the hospital.

When I got out, we were living on the farm, and everybody else was going out and working. All I could do was sit around the house. All I could do was shell butterbeans and peas.

I became good at it. I would sit outside the back door in the hot summer time with a big old wash tub filled with butterbeans or peas, whatever they had picked from our garden. I mean you start shelling a wash tub full of beans you feel you are never going to get through.

I can remember doing that as a kid.

I know they felt exercise was something I wasn't supposed to do. They felt like I never was going to be able to run.

I had two cousins. Jerry Reeves was born in September and Bob was born in December and I was born in January. All three of us started school the same time. I wasn't supposed to start that soon. Jerry was the only one really that was supposed to, but Bob and I did, too.

We were first cousins. Our dads were brothers, but they were double first cousins: their mothers were sisters.

So we started out in first grade. Basically they did that because since I was just sitting around, they felt like they would go ahead and start me to school.

My mother later told me I also had rheumatic fever, but I swear I don't ever remember that. That wasn't what I was getting shots for.

She carried me in her arms until the medicine finally killed the infection. I don't know how long that went on. Months. I remember laying in the hospital a long time, and getting shots all the time. And when I came home, I didn't run and play with the other kids.

But I did start first grade, and then it wasn't long until they okay'd me to start playing. But I was basically a year ahead of where I should have been. So I was always the youngest kid in our class.

Bob and Jerry played a big part in my development as an athlete. My dad had two brothers, Uncle Jake and Uncle Doc. Uncle Jake had three boys and two girls. Uncle Doc had three boys and a girl and my dad had three boys and a girl. Each family had three boys in it. And all the boys were basically the same age—the oldest boys were pretty close, the middle ones were pretty close and the youngest were close also. Bob and Jerry and I were the middle boys. We played the same sports.

My dad had two sisters. They had children, too. So the whole clan used to get together on Sunday. After church you would go to somebody's house and play basketball if it was basketball season, baseball if it was baseball season and football if that was in season.

From the time we started in first grade we went to a little country school named New Era. A very small school. When I graduated from eighth grade we probably had only six players on our basketball team. We could only have one guy foul out. If we had two, we went with four.

But in that little country school we had some good athletes. We all were very competitive, good athletes, and we played all the sports. We started playing organized ball in basketball and baseball. We didn't have enough to play organized football.

I remember in the sixth grade we went over to Plains, Georgia, where Jimmy Carter is from. We played them in basketball, and we beat them 65–2.

That was our first organized competition where we got on a school bus and traveled to play somewhere.

We didn't have an indoor court. We played on a dirt court, outside, and we had the basket on a big post. You had to learn to shoot around the side. You couldn't go right underneath or you'd run into the big pole.

So we played them. We did not get beat in basketball. We even beat Americus Junior High School. It had several hundred kids. We did not lose a basketball game in the sixth grade. We had Bob and Jerry and me and several other good kids from the country. We didn't have but six or seven players.

In that 65–2 game, it got so bad we were gonna let them score.

They couldn't make even a layup. We had them 65–0. Finally the kid scored from midway between the top of the key and midcourt and it went in. It was toward the end of the game.

Plains always had a good high school basketball team. They were like Class B and Americus was Class A. It had more kids. When I graduated from Americus it was Double A and Plains was still B. But it always had a good basketball team.

We won the state basketball championship my senior year at Americus, and Bob and Jerry and I were all on that team. Three guys from a little bitty country school. And we played Plains, and it was the first time we had ever gone over 100. The score was something like 100 something to 90 something.

Those same kids we had beaten 65–2 in the sixth grade had a real good basketball team by the time we were seniors in high school.

One of the funny things about going to school in New Era was Mr. Dow Burk, the principal. He was a tall lanky man who talked real slow. He was a disciplinarian. He was also a great math teacher. I mean I didn't have to open a book when I went to college because I started out with a good math background.

He was a great believer in giving homework. After turning it in, you'd go up to the blackboard and do work before the other students. Which was good, although I didn't realize it at the time. It put a lot of pressure on you. You had to perform, keep up, in front of the other kids.

We probably had only 20 in our class, girls and boys. Behind the backstop of our baseball field was this big cane reed field. We would hit foul balls and they would land back in these canes. We would do assignments and he'd say, "Okay, you got 20 problems today. The first two to finish get to go look for baseballs in the cane field."

Well, you couldn't do your work fast enough because you wanted to be one of the first two finished.

Or he'd say, "Okay, we need the grass cut. First two guys to finish get to go mow the baseball field." We'd break our necks to get to go out and cut the grass. We thought that was great. He would use your school work as sort of a reward system.

And we would have long lunches, long recesses. So we had some great times with 45 minutes in the morning for recess and maybe an hour and a half at lunch and then 45 in the afternoon. If we could get Mr. Burk involved in the game he would forget to blow the whistle and it would go on longer.

We had a couple country stores where we could go and buy candy and cokes and whatever. I'll never forget, if you ever hit a ball good, it would go all the way to the country store. There was nothing to stop it.

So we were always playing sports, but because of the number of students we also got a great education.

It's funny. Not long ago I went back to Americus to be inducted into the Americus Hall of Fame and to talk to the graduating class.

I went by the New Era. And in your mind you have a vision of how big that school was. I was stunned at how small it was. I can remember walking down the halls. Those lockers were huge. Now, they don't come up to my chest.

I couldn't believe they were the same lockers. Of course the school house hasn't been used in years. They consolidated and went to the city schools and so forth.

We used to have fights, piggyback. You tried to pull the other guys' rider off. Bob and Jerry were always partners or Jerry would be my partner. You switched back and forth. He was the smallest of the three, so he was always the rider. And he could be pulled down and almost have his head dragging the ground and still pull himself back up.

We used to do all kinds of things in that country school.

Bob and Jerry and I would play home run derby in baseball. We would take on everybody else. We would never get out. The whole recess we would be up batting, never take the field. We were that good compared to the others. We got a lot of good hitting practice.

Of course after eighth grade we had to go to the city school, and we were in awe. When I walked into Americus High School that first day and saw all those students, all the people in the hall, I was scared to death. I don't know if introverted is the word but I certainly didn't feel comfortable in that situation.

The time you did feel comfortable was the time you were participating in sports. Because of all the chores on the farm, I had to get my dad's permission to play football. He was excited about it and thought that would be great. He and his brother had a road construction business by that time.

The first game I played, I was playing tight end. We had our first game up in Macon, Georgia. It's about 60 or 65 miles from Americus. I probably weighed 145 or 150. I was playing tight end, and I had big feet. And I was slow. I was the slowest guy on our team. There wasn't anybody on our football team, lineman or anybody, who couldn't outrun me.

So I would stay out after practice running 40 yard dashes trying to improve my speed.

Anyway, my first game we go up to Macon. I'm backing up, so I'm probably not going to play in the game. My mother went up for the game. As it turned out, Bill Moyd, who was the starting halfback for us, forgot his shoes. We didn't have any extra shoes. Everybody had to furnish his own.

Because of that, I got to start at halfback. I was the halfback that didn't carry the ball. If the right half carried the ball I played left half. If the left half was supposed to carry the ball, I played right half. So I also ended up playing the corner on defense because that was his position on defense.

I don't remember a lot about my freshman year. We played about four or five games.

I didn't play basketball or baseball my freshman year because I had to work on the farm. I learned to drive a tractor when I was nine years old. I learned to turn land and harrow land and plow peanuts and plow cotton.

After football season was over that year I would ride the school bus, and instead of going home it would drop me off wherever the field was I was going to work that particular day. I would get off the school bus and walk out into the field and get on the tractor. Then I would plow until dark when daddy would come to take me home.

So I knew that after all those years getting off that school bus I wanted to play those other sports, too. In the summers, that's all you did, every day, you worked on the farm.

Between my freshman and sophomore years my high school coach found out I could throw the ball pretty good so he switched me to quarterback. We had a great time as sophomores.

We were undefeated on the B team. We had won about five games in a row. Jerry was the halfback and I was the quarterback and Bob was the receiver.

I almost broke into tears when they wanted me to come to play on the varsity and they hadn't won a game.

We tied that first game, but it was against a first year team. So it wasn't like it was against somebody real good. But it was an improvement. Then the next week we won our first game, 14–7, against a pretty good team.

Then I remember going down to Adel, Georgia. It is right in the middle of the pulpwood country, turpentine. Their football team was tough. We were down like 28–0 at the half. We started to go in at half-time and looked over and they stayed out on the field and played bull in the ring, all these tough tackling and hitting drills.

It was like, "Well, we didn't get enough action the first half. We're going to stay out here and go against ourselves, get some competition."

Well, we end up getting beat bad, 49–0 or something like that. So my sophomore year was exciting from the standpoint I made the varsity as a sophomore. It was unusual for that school, but it was more or less because we didn't have a very good team. It wasn't because I was such a great athlete. I started playing basketball on the B team, but no baseball that year.

Then we changed football coaches. We got a coach named Casey King. He was head coach of a little old bitty Class B school named

Patterson, Georgia. They had been state champs in Class B and he was a real hard nosed coach.

So we had spring practice in February every year, 20 days where you did nothing but hit. On the first day of practice, he told everybody to line up five yards apart and the line probably reached for 120 yards. We probably had 60 kids out, and it seemed for as far as you could see there was the line.

I was the first one in line because I was the quarterback. He took the ball and threw it to me and said, "Okay, turn around and run through that line."

I thought, "Boy, this is strange." I got the ball and the first guy came at me and I kind of faked around him but he dragged me down.

Well, Coach Casey King blew the whistle and he said, "Oh, no, no, no! That's not what I want you to do. I want you to try to run over every one of these guys. When they tackle you, you get up and try to run over the next guy. You get up and try to run over the next guy."

He called it his "losers line." I mean, by the time you got through the line you had been tackled 60 times. That was the way spring practice started off every day for 20 days. And we had sideline tackling where you have a ball carrier coming down the sideline with the ball and he would teach you the right approach. And it was head on.

Then he would have a 2 by 8 board, and you would get one guy on one end and another on the other, and run head on. And that's all we did for 20 days, hit, block and tackle.

Really and truly, that's what we needed. We weren't a tough football team. It was one of our problems the year before.

He was also the one that first started getting me into knowing why you call certain plays. He let me call plays, but he'd get me into situations and say, "This is a good play because of this."

He stressed the fundamentals. To get his point across, that losers line we ran in the spring, every time the next year when we would lose a game, we would have to open practice with that drill every day the whole week.

That kind of gets your attention. We were 5–5 my junior year. But the games we lost were 14–7 or 21–20. We were never embarrassed.

Before the season, Coach King talked our touchdown club into buying us a bus. We painted it up in our school colors, blue and white, and put a big panther on the side, Americus Panthers. It kinda made everybody proud to get on it. We used it for basketball and football and baseball.

But the first thing we used it for was to go all the way down to Waycross, Georgia, to a state park in the swamps and everglades— Laura Walker State Park. They had some screened-in cabins. We were there for two weeks. There weren't any parents around to say "You're working my son too hard," or "You're hitting my son too hard or beating on my son."

Plus if you wanted to quit you were about 200 miles from home. There wasn't any way you were going to quit. It was so hot, so humid, we would get up and practice in the morning before breakfast. We would practice on a little old cut out field that didn't have very good grass on it and wasn't marked off. It didn't have sidelines or hash marks or anything like that. It was just an open field in the middle of these pine trees.

Three other schools were there—Patterson, Moultrie, Ware County, and Americus. And it was illegal. But we would practice against those other schools. We would scrimmage one of them every day. So we had three or four games under our belt before the season started.

What it did was make us hard nosed again before the season. It made us tougher. And you know, we took pride in that. We started getting bigger. I probably weighed 160 pounds and was starting to get some muscle definition.

In the morning we used to have to take turns. We had to put wood in to heat up the hot water heater. Franklin Brewer played guard for us. He goes out one day to put wood in and there was a skunk in there. And the skunk sprayed him.

Nobody wanted to be around Franklin. He was a tough guy, a grade behind us. He was the one the year before started as a freshman. He was that good. A nose tackle.

The state fair used to come around and they had a deal where if you'd go fight this gorilla and could stay in the cage for two minutes they'd give you $200. The gorilla was just beating everybody up.

Brewer ended up winning the $200. But Coach Hightower ended up kicking him off the team for a week for fighting a gorilla.

Anyway, Brewer gets sprayed by the skunk. He ends up having to eat breakfast by himself for a couple of days, and of course he couldn't practice. Nobody could stand to be around him.

Coach Hightower was our coach my senior year. Coach King had made the mistake of calling the son of one of the school board members a son of a bitch during practice one day and they fired him.

Coach Hightower, even as I went on through high school and college and into the pros, was the type of coach you remember because he was fun to play for. He made football fun, although he was also hard nosed and tough. I still think a lot of him. He meant a great deal to my career.

Going into my senior year we had a good team. We lost a game early in the season to Bainbridge 28–21. It had two great running backs named Ed Varner and Fred Barber. Ed ended up going to Georgia Tech on a scholarship and Fred played fullback at Georgia and was captain.

The fourth game we were playing Sylvester and I went back to pass and got tackled and then got piled on. As I started to get up I tried to push up with my left hand and something burned in my shoulder.

I reached under my shoulder pads and it didn't feel right. It turns out I had a compound fracture of my clavicle. So I missed four games, actually missed five weeks with an open date. In that time we lost a game 7–6 to Brooks County that kept us out of the playoffs.

When I came back we played three games. We played the team that won the regional championship, Ware County High School, who beat Brooks County, and we beat Dublin in Dublin, where they had a 40 game winning streak. It was probably the most exciting high school game that I'd ever been associated with. They were the eventual state champions.

In the last game of the season we beat Cordele, another Double A school. We ended up 8–2. We beat the state champions and we beat the regional champions. But we were out of the playoffs because of the subregion loss to Brooks County while I was hurt.

That last game of the season against Cordele, right before the half I went back to pass and got tackled and somebody fell on me, and I really felt that clavicle burn.

But I wasn't going to tell Dr. Robinson or anybody. I had had a hard enough time getting back into the lineup. No way would they let you play if they thought you were hurt.

So we finished the game, and next week we started basketball practice. I couldn't lift my arm all the way up. The pin they put in when I hurt my shoulder would move in and out just a fraction. It would hit the clavicle joint right near the neck. It really did hurt.

Dr. Bud Robinson said, "You really don't need that pin in there. Why don't you just come by the emergency room at the hospital. It really won't take but a minute or two and I'll get that thing right out.

"But be sure and bring somebody with you. I'm going to give you some anesthetic to kill the pain, and you need somebody to drive back in case you get a little woozy."

So I took my cousin Bob Reeves with me. We were both in study hall—we had an hour. That was plenty of time to run to the hospital and get this pin out. So we drove to the hospital, and I remember sitting on the table. Dr. Bud was talking to me and fooling around and seeing where the thing was.

His nurse was there, and they shaved the area and kind of deadened the area with novocaine. Then he just took the scalpel and cut, and when he did, blood started running down by chest.

"Wait a minute, Doc. I can't handle this. Let me lay down on the table so I don't have to look at this." So I did. And I don't have to see it. Well, he takes a pair of pliers, and he grabs on the end of that pin, and he pulls on it.

It doesn't move. When I had gotten hit it had kind of bent the end of it and therefore it wouldn't come out. He had Bob grab my feet, and two nurses grab me by the arms, and it took him about 15 minutes of just pulling and pulling and I could feel that pin come out slowly like you were pulling your foot out of the mud.

It wasn't like I was in a lot of pain—I wasn't comfortable, and I could hear all that stuff going on—but I wasn't in pain. The funny part was I had to drive back to school. Bob was white as a sheet. He couldn't drive. He was too weak from watching all that blood. But I never had any more trouble with it. My mother still has that pin in a bottle at home.

We went on my senior year to win the state championship in basketball and baseball. Had we won the football championship, it would have been something no school had ever done in the history of the state—win all three major sports titles.

Jerry was the most valuable player in Class A in football. He rushed for over 1,400 yards and scored 20 some touchdowns. He went on to Troy State. Bob Reeves was the most valuable in basketball. He and I both made all state in basketball. The closest we came to getting beat in basketball was the first playoff game of the subregionals.

They had consolidated several county schools in Thomasville and started a new high school called Central of Thomasville. They had to play all their games up to Christmas away from home.

They seeded you at Christmas. We had the best record at Christmas and Central had the worst record. But after Christmas they started playing some games at home and started playing together and had a 10 or 12 game winning streak going.

We opened up the subregional against Central, and I remember them coming out for the warmup, and they had like the first four players dunk the basketball.

Our tallest player was about 6–1. That was Bob.

They had us down at halftime by six or eight points. Then, most of their starters fouled out and most of our starters fouled out, and it ended up our bench beating their bench in a very close ball game.

We had no trouble from then on. We went straight through and won the championship game by about 12 points. We were a very disciplined team that ran plays which were unusual for high school. We ran plays against man to man and plays against zone and were very well coached. We full court pressed.

It was the first time Americus had won a state championship in basketball in quite a while.

So we went into baseball. I had been a leftfielder. I had a pretty good arm. We had a pitcher named Loveard McMichael. He was the backup quarterback who had come in when I was out with the broken collarbone. He was an excellent pitcher. But other than that we didn't have a pitcher.

We had gone to the state tournament the year before. So Coach Melvin Kinslow decided he was going to make a pitcher out of me.

He would bring me out every day. He had this gadget built that had two poles on either side of the plate and strings across to define the strike zone. I could throw the ball hard but I had no idea where it was going.

The first game I pitched was against Cordele. It was the opening game of the season. It was drizzling rain. It was cold. I gave up just one hit, but I walked about 12 and I hit about four or five other guys. And that was the first inning. They scored seven or eight runs in the first inning.

I came in after that inning and I told coach my arm was hurting. Of course Coach Kinslow was extremely competitive. "I know it's not your arm," he said. "You just aren't competitive," he said.

Well, he might as well have spit in my face he made me so mad. So I went back out and pitched seven innings and I threw every ball as hard as I could throw it.

And to this day I still can't straighten my right arm out all the way.

I ended up pitching that year, and I remember the sports page after one of those games that year said, "Reeves Pitches 1-hitter, a 9–7 victory." I gave up seven runs on one hit. That's how wild I was.

So we go to the finals of the state tournament. It is a double elimination tournament. We had won our first game. Loveard had pitched an excellent game we won 2–1. We were going to play Model close to Rome, Georgia, in the finals. They had great baseball up in north Georgia.

I figured I was going to pitch. I had been the second pitcher all year. Coach came to me and said he was going to let Bob Reeves pitch that game. He was our catcher. He could have signed with Cincinnati right out of high school. He had a great arm, could hit the ball and had good speed. He probably was the best baseball player we had, he and Loveard.

So I had to catch. I'll never forget the first kid that stepped up was probably 5–3, 5–4, something like that. And he stepped up to the plate first pitch of the game and he hits it off the left field wall. Bob threw a fast ball. It was right down the middle and it never moved. The kid hit it, and I can remember Roy Frost, who was taking my place in left field, running back to the fence to catch it.

The ball went underneath the fence. They had a scoreboard there, and that ball went under the scoreboard, and you could hear Roy Frost, banging around underneath there trying to get the ball out.

He's trying to get out and you could hear his head hitting the tin out there, and the guy ended up with a triple to open the game. They end up scoring three in the first and two in the second and they are ahead 5–0.

In the bottom of the fifth he asked me to go in and pitch and I got them out, three up and three down. So we go into the top half of the sixth inning and we score six runs. So I'm getting ready to go back out and pitch the bottom half and as I'm starting to go out to the mound, Coach Kinslow comes up to me.

"You know, I think we've got an excellent chance of winning this game. I think I'll let Loveard finish up."

So I go to left field, Loveard finishes and I end up winning the state playoff game pitching to three guys. We win 6–5.

They win their next game, and came to Americus. We felt like we could draw a big crowd in Americus and they worked out a deal where some of the kids from Model stayed at our house.

I remember they had a catcher named Gary York who was the nephew of Rudy York, the old Yankee. I remember the stadium was packed. It holds 6,500 to 7,500 people. It used to be a minor league park back when they used to have the Georgia–Florida league.

Loveard was pitching the game and this kid, Gary York, was batting. Jerry Reeves played centerfield and I played leftfield when Loveard was pitching. I remember this kid hit a pitch to dead center field, about 435 feet. Jerry caught it on the dead run. He ran right up against the fence. It is one of the greatest catches I have ever seen. That's the kind of speed Jerry had.

We ended up winning the game to win the state championship.

During basketball season a guy named Weems Baskin had come down to see me and I went up to South Carolina on semester break. I had never visited a school before except one game my senior year when Jerry and I and another guy drove down to Florida State to see them play the University of Houston.

They didn't offer me a scholarship because they were looking at a quarterback from Cairo, Georgia, who was also a pole vaulter. They gave him a combination scholarship.

I had never really been a prospect at any college, but South Carolina had a guy named John Caskey who took me out. My dad and I had driven up to Columbia, which is about five and a half hours from Americus. And we were staying at a motel up there.

John Caskey came by to pick me up at the hotel. My dad had given me five dollars to go out. We go to the Martinique Restaurant. It is a big restaurant there. We were sitting at the table, looking at the menu.

"Would you like a cocktail?"

"Oh, no. I don't care for a cocktail." He said he was talking about a shrimp cocktail. So I said, "Oh. Yeah. I'll take one of those."

So I'm looking at the menu, and he said, "What would you like?"

"I don't know. What're you going to have?"

Well, he ordered a filet mignon. I'm looking, trying to figure out which one of those things was the FEE-LAY MEE-NON. I finally figured it was the one I thought was the fi-let mig-non. I looked at that thing. It was like $14. For two.

I thought, "Gosh. I only got five dollars. But that's okay. It's for two." So I didn't enjoy the meal because the whole meal I was sitting there, thinking how I was going to ask him for some money.

I figured I was gonna have to borrow some to help pay my share and to get back to the hotel.

So we finally get through and he orders dessert. I didn't order any because I didn't want to have to ask for any more money. Finally, when he got through eating, I worked up enough nerve to ask him if I could borrow some money until I got back to the room.

"What do you need money for?"

"Well, see, I only got $5 to pay for this meal."

He started laughing. "You don't have to pay for this. The school is paying for it."

Well, I hadn't enjoyed the whole meal—my stomach was hurtin' so much. Caskey never let me forget that. He ended up being captain when I was a sophomore.

The next day we went over to what they called the round house, where they had all the lockers and things like that. Jack Scarbath was the quarterback coach. He had played for the Redskins.

He asked me how I liked the school.

"Oh, I think it's a great school."

"Well, how would you like to go to school here?"

"Oh, heck. I'd love it."

"All you have to do is sign right here," he said.

Well, I couldn't sign that thing fast enough and my dad couldn't sign it fast enough, either. That's how I was recruited to South Carolina.

It was the only school to even offer me a scholarship.

So when my senior year was over they have the Georgia All Star game about two weeks before college starts in the fall. Coach Hightower said, "You got a chance to be on the football or basketball team. Which would you rather play on?"

"If you have a chance to be the coach, I'd like to be on whichever one you are going to coach."

He told me he thought I ought to play football, since that is what I had a scholarship for at South Carolina. They named the teams, and sure enough I was on both teams. As it turned out, he ended up coaching basketball, and the guy that coached football had his own quarterback on the team.

They played it in Atlanta at Grant Field. We stayed on the campus at Georgia Tech. It was a big thrill. I roomed with a big tackle named Dennis Murphy, who was going to Florida.

This quarterback played the first half and we were down by one point, like 7–6. And I came out the second half and played, and drove us down for like three touchdowns and ended up getting most valuable player for the game.

That was a total surprise. Well then all kind of schools started recruiting me. They didn't have the letter of intent back then. So a lot of schools, particularly in the Southeastern Conference, were trying to recruit me.

I had wanted to go to Georgia Tech all my life because that's where my brother, Charles, had gone.

So after that game they said, "Look, we would really like for you to come to Georgia Tech."

But I said no, I had already signed with South Carolina.

Alabama sent a guy who tried to recruit me. "We don't have a quarterback at Alabama," he said. "The kid that we had broke his arm." I was down at Waycross, helping my high school coach at that summer camp, when this coach came around.

I called my brother to see what he thought, should I go over and visit or what? There were bad feelings between the schools at that point. There had been an incident a couple of years before when an Alabama player hit a guy from Georgia Tech on a punt and fractured his jaw.

My brother said, "No. I don't want you to go visit Alabama." I kind of wanted to because I had heard so much about this guy that coached them, Bear Bryant.

Well, as it turned out, the guy who ended up quarterbacking them was named Joe Namath. So I would have gone over there the same year as Joe Namath.

I also visited Florida, and when I got back, Coach Bass was in Americus, along with Coach Baskins and Coach W. L. Strickland. So we all went to lunch at the Lighthouse Cafe, with my dad, and Coach Bass was very honest with me.

"We recruited six quarterbacks," he said. "We need to know what your plans are. We made plans for you to be here, and we kind of took a chance on you when nobody else wanted you. If you start with us, it will be because you are the best quarterback we have got."

And they didn't promise me anything. I had been promised all kinds of things by some of the other schools, that I was going to start as a sophomore and all that stuff.

That kind of impressed me, what Coach Bass said. It was the way my father was. He was blunt and to the point.

Coach Bass gave me that spiel, and my father looked at me and said, "Son, where do you want to go to school?"

I'm sitting there with three coaches from South Carolina. I said, "I want to go to South Carolina."

So Coach Baskin, who was an older coach, said, "That's great. Come with me." He took me down to the telegraph office and he wrote out a telegram and handed it to me.

"Dear Coach Graves," it said. "Please do not call me or contact me. Have decided to go to the University of South Carolina." And he said, "Sign this." So I signed that thing.

I've never regretted it. We never had a great football team but it was fun.

# 5

## South Carolina: The College Years

WHEN YOU break a collarbone and miss four games in your senior year, you don't get a lot of exposure.

Both these things were factors in my getting an offer only from South Carolina until after the summer all star game. Some smaller schools were interested in me as a basketball player, schools like Georgia Southern and Mercer. I really thought, until I heard from South Carolina, that there was a chance I might go to some small school and play basketball and baseball.

I didn't think I was a good athlete, anyway. I was a little behind everybody in maturity, and it wasn't until the all star game, when I threw a couple touchdown passes and made a couple runs, that I seemed to catch up.

I was the kind of guy who did a lot of things, but nothing very well. It was the same at Dallas. Dallas was one of the few teams even interested in me coming out of college. That was the way my career went through high school and through college, too—I was always just barely holding on.

Just going away to college was an experience for me. My brother was going to Georgia Tech, and I was a big Georgia Tech fan. I used to go to a lot of their games as a child, and I used to fantasize about playing for them. When I got that opportunity after that summer all star game, it was really hard to pass it up.

But South Carolina had committed to me early, and I felt an obligation. Coach Marvin Bass had gone there from Georgia Tech, and he did a good job, I think, of pairing me with a guy named John Breeden. He was from Columbia, South Carolina, and had a football scholarship. His mother was Jim Tatum's sister. Tatum was coach at Maryland. Coach Bass knew it was a good solid family. So I had a place to go when the weekends came around. We spent most of our time over at the Breeden's house. I didn't get homesick like a lot of guys.

My freshman year, I was excited to see how I would do. We had six or seven quarterbacks that fall. They were from Virginia and all over. But I ended up being the starter for the freshman team. We played five games. We were 3–2, and the two we lost we could very easily have won.

I remember my first game in college, we drove up by bus to College Park, Maryland, to play the University of Maryland. My mother flew up for the game, and that made it exciting.

I was captain. I remember going out to meet the Maryland captains. I couldn't pronounce a single one of the guys' names. Falderano and Scrapatatin, names like that. This was weird. I had never heard names like that.

We ended up getting beat, but I was thrilled to be the starting quarterback of a major college team. A couple years earlier I didn't dream it was possible, and now it was coming true.

We had a good freshman team. It was Coach Bass' first recruiting class. When the season ended, he wanted me to room with another guy from Georgia who was going to be a senior that next year. He was a great player—Billy Gambrell.

He later played for the St. Louis Cardinals. He was probably as good an athlete as I ever played with. He was 5-10 and he could dunk the basketball. Nobody could outrun him. He had great physical talent—a natural athlete. He could play pool, golf, tennis, any sport. He had had a tough home life, and Coach Bass wanted me to room with him.

Again, it was a good move. I got to know Billy pretty well. He was a star on the varsity, and it helped me as far as leadership was concerned because I did take over as starting quarterback as a sophomore.

I hurt my knee in the spring, stretched and partially tore a ligament, but it healed all right. As a sophomore, we probably had the best team we had while I was in school. We were 4–5–1, but we lost a lot of close games, and it was a fun season. I was one of the few sophomores that started that year, and we opened at Northwestern.

I was the youngest major college quarterback in the country that year. A coach by the name of Ara Parseghian had just taken over at Northwestern. He had a young quarterback by the name of Tommy Myers, but he was a few months older than me.

The year before Ara took over Northwestern had run basically 85 to 90 percent of the time.

Tommy Myers broke Otto Graham's school record that day. He hit about 21 of 25 passes.

We had kicked off, and on the first or second play, they had fumbled and we recovered on about their 25 yard line.

I went in to run my first play in college. It was a sweep, and in our offense, you pitched the ball back to the halfback and then you led the sweep. You had a blocking responsibility. I remember making a block on the play, and Sammy Anderson scored on my first play in my college career.

I thought, "Boy, what was I worried about? This is really easy."

Then Tommy Myers got warmed up. I watched. He had a receiver named Paul Flatley, who later starred for the Minnesota Vikings. Another great back by the name of Ken Willard killed us in North Carolina. He ran the kickoff back 80 yards after we had taken a 7–0 lead. That was a game that finished with us on about their one inch line because we couldn't line up fast enough to run off a play. I had thrown a pass that got us down that far.

Our final game was the first one played on Saturday in what they call "Death Valley" at Clemson. Up until that year, it had always been played in Columbia and been tied into the state fair. They had always called it "Big Thursday."

Clemson was heavily favored. We almost upset them.

The year before, when I was a freshman, a fraternity at South Carolina had dressed up like the Clemson team. There was a high school in South Carolina that had uniforms just like Clemson's, and this fraternity had got hold of them. They had somebody dress like Frank Howard, the Clemson coach—with the hat on, with the big jacket and tie and chaw of tobacco. He even had a pillow in his stomach. He looked just like Frank Howard.

So, when that team came on the field, the Clemson student body stood up and started cheering. This fraternity bunch lined up and did exercises, but then they went over and started acting like they were milking a cow. Clemson was known as a cow college. One guy would hold his thumbs down and the other guy would act like he was milking his thumbs.

The Clemson fans came out of the stands and a fist fight broke out. It was all over the country the next day. That's when I knew it was a big rivalry. Until then, I was just a country boy from Georgia and I had barely heard of Big Thursday.

My sophomore year, we played that game in Death Valley and were ahead 17-10 at half. Early in the third quarter, I scrambled around and hit Sammy Anderson for a touchdown that would have put us ahead 24-10, but they said there was an ineligible receiver downfield and called it back. Of course, when we looked at the film later, he wasn't downfield.

We ended up getting beat 20-17. Billy Gambrell made a great run near the end that got us down in field goal range. We could have tied, but we wanted to win, so we gambled and I threw an incomplete pass on fourth down.

But those were the kinds of games we lost that year—take the Duke game.

It was early in the year, and it produced one of the strangest calls I have ever seen, even now. We drove and scored and went ahead 6-0 when we missed the extra point. Duke kicked a field goal. They had a guy that kicked off for them named Mike Curtis. He was a great linebacker for the Baltimore Colts. He had a bad knee, but he kicked off.

We returned the ball to about the 25 or 30, and I went in to call the first play, and the official came over to me and said, "It's Duke's ball, first and 10."

I just looked at him. "Duke's ball? First and 10? We didn't fumble or anything. How did it get to be Duke's ball?" They called us for holding while the ball was in the air.

And, while the ball is in the air it is a free ball and if you get a personal foul penalty the other team gets the ball.

It had never been called in the history of college football. But it was called against us and they got the ball. I don't know. Maybe it is still a rule in college.

Coach Bass likes to tell the story that Bill Murray, the Duke coach at that time, was on the NCAA Rules Committee and they were going over rules and he made the comment that he had never heard that rule. So it was called against us the next season.

We had a good football team, an extremely good first team but we didn't have a lot of depth. We had a chance to have an excellent team. That was by far the best of the three teams I played on at South Carolina.

I ended up being second team all Atlantic Coast Conference at quarterback. I think Dick Shiner of Maryland was the first team quarterback or maybe it was Gary Cuozzo of Virginia.

The next spring, I really tore up my knee in an intramural basketball game. I planted to grab a pass and it sounded like a rifle going off. They operated on me that night. Back in those days, they gave you spinals, and I watched them operate on my knee. I wouldn't recommend that.

I stayed in the hospital about four or five days. They took the cartilage out, and the ligament had been stretched. They kind of overlapped it and sutured it and tightened it back up.

On the day I was getting out, Dr. A. T. Moore, who did my knee, said, "I'm operating on a guy today who has got the exact same problem you had. Would you like to watch?"

Well, you know, I hated to say no but I really didn't care to watch. They put a gown on me, the mask, and here I go, walking into the operating room on crutches, just out of bed from my own operation.

I had worked on hogs all my life on the farm, but I had never watched a human other than myself be cut on. I got a little woozy.

The next season was probably the most miserable year I ever went through. We were 1–8–1 or something, and it wasn't something you want to remember. I played every game with both knees taped. I ran the option against Virginia in Charlotsville and got hit and hyperextended my left knee.

Against North Carolina the next week, they left two holes in the tape where they could deaden it. They don't do that now, but back then, there was nothing wrong with it. I certainly wasn't against it. I wanted to play.

They would tape me in practice, and I would strip the tape, and some of my skin would come away with it. The skin was becoming irritated. They had to order non-allergenic tape. It wasn't a fun year at all. It was miserable.

Ken Willard had beat us in football, and in baseball that spring, North Carolina went on to the College World Series. They beat us two games, and he beat us in both.

I was really looking forward to playing baseball my senior season, but Pam and I got married between my junior and senior years, and we ended up living in the married dorm.

Lide Huggins was the safety on our football team. He is now our pro personnel director. He was married and had two little girls. They lived right above us. I remember I would try to sleep and these two little girls would be running up and down the steps. I used to give them a quarter if they'd stay out in the yard or something. It's funny how you remember those things. They are both grown now and beautiful.

My junior year, that awful one, we ended up losing to Tulane, which had the losingest team in the nation at that point. When they lost, Wake Forest had the losingest team. We lost to them, too. A guy named Brian Piccolo kicked the extra point that beat us 20–19. Their quarterback that day was John Mackovic, who took my place at Dallas, and later coached the Kansas City Chiefs. He is now at Illinois.

My senior year, we missed a field goal from extra point range and tied Georgia, and in the next to last game, on a quarterback sneak, a guy fell on my left leg.

They diagnosed it as a broken leg and put an air cast on it, but it turned out to be a severely sprained ankle. There was one game left, up in Death Valley, against Clemson. I wanted to play my final college game.

I shouldn't have. They shot the ankle, and did it again at halftime. Sometime in the second half we have the ball down near their goal, inches to go. The snap is like on one, and I pull out, and Mike Johnson, our center, snaps the ball late.

I jumped to get the ball and somebody hit my ankle.

Even with all that novocaine, I felt it, and I knew something was bad wrong with that ankle. I came out, and our backup quarterback led us to victory.

But that's not the point. Mike had had a couple similar situations that year, but nobody thought anything about them. He snapped the ball over a kicker's head down in Florida once. He would come over to our apartment and we'd be listening to Hank Williams records— we both liked country music—and the next thing you knew, he'd be asleep.

During Christmas holidays he went home to Tennessee and his parents thought something was wrong. They took him to the Duke Medical Center and learned he had three different cancers. He died in a couple months. They named the dormitory for him at South Carolina.

Anyway, driving back from that game, I was in a lot of pain. Pam had driven up, and I was riding and the novocaine was wearing off. We stopped in Greenville, which is right in the middle of the Bible Belt. The ankle was all swollen.

I don't drink, but I sent my brother up to one of the hotels. "See if you can find me a pint of bourbon or something. I have got to find something to deaden this pain."

I don't know how, but he found something, and I drank it all before we got out of town. My ankle didn't hurt by the time we got to Columbia. I didn't feel too good the next day, but the ankle quit hurting.

It wasn't the best way to end a college career, or to look forward to one in the pros. The baseball coach came up that spring, when I was about to sign a free agent contract with Dallas. He wanted me to wait until after the baseball season to sign, but Pam was expecting our first child and Dallas had offered $1000 to sign.

I needed the money.

One last college story. Pam and I got engaged at Christmas of my junior year.

That spring, Larry Gill, a halfback, and I go down to Athens, where Pam is in school. I am going to date Pam and Larry is going to date a girl from Americus named Carolyn Kinnebrew.

We take them out and bring them back for the midnight curfew. Then Larry and I went to The Varsity, a fast food place where you can get a hot dog in a hurry. It's like 12:30 A.M.

The Varsity had these little desks, like school desks, where you could sit and eat and watch TV. So I went through the line and got a couple hot dogs and went back in the corner and started watching TV, and all of a sudden I hear somebody say, "Aw, you're nothing but a high school punk."

I turned around, and Larry is talking to this big guy, this really big guy, and I realize who it is, and that there are four or five other big guys with him.

The guy plays for Georgia. He's a lineman. I've played against him, against all of them. They all play for Georgia, and this guy is Ray Rissmiller, an all American tackle from Pennsylvania, and this is the guy Larry is calling a "high school punk."

They've all had too much to drink. Larry came over and sat down.

"God, you can't believe those guys. They're just a bunch of high school punks," he said.

I was almost choking on my hot dog. "Larry, do you realize who those guys are? That's Ray Rissmiller. All those are guys we played against from the University of Georgia.

"I didn't know that. I thought they were in high school."

Well, about then, here we are, sitting in a corner. And here come these five football players, and they sit right in front of us, and one of them is egging Rissmiller on, trying to get him to punch Gill out.

And I'm sitting there thinking "We're gonna get killed. There's no way out. We're backed into this corner." But I knew a player who went to the University of Georgia, so I said, "Do y'all know Lee Roy Dukes?"

"Oh, yeah," one said. "We know him. How do you know him?"

I said, "We play football at South Carolina. We know who you guys are. We don't want to cause any trouble."

So we ended up being big buddies that night, patting each other on the back and going over to see this guy I knew.

Gill apologized.

# 6

## Americus: A State of Mind

I DON'T know exactly what I felt. I was a rookie, going to Thousand Oaks, California. I was a brand new professional football player, leaving the South for the first time.

And to say I was nervous would probably be understating things.

It was 1965. This was the height of civil rights action—voter registration, the march on Montgomery, growing protests, all of that.

Martin Luther King had been arrested during a voter registration drive in Americus, but they took him to Albany, Georgia. They weren't sure they could protect him in Americus.

Americus was my home. That's how people thought there when I was growing up. It was one way.

I had grown up with black children on our farm, played with them. But I had never been on an organized team with a black player or even played against one all through high school. There were no blacks on the team while I was at South Carolina.

And here I was, a rookie, from Americus, Georgia. It is about as deep South as you can get. We still get our mail from Andersonville, and if you remember your Civil War history, that was the site of the notorious Confederate prison.

It would be my first experience playing with blacks. I wondered:

What were they gonna say about playing with a kid from Georgia? And what was I gonna feel when I was dressing in the same locker room with a black player? How was that whole situation going to be?

I shouldn't have worried. When I got on the plane in Atlanta to fly to California, the first guy I saw was Jethro Pugh. I sat down next to him, and we visited all the way to California.

At Thousand Oaks, I met Cornell Green. He lockered right next to me. I was No. 30 and he was No. 34.

Now, as a rookie in almost any pro camp, you go in and there's a certain amount of hazing. They make you do all kinds of things. At evening meal, for instance, you gotta stand up and tell them who you are and where you are from and then you gotta sing a song. So every night that summer I'm standing up and saying, "I'm Dan Reeves, and I'm from Americus, Georgia, and I went to the University of South Carolina."

So they all knew. "Hey, here's a guy from the deep, deep South."

Three incidents that summer really brought home to me the racial climate of the time.

I was going to breakfast one morning, and I picked up a *Los Angeles Times,* and the headline said, "Riots Break Out in Americus, Georgia." It was during the voting registration drive, and somebody was driving through town and shot into a crowd and killed a white kid.

Some people were arrested, there was a trial going on, and my wife's dad ended up being foreman of that jury. So I'm walking to breakfast and reading about how W. D. White, foreman of the jury, says blah, blah, blah.

Well, everyone by then knew I was from Americus. I really started getting kidded for it. It wasn't vicious or anything, but I kept thinking about what was going on back home.

When our first preseason game came around, we were supposed to play the Rams in the Los Angeles Coliseum. They postponed the game.

The Watts riots had broken out, and the Watts area is right around the Coliseum. So they delayed the game from Saturday to the next Wednesday, and brought in National Guard troops and all.

That Wednesday, we were getting on the bus in Thousand Oaks to drive in to the game when Cornell Green got on and we sat together.

"Hey, Reeves," he said. "I want to make a deal with you."

I said okay.

He said, "You know, my people are causing all this trouble in Los Angeles. So I'll look after you in Los Angeles and make sure nothing happens to you. But, in three weeks, we're going to play the Minnesota Vikings. In Birmingham. In Alabama. I want you to look after me when we get to Birmingham."

Well, I thought that was a pretty good deal. It was a scary situation. Fires were still burning everywhere and only about 10,000 to 15,000 people came to the game. A few things were shouted from the stands, but it went all right.

In three weeks, then, we went to Birmingham to play the Vikings.

And, in my 16 years with Dallas, it was the only time that Coach Landry had everybody go to a movie together the night before a game. He wanted to make certain we all stayed together.

Birmingham was as scary in its way as Los Angeles had been. The summer prior to that one, Sam Cooke, a black artist, was doing a concert in Birmingham and people came on stage and beat Sam Cooke up. Right on stage.

Now, here we were, two professional football teams that had black players, coming in, staying in hotels in Birmingham.

So our black players were understandably scared. It was a bad time.

We got on the bus, and Cornell and I are sitting together, as usual. He really had taken me under his arm in Los Angeles, and we had developed a good friendship.

I didn't smoke too much, but I did smoke a cigarette at halftime. And if I got to the locker room first, I'd light two and have one ready for him when he got there. He'd do the same if he got there first.

I'm sitting on the bus, sitting next to him, and I'm thinking, "I'll look after him like he looked after me and everything will be fine."

We're driving to the movie. And we have a clown on the team by the name of Buddy Dial. We stop for a red light, right in the middle of downtown Birmingham, Alabama, with all these people walking around us in the city where they attacked Sam Cooke on the stage.

And we're waiting for the light to change. And Buddy Dial stands up, and he starts singing at the top of his voice, "We shall overcome."

Pretty soon, everybody on the bus joined in. I looked out. All these people are staring at this unmarked bus where people are singing "We Shall Overcome" in the middle of downtown Birmingham.

I turned to Cornell.

"You're on your own, Cornell," I said.

We got to the theater okay, of course, and there were no incidents except, like in Los Angeles, some loud mouths from the stands on game day. At the theater, we all had to sit in the balcony, the whole team, because they wouldn't let the black players sit downstairs.

Our black players even felt uncomfortable in the stadium the next night.

It was a strange summer.

It was also part of the way I began changing the way I regarded blacks. Back home, on our farm and in Americus, we didn't come in contact with blacks who had been to college, had degrees.

Our farm is six miles out of town. Americus itself had maybe 12,000 people in those years, the end of the 1950s, early 1960s. It has about 16,000 now. Americus is 140 miles south of Atlanta, 60 miles east of Columbus, 60 miles south of Macon, and 30 miles north of Albany.

It is right in the middle of the state, and like I said, we lived between Americus and Andersonville, and got our mail from the old Confederate prison site—Route 1, Andersonville, Georgia.

My granddaddy was raised in that country, and my dad met my mother in Rome, Georgia. I don't know how far back the family goes in that part of the country.

But, growing up there, on a farm where we mainly raised wheat and oats, plus some cotton and peanuts, I didn't know everybody didn't grow up that same way.

On our farm, we worked side by side with the black people. We had a family that lived on the farm with us. The mother's name was Willie Lou Waters, and she had 11 kids.

Ben Jackson lived on my granddaddy's farm about two miles down the road. He had a bunch of kids, too. He was also one of the smartest men I've ever known even though he didn't have even a first grade education.

He just had great common sense and great natural intelligence. I'm saying that because it was Ben who helped set the way I thought as I grew up.

On Sundays, we played together, whatever was in season. We played all Sunday afternoon until it was dark. It would be my two brothers, Charles and Butch, and my sister, Joanne. She was the best athlete in the family. She was always the first one chosen.

It didn't matter what sport it was. But if it was football season, we played football—tackle football—with no pads, and barbwire fence as a sideline. If it was basketball, we had a basketball goal, and we played on the dirt, and there were little rocks all over. You had to be a great dribbler to keep the ball from getting away from you.

That's how we spent Sundays. During the week, we all worked the fields together, and there were days we'd finish and I wouldn't go home to eat. I'd go to their house, the Jacksons' or the Waters', and eat there, and you just never thought anything about it.

That's the way it was. We chopped cotton, picked it, worked side by side. My daddy owned a road construction company and my grandfather was retired. We had about 275 acres on our farm, and then leased so much from other people we probably had 300 to 500 more, including my granddaddy's.

Ben helped run it. He had been raised in Milledgeville, and he was like a legend. He was about 6-1, and 235 pounds, and the strongest man I have ever known.

He was a great athlete. When I was playing ball in high school and was a fairly decent athlete, he used to tease me. He used to run. He'd turn around and be so far ahead of me he'd be running backwards. I'd be chasing him, and I couldn't catch him.

I've thought it was sad, that Ben never got to college, and wondered how great he would have been if he had.

Our farm had a creek running through it. There is some swamp land and some real rough country outside our boundary line. If a big rain comes, the debris coming down the creek washes the fence out, and your cattle or hogs or whatever would get out and go into the swamps, and you'd have to go in and get them back.

We'd have to spend a lot of time hunting, and sometimes you didn't get them all in. It was not uncommon for a steer to be lost in there for six or eight months, and they'd go a little wild on you in that time.

I remember once, I was about seven or eight, and we had caught a steer that had gotten away and gone half wild. It had short horns, probably five or six inches. We were going to take him to the sale barn for slaughter. My granddaddy and Ben have him in the loading pen, trying to get him to go up the chute and into the truck. They were loading this steer, and it gored my granddaddy, rammed him against the fence.

Ben ran over and grabbed that steer around its neck, and he started beating that steer with his bare fists, right in the middle of its head, right between its eyes.

Blood started shooting out the steer's nose. Ben killed that steer with his bare fists. Nobody messed with Ben. I mean, nobody messed with Ben.

From the time I was eight, I learned to drive a tractor, work with Ben. My granddaddy had started farming with a mule, and my daddy still had one, and he figured it would be good for me to know what it was like in the old days. So he made me plow with the mule all one summer.

I never thought that was fair, two legs against four. I remember the mule's name was January, because that's the month I was born. Mules are funny animals. You could start plowing, and if my dad was in the field, this mule would be fresh and step almost like it was running. I mean, you could hardly keep up with it.

Then my dad would drive out of the field, and it was like the mule knew. It would start slowing down, real slow, and whatever you did, it wouldn't go any faster. Then my dad would come back, and that darn mule would speed up.

And my dad couldn't understand why you hadn't plowed any more ground than you had. He figured you weren't working as hard as you should.

Ben, because of the way he treated me, he probably set the foundation for the relationships I have always had with black players. I learned so much from him, common sense, how to treat people.

So this is the way I grew up, not knowing there were other ways. We worked together during the week and we played together on Sundays, and that's how it was.

It began to change when we all got into organized sports. Playing at Americus High School, I never played with or against a black athlete, and it was the same in the summer leagues.

We had our first integration incident when I was a senior. A white family down on the other side of town owned a place and they had black families who lived on it, and they all ate together. There was a big deal about that in Americus. It was written up in Life Magazine.

And there was a boycott against that white family. They couldn't buy groceries in town or things like that. Also, at that time, if you didn't actually live in Americus, you had to pay tuition to go to the high school. A court order said the children of that family had to be allowed to go to the high school there.

They were escorted to school, and I can remember standing out in front of the school, watching this, hearing people hollerin' at them, and how badly I felt for them. Here were two kids the same age as me. I ate with black families all the time. I couldn't see what the whole thing was all about. I kind of ached for them.

So that was the first outright incident I can remember. When I went to South Carolina, again there were no blacks. I played against them for the first time when we played Northwestern the opening game of my sophomore season.

That would be 1962.

And again, because of those Sundays on the farm, I thought nothing of it. But there were a lot of things said on my team. You know, "We're gonna play these black guys." Only they didn't say black. They said, "We're gonna play these niggers, and we're gonna show 'em they don't belong in this game."

I can remember the opening kickoff they had a black guy who kicked off.

Most of the time nobody messes with the kickoff guy. We had one of our guys from North Carolina was gonna go after him. And I can remember a tremendous lick on this black guy that kicked off.

The University of Maryland recruited the first black player in our conference and we played against him a couple of years. And of course Nebraska had a number of blacks when we played them. But I don't remember anything being said after that first game.

One thing I do remember, though, is going to Maryland one year. One of our coaches had played at South Carolina, and we walked into the cafeteria and saw blacks and whites socializing, sitting together, eating together, and he couldn't handle it.

We had to put him on a bus and send him home before the game. He couldn't stand it.

Those were the barriers we had to cross in those years, the mindsets.

Probably half the Waters family still lives in the area. I just didn't see that old south mentality on our farm, and maybe Ben was part of that.

There's still a lot of people in the deep South have never seen a very educated, intelligent black person. But there also are a lot of white people who don't have high school diplomas or college degrees, either. It's both sides of the spectrum, and it's why, when you get into a wider environment like pro sports, your perspective changes.

It is what happened to me when I got to Dallas.

Because of Ben, I had been around very intelligent people, even if they didn't have a degree. But I had to get to Dallas to realize that. So you change your view from how you were raised.

I spoke at Kentucky State not too long ago. The president of Kentucky State is a black man, studied at Oxford, graduated from Harvard Law School. As a matter of fact, I went to Kentucky State because there's a woman from my home town, a black woman, who called me. She is Shirley Reese, a doctor of physical education.

Things don't heal overnight. You have to meet people and listen and become friends with people whose concepts and backgrounds are totally different from what you grew up with before your views are going to change.

Mine changed drastically when I went to Dallas.

You get into the world, and you see these things, and you change.

The perception of blacks in the South was they would always work on the farm and that's all they would ever do. And then you get out in the world, and all that changes.

If you look at your parents, their perceptions have probably changed, too. My dad's have. But he believes—and I agree with him—that blacks and whites put an awful lot of pressure on themselves where interracial marriages are concerned. You are putting extra pressure on your kids. But if it happens, if two people of different races fall in love, it doesn't make me mad or anything like that. It is just something I would advise against because of the eventual pressures it brings on the children.

The pressures *you* deal with are one thing. But to bring someone else, a child, into that, I don't think it makes sense.

But I would never hold it against anyone. You don't have any control over who you fall in love with. That's the tough part, the pressures that some unfair social problems can create.

But my folks have changed, and I have changed, and I think a lot of the South has changed.

We used to have an annual Halloween party at Dallas. One year, Lee Roy Jordan and I thought it would be funny if we made our own Ku Klux Klan outfits. We would come as dragons of the Ku Klux Klan.

We rode down the freeway without the hats on, but with the sheets around us and people were looking at us strange.

A lot of people—Cornell, Jethro, Bob Hayes—thought they were real. The reaction was funny. I don't know if they objected. Looking back, it was an insensitive thing to do. But on our team in those years, the kind of situation we had, we could do that.

We had a party after every home game. In those same years, about 1966, I was asked to speak at a Cleveland Touchdown Club function so I had to stay over after the game. I can remember going to their team party, and they were totally segregated. Blacks went in one room and whites went in another.

I thought to myself, "This is Cleveland, which is up north where everything is supposed to be integrated, yet these guys aren't getting along together."

The same thing happened the next year, in St. Louis. Blacks in one room, whites in another. Later, it came out there were real racial problems on the Cardinals in those years. I was an outsider, but I could feel the friction.

We didn't have that in Dallas. I'm not saying that everything was lovey-dovey, but we got along. We went to each others' homes.

It wasn't like we went out together every weekend, but we did occasionally. It was a social thing of the times, and they were changing. Schools were being integrated, there was still a lot of unrest, and we had black players who still, even then, were scared to drive, say, from Georgia to Texas because it meant having to go through Alabama and Mississippi.

You had to be able to sit and talk to start to understand. I think athletics really and truly have been one of the things that helped eliminate some of the barriers that were so strong. Not that we are where we want to be or should be, but certainly we have made progress, and I think sports has been one area that has served as a bridge.

I think it happened for some of the black players, too. They saw this kid from Americus, Georgia, who was supposed to hate blacks and make slaves of them and so forth, and learned we weren't like that. That when Willie Lou cried, we cried. She helped raise me.

She was in charge when mother wasn't around. She disciplined us just like mom, and we took it for granted.

I suppose it is the basis for how I have approached hiring since I have been a head coach. I won't hire a guy because he is black or white. I hire mostly from college staffs, because I want a guy first of all who is a good teacher, and I think that is the way we are eventually going to get more good black coaches in the National Football League.

We have had three blacks on our staff at Denver. Charlie West and

Charlie Lee were the first. I hired both of them out of college, because they were the best guys I could find for their positions. I didn't hire them because they were black. Charlie Lee was a running back coach from the University of Texas, and Charlie West was a proven pro, had been coaching at California, and had played here for Joe Collier. He knew our system, and, like Charlie Lee, he was the best guy we could find, the best qualified. So is Mo Forte. When we lost a number of our offensive coaches this spring, I hired Mo out of North Carolina A&T to coach our running backs. I did not hire him as a black coach. I hired him as the best coach I could find.

They were good coaches, good teachers. But to deny there is something to the Good Ol' Boys Network is wrong, too. It is part of it.

You are going to hire people you are comfortable with. In a lot of situations here, I have hired people that I didn't even know. I've got scouts out in the field, and they aren't just looking at players. I ask them to keep an eye out for good, qualified coaching candidates. If I lose one, who do you recommend?

I want to know who is doing a great job of coaching, of teaching. That's the way I'm going. I've had more success hiring college coaches than I have interviewing people who have played pro ball.

To me, college coaches teach. Pro football players have to be taught just like college players. If you are assuming pro players know all the fundamentals you are making a big mistake. You have to go in and teach every year.

I was very fortunate in the way I was brought along, in getting to work and watch a great coaching staff and Coach Landry.

You hire people because you are comfortable with them and because they are qualified. It's very hard to hire someone because of their race. I have had white coaches who have not done the job I wanted done since I have been here. I don't want to hire those kind. It is easy to hire them. Firing them is the hard part, no matter the color of the skin.

I don't deal with players that way, either. We have quality people. You couldn't have the feeling this tcam does if we had black and white problems.

There aren't any barriers here. I think that all started with Ben.

# 7

# Pam

OKAY. I can remember the first time I ever saw Pam. We were out practicing, getting ready for the football season. I was on the B team. I was brought up about midseason that year.

It was my sophomore year, Pam's freshman year, and the head cheerleader was the one that told me about her.

She said, "I got this girl that I want you to date. She's a cheerleader this year, a freshman." This head cheerleader and I rode the school bus together. She lived out in the country, too. Wadean Bradley was her name. You don't know many Wadean's do you?

Anyway, that was the year we were practicing in preseason one day and the cheerleaders walked across the end of the practice field to go over to the stadium to practice cheering. I saw Pam for the first time and I remember thinking what a cute girl she was.

And of course the furthest thing from my mind was being able to date her. She was too purty, too good lookin' for a country boy like me.

And I was on the school bus one day and Wadean and I had gone to the same country school and she said, "Hey, I've got a real cute girl I think you ought to date. Her name is Pam White."

So I said, "Gosh, that's the same cheerleader I saw at practice that day." It took me, I don't know, maybe a week to work up the courage to call her. I remember calling her and said, "Pam, this is Dan Reeves. Do you have a date for this Friday night?"

And she said, "No, Tuck, I don't." Everybody called me Tuck, but I didn't think she knew me well enough to know my nickname.

So we had our first date. My dad and my older brother weren't real helpful to me. Her dad was a former state trooper. They told me how tough he was, so I was already scared to death when I walked through the door. Her dad by then was head of the housing authority.

I remember knocking on the door and sure enough, her dad came to the door and he didn't have a smile on his face or anything. He introduced himself and I introduced myself, and then the first thing he said was "I want her home at 11 o'clock. And she better be here at 11 o'clock." I guarantee you, I always had her home on time. He had that effect on me when I first started dating Pam. But after I got to know him, I learned to love and respect him.

I was a year younger than anybody else in my class. I was too young to drive, so I had to double date all the time. I can't remember who we double dated with that first date. It was with some guy I played football with.

She lived about two blocks from the school and yet she drove to the school. I always thought she was wealthy. I didn't realize until we got married she wasn't. That's a private joke.

The first date we had we went to a sock hop. All the boys were on one side of the room and all the girls on the other, and we never did dance all night. The boys would talk about huntin'. I don't think she was interested in hunting at all.

She was a cheerleader and yet she didn't know a heck of a lot about football. She knew enough to know when to make the yells whether we were on offense or defense, but not a lot more than that.

I can remember it was like the fourth date before I ever kissed her. I remember taking her home, double dating with somebody, and we were in the back seat and I was working up enough nerve to finally kiss her right in front of the high school.

Like I said, that was only two blocks from her house and time was runnin' out. It was one of those real quick kisses.

We dated all through high school. It was one of those deals where we never necessarily went steady. We both dated other people. But whenever it was something special we both kind of assumed we'd go together.

We had some arguments and some bad times. I can remember talking to her on the telephone. You call every night. It was nothing to have a minute or two minutes of silence, nothing being said, just silence on the phone trying to think of something to say and she was trying to think of something to say.

There wasn't a lot to do in a little town like that. You basically went to a movie. And it had a putt putt golf course and a place where we all went for soft drinks and milk shakes and stuff like that. It was called The Varsity, and it was where everybody hung out.

We had some great times.

I wouldn't change those times for anything. When I went off to South Carolina she had another year of high school, and of course that was part of the decision.

I knew I was going to be a long ways from her. I knew as pretty as she was—she was Miss Everything there, Miss Americus High School, most popular—so I knew that was going to be tough. Long distance romance. I am not a great letter writer but I wrote to her pretty regular and she would write back. We dated when I would come home.

After my first year at South Carolina I came home in the spring. Americus was playing in the state baseball tournament. Somehow I found out Pam and her best friend, a girl named Frances Hogg, had gone to the beach the summer before.

The guy that was coaching the other team was down at the beach, and they had told him they were in school in Auburn. That really bothered me, that she was trying to date an older man.

I was driving home from the game, and I was daydreaming. I was thinking about that. You know how your mind just plays tricks on you. I had made that six mile drive so many times before it was almost automatic. I'm behind this big semi-trailer, and there is a curve we used to call the Cancer Curve.

I said to myself, "I'll pass this truck once I get past this curve." Now, as soon as you get past the curve there is a hill.

I started around the truck and I'm about even with the truck and I look up and there is a car coming at me. I mean dead at me. So I slam on the brakes. The car spun all the way around, headed back the way I had just come. It hit the shoulder of the road. The dirt and grass and all came flying through the window.

I was facing back the other way when the car finally came to a stop there in the grass, down in the ditch at the side of the road and I can remember sitting there, holding the steering wheel, and somebody came up to the window. They knew me. I can't remember who it was. To this day, I do not know who it was that was driving the car I almost hit. They had seen me coming and stopped.

If the car had kept coming we would have hit head on. To this day I don't know who it was. They asked me if I was all right. I remember how tight I held that steering wheel. I could have bent that steering wheel.

And I was thinking that was a heck of a way to get killed, thinking about the girl that you're dating, daydreaming.

As I said, we both dated other people. I had been elected president of Boys State. And to be elected is one of those political type things, you have to know people from other schools and all. I had met people from Hi Ys across the state. It is a Christian organization in high school.

One of those I met happened to be a girl from Dawson, Georgia, about 25 miles from Americus. She was a basketball player and a pretty girl. I had met her and dated her a couple of times. My freshman year at South Carolina she called me. Her mother was seriously ill and was in the hospital at Augusta, Georgia.

The girl was going to nurses school in Augusta. She was really upset. I was about an hour or an hour and fifteen minutes from there. So I drove down to see her and see how her mother was doing. And while I was there somehow it was mentioned she was going to be home for Christmas.

I said great. "When you get home and I get home, we'll have a date the Friday night we get home." She said good.

Several weeks later I go home for Christmas, and while I am home, like I said, it was assumed Pam and I would go to the big things together. There was a big Christmas dance. I had forgotten about it until Pam's mother mentioned one day, "Are you going to ask Pam to the Christmas dance?"

"Oh, sure." So I called Pam and asked her. She was a little mad because I hadn't asked her the first chance after I got home. But she said no she didn't have a date and I said, "Good, we'll go to the Christmas dance."

So my cousins, Jerry Reeves and Bob Reeves and I are out hunting one day. Quail hunting. And we're talking about the Christmas dance.

"Who're you taking?"

"Oh, I'm taking Pam. Who're you takin'?"

And I said, "By the way, when is that Christmas dance?"

"Friday night."

"Friday night?" Then it hit me. "Gosh. I have a date with another girl Friday night." So now I am in a dilemma. I have two dates and I'm trying to figure out what's best. So I figure Pam will understand if I tell her I didn't realize it was Friday night.

Well, that was a big mistake. I called, and I mean it was all over. "I'm never dating you again. Come by and take your pictures. And take back your charms and everything else you ever gave me."

I did, and boy, her daddy was mad. "You hurt my daughter. Don't you ever come by here again." I mean, it was bad.

And I felt bad because I was the one who really made the mistake. That was the first time we really broke up. So we didn't date for an entire year before we started dating again. We got engaged between my junior year and senior year. She was going to the University of Georgia by that time.

I can remember the first time I saw her after we had broken up. She was going to Georgia Southwestern College, a junior college in Americus, her freshman year. Then she transferred to the University of Georgia.

My junior year, the week before we played the University of Georgia, I got hit in the eye. I had gone back to pass and got hit and the ball came loose and I dove for the ball and this guy from Maryland dove on me and his face mask came through and hit me in the eye.

When I got up I could see blood. But when I wiped my eye, I couldn't see blood on my hand. I stayed in on defense and they ended up scoring just before the half. We went in at the half and I kept wiping my eye but I couldn't wipe it off.

I had hemorrhaged on the inside of the eye. So they hospitalized me for the week before the Georgia game. For the entire week I lay in the bed from Saturday night to the following Friday. They blindfolded me. I couldn't see anything for those six days. It was my left eye. They took the bandages off and it was just like you see in the movies.

They take them off, unwind them, and you're going, "Oh, gosh! I hope I can see!" It was that type thing.

When they took them off I remember looking out my window. It was October and all the trees were brown and yellow and all the beautiful colors. There was a tree right outside my window. I can remember that was the first thing I saw, that tree. I can remember thinking how beautiful the colors were. It was one of those things you took for granted until you were blindfolded for six days.

Anyway, I got out of the hospital and got permission to make the trip with the team. This was the first time since I played in the Georgia High School All Star game that I was able to play in the state of Georgia.

In my four years at South Carolina, that was the only game I missed. I can remember going down and wanting to play very badly. Coach Bass was the coach. He's on the staff here in Denver now. He said that if I exerted myself I possibly could cause that eye to rupture again and possibly lose sight in that eye.

The eye felt fine. I didn't have any problems with it. So I got my roommate, John Breeden, who was a tight end, and he and I wrestled in the room for about 45 minutes. I mean we were wringing wet with sweat. We rolled over the bed there, the floor, wrestling because I wanted to check my eye out, see if it was all right.

So, sure enough. It didn't bother me at all. So I went running down to Coach Bass' room and woke him up. "Coach, my eye doesn't bother me and we been wrestling for 45 minutes to an hour. I know I can exert myself. I want to play tomorrow."

And of course Coach Bass wanted me to play, too. So he gets the doctors up. The doctors come down and say, "No way. We aren't going to be responsible for his eye. There is no way we are going to okay it."

So we go to the game, and as I walk on the field I look up, and there was a walkway across the end of the stadium and I said, "That's Pam."

So I walked up and that's the first time I had seen her in the year since we had broken up.

I could tell that was her even though it was a long ways away. I knew that was her. So I walked over and started talking to her. That season right before Christmas, every night I dreamed about her. For about a solid week. I got up enough nerve to call her at the University of Georgia, and found out when she was going to go home for Christmas.

She was going home a week before I was. It was like five hours from Columbia to Americus, Georgia. I said, "Could I come by and pick you up and take you home?"

She said sure. So I went by and picked her up and took her home and had a date with her. First date we'd had in over a year. And then we went out and I asked her to marry me. We were engaged that Christmas and planned to marry that June.

We got married in June and then found out at Christmas that she was expecting. I signed with the Cowboys and went to training camp that year and by the time I made the team she was too far along to go to Dallas. The doctor wouldn't let her travel. So actually Dana was born in Americus.

It was after we had played the opening game of the season. I think it was a Wednesday.

I can remember Pam calling me and she said, "I just want you to know that you are the father of a little girl. Goodbye."

"Wha...?" That was it. But she was still all doped up. So her father got on the phone and told me we had a little girl, everything was fine and Pam was doing great. We played our next game against the Washington Redskins.

We were going to play the St. Louis Cardinals next. I went to Coach Landry and asked if I could fly to Americus after the Washington game and see Pam and Dana and then fly back.

He said, "Well, that's fine. We aren't going to practice tomorrow, so why not stay the extra day and just come back to start practice the next day?"

So I go home. We had won the game. I had played a little bit, completed a halfback pass. I had scored a touchdown. I was excited, and had made the team as a running back, which I had never played before. I was excited flying to Atlanta but I was more excited about the baby.

I drove to Americus from Atlanta and got there about three o'clock in the morning and awakened Pam and the baby. I got to bed about seven o'clock that morning and finally got to sleep and the phone rang.

It was Coach Landry. His secretary was calling. We were going to have a meeting and I needed to get back. So I turned right around and flew back to Dallas. I had gotten to see Dana and Pam just briefly.

Then, in about three weeks she and her mother drove to Texas with the baby and we got a little apartment in Dallas where a lot of the Cowboys players and their wives lived. Lee Roy Jordan, Dave Manders, Perry Lee and Lila Jo Dunn lived in this complex. You can tell they were from the South.

I can remember one Saturday morning we had practice and I came home and Pam wanted to go shopping. She left me there with Dana. It was the first time I had her alone. I fed her, and then I can remember lying on the floor, playing with her, throwing her up in the air and she just threw up all over me.

And I had to change her diapers. She was crying. I had never changed her before and they were messy. So I put her underneath the faucet in the sink and held her in one hand and washed her off. It was the only way I could figure it out.

That was a long Saturday. I felt like Pam was never going to get home that day.

# DALLAS
# YEARS

## Part III

# 8

# 1965–1966: The Apprenticeship

I EXPERIENCED basically the same things going into pro football that I had coming out of high school and going into college:

I was ignored.

There wasn't a lot of interest in me. I was a quarterback, a rollout type quarterback. Teams that talked to me before the draft were more interested in signing me as a defensive back.

Or perhaps trying me at running back or wide receiver. But none of them mentioned me being a quarterback. And after being a quarterback all my life I would have loved to have had the opportunity to be tried as a quarterback. You always think you have the ability to do those things. But, also, I just wanted the opportunity to get to play pro football.

I thought I would be drafted. There's a story out that the Los Angeles Rams started to draft me, but their owner was named Dan Reeves, and he thought that people would think it was a publicity stunt. So they didn't. I ended up a free agent.

Right after the draft, I was contacted by the San Diego Chargers, and they sent a guy down. His name was Bud Asher. His brother, by the way, was a sports writer for the *Atlanta Constitution*. His name was Gene.

Bud Asher owned the Thunderbird Motel at Daytona Beach, Florida, but he also had a semi-pro team down there, the Daytona Thunderbirds, and he had this association with the San Diego Chargers. So he came in and took me out to dinner. He said he couldn't take Pam out, too. I didn't care for that, but I ended up going out with him. He said they wouldn't try me at a running back. They already had Paul Lowe and Keith Lincoln, and they were the best in the business. They had just won the American Football League championship, and if I made the team, it was going to be strictly as a defensive back.

He offered me like $500 to sign and a $10,000 contract. I told him I would think about it. I was meeting with the Dallas Cowboys the next day. I would see what they had to offer.

"Let me make a phone call," he said. Well, he wasn't gone but a minute or so. I knew he hadn't made a phone call because he wasn't gone long enough, but he came back and said, "Well, we'll give you $1,500 and $12,000, and that's as far as I can go. That's our final offer."

I told him I still wanted to talk to the Cowboys. I met with a guy named Harvey Robinson. He had coached at Tennessee and was just a neat gentleman. He took Pam and me out to eat, and he was the kind of guy that said, "Look, when you get this money, you need to invest it for the future. You need to think about your life after football." He was just a nice gentleman who made Pam and me feel very comfortable.

They offered us $1,000 to sign and an $11,000 contract. We agreed to sign with them, and it was basically because of the type of person he was.

I also felt that if I tried it in the National Football League and didn't make it, there was a chance I might get picked up by somebody in the younger league, but that if I went to the AFL and didn't make it, it would probably be over for me. So that was another reason for signing the way I did.

The day after I had signed, Detroit called and wanted to sign me as a quarterback. I kinda had that hurt in my stomach. "Boy, I wish I could at least have tried that." But that was the last time quarterback was ever mentioned for me in professional football for a long, long time.

Dallas at that time had signed Jerry Rhome, and he had led the nation in passing. And they had signed Craig Morton, who was No. 2 or something like that. So they had two outstanding quarterback prospects on the team, plus Don Meredith as the starter.

To celebrate my signing, Pam and I bought a bottle of champagne, and iced it down in the kitchen sink. We were living in a little old married students apartment there at the University. A friend of mine named Ira Solomon had a girl friend named Tootsie (I can't think of her last name) and they came over that night to play bridge and drink the champagne and celebrate.

Well, Pam and Tootsie each had about a half glass of champagne and both of them went back in the bedroom and laid down on the bed and went to sleep. Ira and I stayed up 'til late that night, playing gin rummy. And that's how I celebrated by first pro contract.

I worked out that summer with a couple of guys from South Carolina who had played pro ball, Ed Holler and Alex Hawkins. Holler was a linebacker for the Green Bay Packers and Hawkins was a running back and special teams player for the Baltimore Colts. Holler talked me into taking a P.E. class.

He's now an agent, by the way. He represented our former punter, Chris Norman.

We went through and took this P.E. class, and I'll never forget how amazed I was that there were so many people who could not do a sit-up or a push-up. That stunned me. I didn't know there were people like that. I had always been around athletes and that kind of thing was taken for granted.

I had always been in athletic classes. This was the first time I had been in a regular P.E. class with students who were not athletes. It was a great P.E. class. We ran 440s and we ran the half mile, we ran the mile—every day we'd do something. It really did get me in great shape.

I got to work some as a receiver with Alex Hawkins. He helped me on that. I worked some as a defensive back, learning to do both, because I really didn't know where the Cowboys were going to try me.

Dallas had told me when they signed me that, "Hey, we'll sign you as a safety. But we'll try you everywhere. We'll give you a chance." That was another reason I had been intrigued by them, because I knew I would get the chance somewhere.

I roomed with a guy named Jerry Don Balch from Texas Tech. I thought I was country until I met Jerry Don. He talked more Southern than I did. He led the mile, and after we got through running the mile, Jerry Don went over and ran alongside a running back named Jim Zanios from Texas Tech, trying to get him through the test, too.

Jerry Don smoked Marlboro cigarettes. I thought, "My gosh. How can this guy be in this kind of shape and still run like he does?" He could run forever it seemed like.

But he got cut pretty early. We roomed together for like 10 days. Then I roomed with a guy named Obert Logan, who ended up making our team. He was a free agent from Trinity University. He ended up starting that year as a rookie at safety. He played two or three years and was a very popular player with Dallas. "Little O" they called him. We roomed together, and of course we thought somebody was going to knock on our door every day. I just knew it.

First of all, they had me as a defensive back. I was playing defensive safety and I would get up there in man to man coverage and I mean it was difficult for me to cover anybody. I didn't have that kind of speed. In college I had been more or less a free safety and they had me at strong safety. I was about 207 pounds and they felt like I was the size for a strong safety.

So I worked there, and we went over and scrimmaged the Los Angeles Rams that first week. They hadn't cut anybody that first week. The first time I worked as a running back was getting ready for that scrimmage. We were going to work strictly on defense in that scrimmage, and then later they would come to our place at Thousand Oaks and they would work on defense and we would be on offense.

So they put extra guys over on offense to run plays that the Rams were going to run. That was the first time I played running back. And I made a couple of runs. So we went over to Fullerton and scrimmaged the Rams. We did pretty good and I had a decent scrimmage. We just had so many players you were scared to death. We must have had a hundred rookies in camp that year. You worried about getting cut, and there were a lot of guys did get cut next day.

So that made you even more frightened. I would call Pam every night. She was expecting our first baby and I was trying to keep up to date. So as soon as the meetings were over at night I would call her and let her know how I was doing and find out how things were with her. And of course I was homesick and scared to death and all those things.

All those fears everybody talks about—you have 'em. Your stomach doesn't feel real good all the time and you are trying extra hard all the time.

So then, the next week, the Rams are coming to Thousand Oaks, and we are going to be on offense all the time and they are going to be on defense. We had a lot of injuries, so I ended up being with the first unit on offense as a running back. We scrimmaged 15 plays and didn't do too good. We didn't move the ball much.

So I go out and the next group comes in and they go 15 plays and they don't move it much, either. We've only got about three running backs. Jimmy Sidle was the third running back. He was a high draft choice and a quarterback from Auburn. Dallas was going to try him at running back, too.

I remember the first day, when we went through the mile tests and the other things, they paired me off with him. I outran him in the 40. He had been drafted in the fourth round and I had been a free agent.

I ran a 4.6 in the 40. And that's an interesting story itself. That's the fastest time I ever ran it. Most of the time I was 4.65, something like that. After that, Gil Brandt, who was in charge of personnel, called me into his office one day.

"We've got a time of 5.2 on you from college," he said.

"Nobody ever timed me in the 40 when I was at South Carolina," I told him.

"Have you ever met a scout named Hamp Poole?"

"No, I never have." Well, this scout supposedly timed me in the 40. He must have timed me when we were running after practice, sprints or something.

So I ended up running a 4.6 at the Dallas camp that summer, and Poole's wrong time ended up costing me a bunch of money. I probably would have been drafted. Not high, but I probably would have been drafted except for the fact that the 5.2 in the 40 probably got circulated around, like it does.

So that's one reason that now that I'm coaching, I have my scouts time everybody. And if something like that happens, that scout won't be with me very long. It hurts the kid. And it gives you wrong information you might use to evaluate him.

So, anyway, Jimmy Sidle is the third running back. So they told our group to loosen up. Now, you've got to realize that at Thousand Oaks it is cool. There is an opening in the mountains that leads to the ocean, and that ocean breeze comes through there all the time. The wind is blowing all the time and you can sit around and get stiff awful fast.

So that group goes on the field and like the first or second play, Jimmy Sidle gets hurt.

"Reeves!" they holler. All I can do is kind of stretch and loosen up while I'm in the huddle. The first play they called was a pass, with me running a little shoot route, a little pass out in the flat. So I ran out in the flat and the defensive linebacker tried to intercept the ball, cut in front of me. He barely missed it and I ended up catching the ball.

I turned down the sideline and the only thing left is the secondary people. The guy misses me, and I go like 65 yards for the touchdown. But as I get around the 10 yard line, the only time I had a pulled muscle the whole time I played football, I tore my hamstring. I mean, I could hear it pop just like a rifle going off.

I fell into the end zone.

That really frightened me. I knew the chances of coming back from an injury. Every day you miss really hurts you.

I was 207 pounds at the time. Don Cochren and Larry Gardner were our two trainers, and they were great trainers. That was their first year. They put me on a treatment program. I got in the whirlpool about four times a day.

I came back and started practicing seven days later, after a real bad hamstring pull. I mean, everything had turned black, all the way from my rear end all the way down to the back of my knee.

It bothered me the whole year. Every time I started to jump over somebody, every time I started to kick my leg it bothered me all that season. But I was able to come back and practice.

And after that scrimmage, Dallas started to move me around. They moved me to outside receiver. Then I would play three or four days there and the next thing I knew they would move me back to defense. Then they would move me back to running back.

I had two play books, the offensive and defensive play book. And I just kept moving around. Come to find out later, every time, Ermal Allen the backfield coach would say, "Well, I don't think he can make it as a running back." Then Dick Nolan, who coached the defensive backs would say, "Well, I think I can use him as a defensive back."

Then he would use me for a couple days on defense, and they would come down to another cut, and Red Hickey, the receivers coach, would say, "Well, let's try him as a receiver."

They were trying to keep me around. They thought I could play, but they didn't see any place in particular that I could play. That's kind of how I hung on. I played on special teams. We played the *Times* Charity game, the one postponed by the Watts riots. Then we went back to play the Salesmanship Club game in Dallas, and that was the biggest crowd I had ever played in front of. There were almost 70,000 (67,954) people in the Cotton Bowl for the preseason game against the Packers, who were one of the strongest teams in the league.

I made a couple tackles on special teams and we beat them 21-12. That was a big lift for us. They were a championship team and we played it like it was a regular season game. So I made a couple tackles covering punts and was really getting to play a lot of special teams but not as a running back.

Then we went to Birmingham to play the Vikings. As we were getting off the bus, Coach Ermal Allen said, "Tonight, we're going to find out whether you can play or not. You're going to play the first and third quarters, and Amos Marsh is going to play the second and fourth quarters."

You talk about butterflies. I must have gone to the bathroom 15 times before that game ever started. I was nervous and excited. My folks had driven over from Georgia. Pam came. Her mother and daddy came.

Minnesota played its first team virtually the whole game and we played mostly rookies. They beat us to death. In the second quarter, Amos Marsh got hurt, so I ended up playing the whole ball game. The only good thing about the ball game was that, again on the same basic play where I scored in that Ram scrimmage, I went out in the flat, the linebacker tried to intercept, I caught the pass, turned down the sideline, made a couple good moves to get past the secondary, and I scored.

Well, when you get beat 52-17, you don't think a lot about what you did. You are not too excited about your chances of making the football team. I just knew I was going to be cut that next week. We were getting down to 44 or 45.

I remember getting on the bus after the game. I was really disappointed, and knew I was going to be cut, and I was really low. Because Pam and my folks were there and we had stood around outside talking, I was the last one to get on the bus. There was only one seat left.

So I sit down by this man and I have no idea who he is. We ride back to the airport and everything is kind of quiet. This guy says, "God. I can't believe we get beat that bad. I worked so hard to get this thing, finally get them to agree to televise it back to Dallas, and we play like that."

I am furious at this guy. I had never seen him. He had never been around. So when we got on the plane, I asked Meredith, "Who is that little bitty guy back there? He really made me mad on the bus."

"Why, that's our owner. That's Clint Murchison. What'd you say to him?"

I hadn't said anything. Thank goodness.

We had played as hard as we could. We played a lot of rookies. We knew we probably weren't going to win the game. We weren't happy with the score, either. But they played Carl Eller and Marshall and Tarkenton and Mason and Brown—all those guys played the whole ball game. And we were playing Craig Morton and Jerry Rhome and me and all the other rookies. We must have had 16 or 17 rookies make the team that year.

After the game Norm Van Brocklin had said Dallas was about where Minnesota was three or four years ago. Well, that made Coach Landry so mad. We had come into the league the year before Minnesota. And here was Van Brocklin saying Dallas was about where Minnesota was three years ago.

They didn't beat us for five years after that. That article appeared on our bulletin board every time we were going to play the Vikings. It got us fired up. It made us mad, too.

After Birmingham, we flew home and I just knew I was going to get cut. We were going to play our last preseason game against the Chicago Bears in Tulsa, Oklahoma. They had had an excellent preseason, and they also had two rookies everybody was talking about— Gale Sayers and Dick Butkus.

I ended up alternating every other play, bringing in the play, alternating with Perry Lee Dunn. I made a couple tackles again, but the thing I remember most was, that on one of them, Jon Arnett was returning a punt.

I'm the end man. As I come off the line I try to get away from the first guy and he cuts me on the ground. I get up and they are double teaming what we call the gunner (end man) on punt coverage—that's me. I get up off the ground and he knocks me over about four or five yards. I fight him off and I'm getting closer to the sideline. And all of a sudden the next guy, the guy that cut me originally, hits me and knocks me out of bounds.

He knocks me into the Chicago bench. And here comes Jon Arnett, getting in behind the wall. And I really don't know. Can I tackle this guy or not? Am I allowed to come back into the play from out of bounds?

Am I eligible to come off the sideline and make a tackle? I figure I might as well make a tackle if I get a chance. I finally made the tackle, but he had made a 30 or 40 yard run. All I am thinking about flying back after the game is, "They are going to see that on film. Is that going to end up getting me cut?"

I make the team. I am really excited. I call Pam and I am really excited. We are going to open up against the New York Giants. It's funny, how you know you have made the team.

Nobody called me. That's how you learn. It was by going to the first meeting and still having your playbook and nobody had said "Bring your playbook and go see Coach Landry."

So there you are in the meeting on the first Tuesday morning of the regular season, with your playbook, and you know you've survived.

I was scared to death that morning. They had cut up to 9:30 or 10 that morning. I was sitting there, on the edge of my bed, just knowing there was going to be that knock on the door and that was going to be it.

I hadn't slept the night before, and I know I didn't eat. I have never been able to eat a pregame meal. My stomach gets too nervous. So as we go through practice I can't wait to go call Pam and tell her I made the final cut.

I didn't know a lot about the Dallas Cowboys. Being from the South, I'd watched the Washington Redskins, and I knew the Giants and I knew the Colts and I knew the Packers. But Dallas was a new team I didn't know a lot about. When I got there, they had never had a winning season.

There were a lot of new players there that year, and some of their veteran players were old guys they had gotten from other teams. But they had moved the football, always had a great offense. And they had been picked by *Sports Illustrated*. Every year they were picked to win it and never even had a winning season.

The rumors the year before all had Coach Landry being fired, but Mr. Murchison had given him a 10 year contract instead. That's the kind of owner Mr. Murchison was.

We were getting ready to open against the New York Giants that week, and I am scheduled to play some. I'm going to alternate some, bring in plays. We play our first game, and we beat them, 31–2. I threw a halfback pass to Frank Clarke, ended up scoring a touchdown.

We get ready to play the next week, and I get a call on Wednesday morning that Dana was born. Pam was on the phone. I had gone ahead and gotten an apartment for us. I had gone out with Biddie Jordan, Lee Roy Jordan's wife, looking for a place for us.

We picked out a little duplex with an upstairs-downstairs apartment in it. I was there when she called that morning.

That's when she said, "I just want you to know that you are the daddy of a 7 pound, whatever it was, 15 ounce, little girl. Bye." That's when I got permission from Coach Landry for a short trip to Americus that was cut even shorter than I expected.

About the third or fourth week of the season, Dallas cuts two players, two rookies, who have made the team. This is about the time Pam comes out with the baby.

I mean, it scared me to death. I didn't realize they cut people after the season started. Most people don't. But Dallas was still in kind of a transition period in those years and they were trying to pick up players here and there where they were weak. So they released two players. Two rookies. And I mean it scared me. I went through the rest of the season scared to death, just like training camp.

We made it through the year, and went to play the New York Giants. And if we can win, we finish second and go to the Playoff Bowl, that game they had in those years for teams that finished second in the two conferences.

Sure enough, we ended up beating the Giants. Jethro Pugh blocked a field goal and Obert Logan ran it back for a touchdown. That clinched a 7-7 record, the first time ever that Dallas had reached .500. And it clinched second place in the Eastern Conference, behind the Cleveland Browns.

So we played the Baltimore Colts in Miami in the Playoff Bowl. After a couple of times in that thing we started calling it the Toilet Bowl, because that's really what it was, a nothing game. But that first time it was exciting for us.

The wives come down for the game, and we think we can win. They don't have Johnny Unitas as quarterback. Tom Matte is going to play quarterback. He's a running back, and he's got the plays written on tape on his wrist.

They beat the heck out of us. They beat us 35-3. I mean they shut us down. They didn't only beat us, they embarrassed us. Through the latter half of the season we had gone into a four wide receiver kind of thing with Don Perkins the only running back and Don Meredith rolling out. It was almost like the run and shoot, passing on every down.

Baltimore blitzed us. We didn't have it protected. They almost killed Meredith in the ball game. In the second half we went back to a normal set but that didn't help. Their defense was so fired up. They felt like they should have beaten the Packers for the championship and they wanted to prove it and they did.

So the year kind of ended on a sour note. Really and truly, we didn't have a running game. And now I am worried about how long a career am I going to have in this league.

Going into the next season, Dallas decides to move Mel Renfro, a defensive back and the league's leading punt returner, to running back. They move him to offense, and I don't even get a call from them.

Instead, I get a letter that offers me 90 percent of what I made the year before. I didn't sign it. I said, "I can't believe they are offering me less." I didn't sign it. I started to. I wanted to play.

We go to training camp in the summer of 1966, and I am working behind Mel Renfro at running back. They had really done some interesting things to try and use the skills of Mel. They put him out at wide receiver, put him in motion a lot. They moved him around and tried to cause the defense some problems.

Because I was backing him up, I was working in those same areas and it really kind of suited me. I could do a lot of things—I could catch the ball, I could run routes. We were gonna move Bob Hayes inside at times and split me outside. We had a lot of things that were really gonna cause the defense problems.

So we had it all set up for Mel Renfro to be the starting running back, and he was averaging like 5.7 a carry in preseason. Then he gets his ankle hurt. Mel was only about 5-10 and 175 or 180 pounds. But he gets his ankle hurt against Minnesota in a preseason game in Dallas.

I go in to take his place. I had a pretty good game and ended up getting the game ball. It was really uncertain at that time whether Mel was going to be able to come back off that ankle injury and be able to open the season against the Giants.

As it turned out, he made it back and ended up starting the game. But he got hurt early in the ball game and I went in. We beat the Giants 52-7. I've still got a watch I got for that game. I scored four touchdowns. It was a record for Dallas at that time. I got an engraved watch with the score and everything.

Now I am playing some because Mel is hurt. I scored a couple touchdowns against Minnesota the next week and after two weeks, I am leading the league in scoring.

So, when Renfro got well—well, wait—there are some things about the Minnesota game I remember. They were picked to win the Western Conference going into the season. They had a good team with Tarkenton and Mason and Brown and Eller and Marshall and Page and Hilgenberg and Warwick and all those great defensive players.

We played them, and they never played an even defense the whole ball game. They played an overshift or undershift defense the whole game. But, right before the half, Meredith hit Bob Hayes on a long touchdown pass that kind of got us back in the game. So we go in at halftime and make some adjustments. And I remember it was a hundred and some degrees at the Cotton Bowl. Because Renfro was hurt, I was playing every offensive play.

I was also covering kickoffs, covering punts. I lost 13 pounds in that game. Now, 13 pounds on a big lineman are not very much. But 13 pounds on a 200 pound running back is a lot of weight. I remember it was so hot they didn't even have a halftime show. People in the band with their uniforms on were passing out in the heat.

When I scored the third week in a row, and Renfro was close to coming back, that was when they made the decision that Mel was going to play defense and I would be the starter. I had been figuring I would be moved back to second team, so that was a helluva thrill.

I was winning the job over an all pro who they had really set the offense around.

Some funny things happened that year. It was like the sixth game of the season, we were undefeated and we played the Cleveland Browns up in Cleveland. They were the defending Eastern Division champions. Meredith threw about five interceptions and we got beat 30–21.

We get home, and I got a call from my dad. The game wasn't televised or anything, so they don't know anything but the score, and the fact that I hadn't scored. He wanted to know if I had got hurt.

"No, I didn't get hurt. Why would you think that?"

"Well, you didn't score a touchdown so I figured you had got hurt." I had scored one in every one of the games prior to that.

We went through the season, and we ended up playing in one of the most exciting football games I have ever played in. In all the years I have been in football now, only that Cleveland game for the American Football Conference championship in 1987 might top it.

We played the Browns, in the Cotton Bowl, on Thanksgiving Day. It was the biggest crowd ever to see a Cowboys game in Dallas, and it is still the record today—80,259, Nov. 24, 1966.

We had a half game lead in the Eastern Division, and the Browns were the team that was trailing us. We had tied St. Louis 10–10 earlier in the year to create that half game edge. If we could beat the Browns, we would have a game and a half lead with three games to go in the regular season.

We had never beaten Cleveland, so I mean it was a big, big football game.

We took a lead early. I ended up taking a pass out in the flat, and by the fourth quarter, we have a four point lead. If we can drive in and score a field goal it would pretty much clinch a tie, and if we score a touchdown it is going to pretty much win the ball game.

I remember Meredith went back to pass, and I flared out of the backfield. He couldn't find anybody open and he hit me with a little old pass out in the flat. I cut down the field, and I got tackled by Erich Barnes, a defensive back, and Paul Wiggins.

Paul Wiggins went on to coach at Stanford and the Kansas City Chiefs, and he is coaching on the Minnesota staff now. He was a great defensive lineman for the Browns.

I am laying in the pile, and Paul Wiggins grabbed the inside of my leg and just pinched the fire out of it. I mean, it really hurt. I had a big ol' bruise on it afterward. It made me mad, and I kicked at him.

The pile was right in front of our bench, and Coach Landry was screaming at me:

"Reeves! What in the world are you doing? You're gonna cost us a penalty! You're gonna get kicked out of the game!"

I jumped up off the ground. "Coach. The guy pinched me."

Well, Coach Landry just turned around and walked away, laughing. Then the officials started laughing. I am walking back to the huddle and one of them says, "Reeves, we got more important things to worry about than somebody pinching you."

So I am mad. I get in the huddle, and guys are waiting on me to get there. They are waiting to call a play. The clock is running. I got in the huddle and said, "You know what Wiggins did?"

"No. What?"

"He pinched me."

Well, they just died laughing. I've often wondered what the people in that stadium thought that day, seeing a whole huddle break up laughing in a game where we set a record for attendance and it was a crucial time and the stakes were so high for both teams.

Old Don Perkins, who was our fullback, was quiet. He normally never said a word. He had a little grin on his face. He said, "That's all right, Reeves. I'll get him back for you. I'll goose him when he ain't lookin'."

Well, here we are. We're playing in the biggest football game we've ever played in in our lives. And here's a guy, you know, talkin' about gettin' pinched and somebody talkin' about goosin' a guy.

The funny thing about it was, Perkins ended up scoring the touchdown from about 16 yards out. I remember we were in I formation, and we handed off to him over right tackle. And as I'm faking, to make it look like we're going wide, I'm watching him. Perkins was great to watch. He had—they talk about crazy legs—Don Perkins had the craziest legs around.

His legs would kind of go out to the side. He could make cuts on a dime. And I'm watching him, and he makes the damnedest run. It clinched the game for us and really, it clinched the Eastern Division championship.

It was our first championship. I ended up scoring 16 touchdowns that year. Eight running and eight receiving. It is still a record in Dallas, and one I am very proud of. The season was only 14 games in those days. It has gone to 16 since, and it is still the record, which is amazing considering all the great runners they have had since then—Duane Thomas and Tony Dorsett and Calvin Hill and Walt Garrison and Herschel Walker.

We scored 445 points as a team that year. It's the most Dallas ever scored until they went to the 16-game season. I scored 16 touchdowns and Bob Hayes had 14. We had a high scoring team.

So there I am, my second year in pro football, and we are getting ready to play the Green Pay Packers in the Cotton Bowl for the right to go to the first Super Bowl.

I remember the game very well. We had a great game plan. I think our football team was confident that we could beat the Packers. Then they took the opening kickoff and drove 80 yards and scored when Elijah Pitts caught a pass on a circle route.

Now they kick off. Mel Renfro receives the kickoff, gets hit, fumbles the football, and Jim Grabowski picks it up and runs it in for the touchdown.

We're down 14–0 and we haven't even been on offense yet.

Finally, we get the ball, and we drive right down the field. We don't make any mistakes. It was a beautiful drive, and I ended up scoring from about five yards out. It was a hole big enough to drive a truck through. I've seen pictures of that play, and there isn't a Green Bay defender anywhere in the picture.

Several other things happened that stand out. We battle back, and we've got a chance to score or go ahead when the score is like 17–14, something like that. We have a play with me lining up in what we call Trips formation, with three receivers on one side and Bob Hayes on the other side.

I lined up next to the tight end. We knew that forced Green Bay into a certain coverage. In that coverage, Ray Nitschke is going to have to cover me. Bob Hayes is to the wide side of the field, and I'm in the Trips formation to the short side. We know they are going to double cover Hayes.

Nitschke is going to have me, man to man. He tries to hit me coming off the line. He misses me, and I get behind him. I see the thing clear out. I see the strong safety go with the tight end, and I see the cornerback go with the wide receiver.

And I'm free to go to the corner. I look back and see the ball coming.

I've got the ball right on my fingertips. I mean it is almost right in my hands in the end zone. And Willie Wood comes across and knocks the ball down. He was the free safety, the guy who was doubling on Hayes on the other side of the field.

I couldn't understand that. Willie Wood? How could he be doubling Hayes and come that far and make the play?

Later, we looked at the film. Bob Hayes comes off the line about half speed. Willie Wood looks at him. He knows right away he is not involved in the play. If Hayes had come off at full speed and run his route, Willie Wood would have double teamed him. But he sees that Hayes is not involved in the play, and he turns and sees Meredith looking to the other side and takes off and just barely knocks the ball away.

So we ended up kicking a field goal.

Then the Packers went on a scoring spree, and only a blocked extra point by Bob Lilly kept it from being a 15-point lead. Instead, they were up 34-20.

We get the ball back with about five minutes to go, and Frank Clarke runs a corner-post route against their strong safety and beats him for a touchdown. So it is 34-27 with a little more than two minutes left to play.

Our defense holds, and Don Chandler has to punt, and he gets off a poor punt. We get the ball in pretty good position.

We try the same play to Frank Clarke, except instead of going to the post he goes to the corner. He is wide open. Tom Brown is the safety, and he just tackles him because he knows he is beat. So they put the ball on the 2 yard line, first down and goal to go.

We run four plays, and we don't score.

I can still remember all four of them. The first play, we run the same play I had scored on early in the game and get a yard, down to the 1 yard line. On the second play, they faked to me into the line and Meredith rolls out. But on the play, I get hit in the eye.

By Ron Kostelnik. On that same play, Jim Boeke jumped, and we get penalized. So on the incomplete pass, we are penalized five yards, back to the six.

I can remember this like it was the Keystone Cops, like it was one of those speeded up type things on old movies. On the next play, they fake a quick pitch to me, fake a trap to Perkins, and we got a receiver going to the corner and I am out in the flat.

They cover the receiver in the corner. I've got a block in front of me, and Meredith throws the ball. I drop the pass. Because of my vision, I am seeing two of them. That's no reason. I should have caught the ball.

That's not the point. I should have taken myself out of the game. I was hurting the team by being in there and not being able to see. Anyway, I dropped the pass.

Now, it is third and six. We go into a formation where we send the outside receiver on a down and in, a slant in, and the tight end on a shoot route.

On the play, the tight end goes out. Herb Adderley is the corner on that side. Herb Adderley and the safety run together. So Pettis Norman is standing out in the flat, by himself and Don Meredith sees him. He doesn't want to overthrow him. So the ball goes low, and

Pettis had to kneel down to make sure of the catch. He catches it, gets up off the ground, and runs into the end zone.

But Brown, who had collided with Adderley, gets up and just touches Pettis while his knee is still down.

So, of course, they rule the ball is down at about the five.

So, on fourth down, we had the wrong substitution in the game. Bob Hayes is playing tight end. He is supposed to be out of the game on a goal line play, but he has to line up on Dave Robinson, their big linebacker. Robinson weighs about 245 or something, and Hayes is supposed to slam into him and go out to the corner.

Hayes doesn't touch him and Robinson comes through and grabs Meredith by the jersey. As Meredith is being slung around he just throws it into the end zone, hoping somebody will catch it.

Brown intercepts.

They ended up winning the game, 34–27, to go to Super Bowl I.

Several things came out of that game that made a lasting impression on me for when I became a head coach.

First of all was Bob Hayes coming off the line, and because he wasn't involved in the play, he didn't think he was important to the play, that irritates me now worse than anything in a player. I mean, everybody is involved. Even if it is a decoy route, you run that route at full speed.

The other thing was the substitution thing, trying to get the right players in the game for the play that is being called.

As hard as I try as a coach, the same things have happened to me as a head coach as happened to us on the goal line in Dallas.

Other things came out of that game. Since then, Dallas has become so much more efficient at the two-minute attack, not panicking, taking your time, using your time outs.

I did a study when I was an assistant coach. How many times when the game ended did we still have time outs left? Yet we were in our two-minute attack, hurry up, running two plays in a row and blah blah blah. And we still got three time outs when the game was over.

So we became much more efficient. Let's use our time outs. Let's slow down. Let's think about what we're doing. And we won an awful lot of games in the two minute period.

To me, it all boiled back to the starting point in that Green Bay game. We had them on the ropes. I'm not saying we would have won the game. They were a better football team than we were in 1966.

They were more experienced. They had playoff games under their belt. They were a great football team.

But I would have liked to have had our chances had we tied that game and gone into overtime. We had battled back from 14 points down twice in that game.

But they went on to Super Bowl I and a piece of history, really, with that win.

We had a very determined football team going into the 1967 season. We came close in 1966. It was a tremendous experience for me.

I had a pretty good championship game, scored in it, had a great season, 16 touchdowns, led the league along with Leroy Kelly of Cleveland.

I really felt like I was a part of it, not lucky just to be there.

Back in the summer I had not signed that contract, and had gone almost a month into training camp when Tex Schramm called me into his office.

"We can't have you here without a contract," he said. "We need to get you signed. I got two deals I'll offer you," he said. "You can choose whichever one you like.

"You made $11,000 this year. We'll sign you next year for $13,000 and the next year for $17,000. Or we'll give you $15,000 and $15,000." Well, heck. Fifteen was a lot more than thirteen. So I said I'd sign for 15 and 15.

Which we did. So I'm playing, and I'm making $15,000 and ended up tied with Leroy Kelly for the most touchdowns in one season and setting a club record that is still there more than 20 years later. I'm the leading scorer and one of the top rushers in the league, making $15,000. Which is a lot of money, but not for guys who were playing.

That was the time Joe Namath had signed for $200,000 or so my rookie year. All the guys had come in with big contracts because of the war between the AFL and NFL.

So, when the season was over, I went in to talk to Schramm about renegotiating my contract. I didn't have an agent. I wasn't making enough money to have an agent.

I went in, and I told him I thought I was underpaid and I wanted to redo my contract.

"Who do you think you ought to be compared to?" he asked me.

"Well, I know Gale Sayers is making $100,000."

"That's a different situation. Gale Sayers is a No. 1 draft choice.

He was the top running back picked. He ought to be making more money than you."

"Well, Elijah Pitts."

"That's a different situation. Elijah Pitts is a veteran back with a championship football team. You only been in the league for two years. When you've been in the league for eight years like Elijah Pitts, you'll make as much money as he does."

Well, everybody I mentioned was a "different situation." There was nobody in the same situation I was. He wouldn't renegotiate. I was so mad I wanted to fight him for it.

# 9

# Third Season:
# A Son and the Ice Bowl

I WENT into 1967 with a heckuva lot more confidence than I had the year before. I was really looking forward to 1967.

That was the year they broke the conference into the Century Division and the Capitol Division. We ended up winning our division, the Capitol.

We opened up in Cleveland, and we beat them 21–14. They were the team we had beaten for the conference championship the year before, and we had to open up in their place. It was a tough game.

We beat New York in the second game, and I was keeping up with my 1966 touchdown pace and having some good games.

We played the Los Angeles Rams the third game of the season. George Allen was their head coach. We were both undefeated, and they just beat the heck out of us.

It was 35–13, in Dallas. They had a defense they put in especially for us. We would go into that Trips formation, and isolate me on a linebacker or a safety. Then they could come across with the free safety. We had never seen that, what we call a slide coverage. The free safety would come over and the linebacker would actually go the other way, and they were banjoing the three outside receivers.

I was supposed to run a turn in. So I come down the field and Eddie Meador, the free safety, he ran the route better than I did.

So I thought Don Meredith would see that. So I took off. There was nobody back there. But Don had already thrown the ball. They intercepted, and it taught me a great lesson.

As much as you might like to improvise with pass patterns, the quarterback can't read your mind. So you have to stick with the pattern. Of course, I got chewed out real good by Coach Landry when we watched the films about that specific play. But it did lead to a counter play off that pattern when we played them the next year, and we scored off it.

We had a 9–5 record that year, and ended up winning our division.

The highlight of the whole year for me, without question, was Pam expecting our second child. Having not been there when Dana was born, I was excited about it. I was able to be with her the whole time. We were playing the Atlanta Falcons that Sunday, November 5.

On Friday, Pam went in for a checkup. We knew it was close. Her doctor was Doctor Charles Guerriero. Pam still flies down to Dallas to see him for a checkup on occasion. He was the doctor for most all of the wives.

"You're awful close to having this baby," he told her. "If you don't have that baby tonight, you come in in the morning and we'll induce labor because I'm not going to miss the game on Sunday."

That's the way it was. Sure enough, on Friday night, I couldn't sleep. Every time she moved, I thought she was going to have the baby.

Saturday morning, we got up and went over to the hospital. I'm in kind of a waiting area with Pam and then they come to take her into the delivery room.

All I've ever seen are these pictures where guys pace back and forth for two or three hours, waiting. I had seen these movies and figured it was going to be a long wait, so Lee Roy Jordan was there.

"I'm gonna go get a hamburger or something," I told him. "I haven't had any breakfast. I'll be right back."

When I came back, the doctor was there.

"I been looking for you. Where you been?"

"I went to get a hamburger."

"Well, you got a little boy." She had had the baby and everything while I was gone. "You got a little boy, and he's doing good, and he's got all his plumbing."

I was excited. I got on the phone and I called everybody. Pam was doing good, and it was just the idea of having a boy and everything. I called everybody I knew to tell them about the little boy.

I hadn't slept at all on Friday, and didn't get a lot of sleep on Saturday, and on Sunday we played Atlanta. And I scored four touchdowns. There was a big to do about that, having had a son born on the fourth and then scoring four touchdowns. I've got pictures of Lee and me and Pam the next day, me holding the baby up, hoping I don't drop him or something.

We won the division, and ended up playing Cleveland in the conference championship game for the second year in a row.

Let me backtrack a little. We were playing in Philadelphia a couple of weeks earlier, and I ran off tackle and got hit from two sides at once, boom, boom.

My arm went numb. We were way out in front, and I went over to the sideline. They figured it wasn't a separation. I had pinched a nerve in my neck. Finally, the feeling came back to my left hand.

We had this big lead, and they put Jerry Rhome in, and Philadelphia intercepted two passes, and now it was 24–17. So Coach Landry put the starters back, and on the first play I threw a halfback option pass to Lance Rentzel for a touchdown. We ended up winning big, 38–17.

They figured I had chipped a vertebrae in my neck, and I had to go through traction every day to try to relieve that pressure. We went to San Francisco the last game and they beat us.

We played Cleveland for the conference championship, and on the fourth play, I got hit the same way on the same play, and my left arm went numb again. Eventually, it came back, except it didn't come back in my point finger, my left index finger I guess you call it.

I didn't play any more in the game because they didn't need me. We beat them 52–14. Bob Hayes ran back two punts for touchdowns. It wasn't even a contest.

The following week they sent me to a neurologist. He confirmed I have nerve damage because of the chip. So they did the traction, and we were going to go up to Green Bay to play the Packers in the championship game.

It was to be played on New Year's Eve afternoon. I had to wear a neck brace, which I had never done before. There was a new field in Green Bay. It had a heating system underground to keep the field from freezing and so forth.

We went up, and we stayed in a Holiday Inn in Appleton, Wisconsin. I roomed with Walt Garrison. The day before the game, we made the trip from Appleton at the same speed they estimated we'd be able to go with crowds filling the highways on game day. They wanted to know how soon to leave the hotel to get to the game on time, because the traffic was going to be so bad.

So we drove about 15 miles an hour, going from Appleton to Green Bay. We thought we never would get there. It was a miserable trip the day before the game. It was cold, like 15 degrees above zero, but with the sun shining once we started working out and working up a sweat it was fine. The field was in great shape and it was beautiful weather.

That was the forecast for the next day. We were a much better football team that year, I felt, than we had been the year before, simply from the experience standpoint. We had acquired Lance Rentzel. With him and Bob Hayes on the outside it gave us two great receivers.

Our defense was playing good, and we felt like we had a good chance. Plus we were coming off that big win against Cleveland.

We were staying in a hotel built in a kind of rectangle. Walt and I were back in the corner. The restaurant was up in the front. We got up the next morning and got dressed. At Dallas, we had to wear coats and ties on trips. So we put on our coats and ties, and walked out the door to go eat the pregame meal.

And we walked about 10 yards.

"Boy, it's cold! We better go back and get our overcoats," I said. We only had to walk about 50 or 60 yards to the restaurant part of the hotel, across this open courtyard inside the rectangle. We went back and got our coats, and now we kind of jogged over to the restaurant.

It was overcast. We went in the restaurant, and the waitress came up.

"Boy, it's cold out there," we said.

"Well, it ought to be," she said. "It's 17 degrees below zero."

"Are you joking?"

"It dropped 32 degrees overnight."

I had never been in that kind of cold. I was under the impression that once it got below freezing, freezing was freezing. If it was 32, or 15 below, that didn't make any difference. That was the first time I realized you could feel from 15 above to 17 below just like you could feel going from 70 degrees to 102 degrees above zero.

There was a difference.

We had our pregame meal, and went to the stadium at 15 miles an hour. By now, everybody is talking about the cold. It is really cold.

Coach Landry had Dickie Daniels—he's with the Washington Redskins now—and Sim Stokes, he was a wide receiver, he had them hurry and put on their uniforms.

"Go out and test the field," he told them. "See if our cleats are okay and so forth."

They weren't gone 30 seconds. They couldn't possibly have walked any further than the first goal line. They came back.

"Coach, it is frozen and it is cold."

People started to tell us, "wear your insulated underwear, and your feet won't get cold if you wrap them in saranwrap." So we put these baggies around our feet. They didn't work. As soon as you made one move and busted the bag you could feel the cold air coming in.

We went out for warmups, and I was holding for field goals and extra points. I don't think we tried more than four practice field goals. You couldn't catch the ball from the center. It was just like a brick.

Coach Landry had a policy that anybody who touched the ball could not wear gloves. So we were sitting there with no gloves on. Meredith went out to warm up. He may have thrown four or five passes. We said, "This is ridiculous. How can you warm up in this stuff?"

So we went back inside, until it was time to go back out.

They had blowers on the sideline, but it was just miserable, miserable weather. You can't imagine how cold that was. When they started the game, Norm Schacter was the head referee. The first time he blew the whistle in the game, he pulled the whistle out of this mouth and just peeled the skin off his lips.

It was a metal whistle and his lips had frozen to it.

They had to go find plastic whistles.

It was one of those games we knew was going to be evenly matched. But we changed our game plan a little because of the conditions. We didn't play as much man to man as we had planned. We tried to play more zone because the footing was bad.

Everything we had planned for, basically, on defense went out the window. On offense, knowing where we were going had a little bit of advantage as far as standing up, and the defense was at a little disadvantage, just as ours was when they had the ball.

It turned out to be a defensive struggle.

We were down 14–10 in the third quarter. We had taken the ball at about our own 15 and driven the length of the field with a long drive. We had the ball over seven minutes. We got down to about their 15 or 20 yard line, and Meredith went back to pass.

He couldn't find anybody, scrambled out of the pocket, got hit, and fumbled the ball. They recovered. We really had a chance to take control of the football game at that point, until then.

So the defense held, and at the end of the quarter we got the ball again and went on the field. The whistle blew, and we changed ends, and I remember we were standing in the huddle.

"Let's run Pitch 48, T pull," Meredith says. That's a quick pitch to the halfback going left, which was me. We had run it several times during the game and had some success with it.

I don't know whether it was Don mentioned it or I did. "What about the halfback pass off of that?"

I said, "Hey, I think it might be good because we've been running it and they've been coming up. And I can throw it to my left. That's no problem."

"Okay. Let's run the halfback pass off of that play."

In the huddle, I actually kept my hands tucked into the tops of my uniform pants until the last possible second. We came out in an I formation and then shifted to a split backfield and I shifted to the left halfback position.

I was leaning over, but I kept my hands tucked. I just took them out at the last minute.

Meredith pitched me the ball. I had a tackle, Ralph Neely, pulling in front of me. The outside receiver faked a crack back, like he was going to block the strong safety. It was Willie Wood at safety. At that time, Green Bay was playing its safeties right and left, they weren't playing strong and weak.

So Willie Wood was the right safety on that formation, and Gary Jeter was the defensive back. I saw the safety come up, and I looked at Jeter, and Jeter came up.

That was the key for me to pull up and look for Rentzel, who had faked and then broke back to the corner.

And he was wide open. Nobody was close.

I remember stopping, and when I stopped to throw the ball, I heard Jeter cuss. "DAMN it!"

He knew he'd made a mistake. As I let the ball go, the wind was blowing. It was blowing in our face in the fourth quarter. I didn't want to overthrow him. As soon as I threw it I thought, "Oh, my gosh, I've thrown it too long." But the ball was held up a little by the wind and Rentzel ran right under the ball, caught it, and outraced Brown, the other safety into the end zone.

Well, I thought we had the game won right there. You can't imagine how miserable it was, trying to play on that field. You couldn't stand up, and it had gotten worse as the game went on. It had kind of thawed with that heating system under there, but then it froze over as it got colder.

It was almost like being on an ice rink.

In the fourth quarter, we had the ball and we ran a quick pitch to the right side, only it was a running play, not a passing one. They forced real fast with the corner. So I had to try to cut back inside and when I did, I slipped down.

I was laying on the ground. You can get up and run unless somebody has touched you while you were down. Nobody had, so I went to get up off the ground and I saw a player coming at me to hit me.

So I spun back to my inside to get away, and when I did, I met Ron Kostelnik. Actually, I thought it was Ray Nitschke. I met him, head on. Bam. I really took a shot, right in the face. I am laying on the ground, and I look, and my face mask is gone.

I know something's wrong. I started to feel around, to see if I got any teeth missing or anything. It doesn't really hurt, and there is no blood on my hands. So I take my tongue, and try to feel and see if my teeth are there. I can't feel my teeth on the left side because they have been knocked through my lip. My lip was hanging, and I couldn't get my tongue between my teeth and the lip.

I knew something was wrong. I went off to get my helmet fixed, but there was still no blood whatsoever. None. So I go over, they take my helmet, and stand me in front of the blower. When I get in front of the blower, the blood just starts pouring out.

I had busted by lip, busted my nose, just made a mess of things right there. I still don't have any feeling on my upper lip here on the left side. I can't even feel it when I shave, not to this day.

That's how miserable it was.

And for the Packers to take the ball and drive the length of the field and score and beat us the way they did was unbelievable. I can still remember the drive. I can remember on a couple of third down conversions how they ended up getting their backs up field when our linebackers came up and slipped trying to make a tackle.

Chuck Howley missed one time on Donny Anderson and Dave Edwards one time on Chuck Mercein. They had overcome two third down situations, and they ran a sucker play against Bob Lilly. They false pulled the guard, faked a choke block with the center, so Bob starts chasing. It meant there was going to be a sweep the other way. Instead, they handed off on the sucker play to Mercein and he ran down to about the 3 or 4 yard line.

They ran a couple of plays, and our defense held them, but they got down to like the 1 yard line. They called their last time out.

They had no time outs, and they were trailing 17–14. We came over to the sideline to talk about it.

"Well, they don't have any time outs. There are only 13 seconds left. If they run, there is no way they can get their field goal unit on the field after the play if they don't score and the clock keeps running."

We felt like they would do some kind of pass, drop back pass where Starr would throw the ball away if the guy wasn't open.

And they run a quarterback sneak. Of all things. If they don't score, we end up winning. But they do, and beat us 21–17 and go to Super Bowl II.

It was probably one of the toughest losses we ever had. I felt, and I think our team felt, like we could win that ball game. One second, you are thinking about Super Bowl, and all of a sudden your season is over.

My face was all swollen. I had a big scab where my face mask had gouged my nose. I had scabs where my teeth went through my lip. Somebody interviewed me.

"Ray Nitchke's an animal," I said. I meant it kind of tongue in cheek. He is a great linebacker. We played them the next year, in pre-season, and Ray Nitschke was on me on punt coverage.

And I mean, he tried to kill me. Every play. He did a pretty good job of it. By then, I had looked at the films and found out it wasn't Nitschke, it was Ron Kostelnik.

I had blamed the wrong guy, and you don't ever want to blame a linebacker because he's got a lot more chances to get you than a lineman.

But that was an awful disappointment to lose that game. A lot of people remember that game. The cold fascinated them. It's become one of the legendary games in league history, and you hate to be the loser in a legendary game.

As far as I know, nobody got lung damage, although there were some stories printed later that suggested that. If anybody was going to from being all sweaty and then breathing in that cold air, it would have been me. In that third quarter, when we had the ball for seven minutes or more, I was out there the whole time, and I was in motion or carrying the ball or something. I was running on every play.

I ran on every play. I was doing more running than everybody because Bob Hayes never moved out of his steps. He had his hands in his pockets the whole time.

It burned. Most of the burn was right through the trachea.

I did have another situation in that game where I came across the middle and Dave Robinson hit me. It knocked the breath out of me. Then, the next couple of weeks, I started having some problems.

I went by and had an x-ray. I found out I had two cracked ribs. I didn't even know it was that bad at the time. You just couldn't feel. My lip didn't bleed. I took this shot and cracked two ribs and didn't know it.

They didn't even have a halftime show. The instruments froze. Their lips would have frozen to the horns anyway, like Schacter's did to his metal whistle at the start.

We did have four or five guys get frostbite on their fingers. They were the ones that wore gloves. They were the old, brown, cotton gloves, and we suspect the reason they ended up with frostbite was they would go over in front of the blower and get their hands warm. They would sweat a little under those gloves, then freeze when they went on the field.

As for anybody having an advantage that day, I don't think there's any way the Packers had one just because they were from Green Bay.

I know you didn't have to worry about seeing, because nobody was standing on the sideline. They were all back there by the blowers. I told Coach Landry that was the only ball game I've ever been involved in where I was glad when we didn't make a first down. It meant you could get over to the sideline and stay warm.

You hear all kinds of stories now about how the Packers say, "Oh, it wasn't cold," and "we knew we were going to win the game on the last drive."

That is the biggest bunch of crock I've ever heard. There ain't no way they knew they had that game won and there's no way they can say they weren't cold. I talked to them at the time. They couldn't come out and warm up decently either.

So they had no advantage in the ball game. Nobody's used to that kind of weather. Now you hear stories of how they got in the huddle and "the feeling was there, and we knew we were going to score."

There's no way. There had been very little offense generated in the game. There was that one last drive and the half back pass, and otherwise it was a punting duel. You couldn't even stand up.

It was the only time I ever wore that neckbrace, collar. Any time you see a picture of me wearing a collar, it was that game, the Ice Bowl game. It's the only time in my whole career I ever wore it.

The strings broke several times in the game. They would get sweaty, then freeze and just shatter. And I remember looking at my left hand. It was still numb, and the circulation must have been bad because it was almost purple.

The feeling didn't come back in that hand until we were snow skiing up in Ruidoso, New Mexico, in February with Walt Garrison and his wife.

I still have trouble with my neck. My left shoulder hurts all the time and I can't sleep on my back. About twice a month I wake up with a stiff neck. It's calcium building up around that vertebrae. It's just going to be a problem all my life.

Eventually, a Dallas writer, the late Steve Perkins, wrote a book about the Cowboys, *Next Year's Champions.*

That was just the start of it. We had a lot more heartaches to go before we won one of those.

# 10

## The Knee: 1968

THAT YEAR was really a bummer for me. I got hurt.
I had this suspicion at the time, and it grew as the
year went on: Things were changing for me in professional football. I was right.

For one thing, we started our season having lost
two straight championship games to Green Bay,
with a chance to go to Super Bowls I and II.

We still had a good team, with high hopes. But
for me at least, it became an injury plagued season
right off the bat. We played the Rams in a preseason
game in Los Angeles the third week of the preseason. I scored a touchdown, and as I was going into
the end zone, I was laying on the ground. Somehow,
Deacon Jones came over a pileup and he landed on
my foot, my left foot.

Instead of bending the foot the normal way, the
impact bent it the opposite way. I didn't know if I
had broken it or what. X-rays showed nothing was
broken, but it had popped the capsules between
each of my toes on that foot. We were staying at the
hotel right by the Los Angeles airport.

I got up in the middle of the night, and I stood
up, and just fell flat on my face. My foot had swollen up clear down through my toes.

We went back to Dallas, and I got all kinds of
treatment on that foot, but I still missed the last two
preseason games that summer. I still couldn't walk,

but I played in the opening game of the season against Detroit.

It was odd. Running with the football and doing those things didn't hurt. It hurt me worse walking back to the huddle afterward. Anytime I was walking, it hurt.

We beat Detroit 59-13, and the next week in the rematch with Cleveland, I rushed for over 100 yards. My foot was getting better, and I got one of the few game balls I ever got. We beat Philadelphia the following week, and then went to St. Louis undefeated for the fourth game.

My foot had gotten to the point it really wasn't bothering me. We went up to St. Louis, and about the fourth or fifth play of the game, Don Meredith called a play where I was supposed to run a sweep to the right.

It all got jammed up. We were pulling a guard around to lead us. Penetration caused John Wilbur, the guard, to get knocked back. He was so big I couldn't see around him, but I knew I was going to have to cut up, that somebody was coming, from somewhere.

I thought to myself I had to get out from behind him. Just as I planted my left foot and started to cross over, I saw the guy's helmet come underneath. All he was really trying to do was knock the blocker down. I don't think he was really trying to tackle me.

It was Lonnie Sanders, a defensive back who was a substitute in that game. His helmet caught me right in the knee. It was fully planted and I had all my weight on it. It just tore everything in my left knee.

It's funny now. It wasn't funny then. I was there on the ground, and I was looking for anything to grab because the pain was so great. I had had all kinds of knee problems, but this was something I had never experienced. This felt like somebody had stuck about a hundred hot pokers in my knee.

It was on fire.

So, I was looking for something to hold on to. I grabbed somebody's ankle. I was squeezing it as hard as I could, and every now and then the guy would try to yank his ankle free. I was squeezing so hard it probably hurt him.

After a minute or two—it seemed like years—it was almost like somebody took water and cooled the joint off. I was laying there, and the trainers were looking at my knee, and I remember looking up to see whose ankle I had been grabbing.

It was Norm Schacter, the referee.

I got up. My knee wasn't loose on the field. I guess because of the pain your muscles tighten up. So when they checked the knee on the field, the muscles kind of supported it and the knee was fairly decent as far as stability was concerned.

I was helped off. I could put my weight on it, but I knew it was something bad. I knew this was different from anything I had had in college. They iced it down on the sideline, and I sat through the rest of the first half.

Ten thousand things go through your mind. The biggest is, "Is this the end?" You feel like your career is over. You are young, you feel like you could play forever. Then, all of a sudden on one play, something you have dreamed about all your life is all of a sudden taken away from you.

Dr. Marvin Knight is our team physician, and when we go in at halftime, he tells me to get up on the table in the training room. He cut my pants off, tested the knee, and it was obvious. "It's torn," he said. "We'll operate on you as soon as we get back to Dallas."

He said, "Don't drink anything. Don't eat anything."

"Fine. I'm a little thirsty. Just let me have a glass of water or something and I'll be fine." I had gone out in the pregame warmups and then played a little before I got hurt, so I was thirsty.

"No. You can't have anything to drink. No."

It was tough to go through the rest of the game. They gave me something for the pain, because by now there was a tremendous amount of pain.

Afterward, we got on the plane, one of those Electras with a lounge at the back. There was more room there to put my leg out straight, so they sat me back there. All I got on is my underwear. They gave me a blanket to put around me.

I remember calling the stewardess over, and pointing to Dr. Knight across the aisle.

"I can't have anything to eat or drink," I told her. "I have to have surgery as soon as we get back to Dallas. And he's the guy who is going to do the surgery. I want you to make sure he doesn't have anything to drink. If he even goes in the bathroom, I want you to follow him. I don't want him operating on me if he's going to have a beer or a drink or anything."

She followed him everywhere he went that trip home. As soon as we landed at DFW, they had an ambulance there and they took me straight to Baylor Hospital.

There's nothing worse than having a cast on your leg from the hip to the ankle. You have a difficult time getting to the bathroom, and when you do, you can't go. It's just a miserable feeling.

I knew that Dr. Knight was not going to let me out of the hospital unless I got up and started walking around. So, on Wednesday, I remember telling myself, "You have got to get up and do something."

The nurses' station couldn't have been more than 20 or 30 yards from my room. As soon as I stood up, the blood rushed down and into my knee, and it felt like it was ready to explode. I made myself walk from my room to that station. When I got there, I was wringing wet with sweat.

It must have taken me 30, 45 minutes just to go that short distance. I fell back into bed, and Dr. Knight came by that afternoon.

"Doc, when am I going to be able to get out of here?"

"Soon as you're up and around, you can leave," he said.

"Well, I walked all the way to the nurses' station and back today already," I told him.

"Oh, well, if you did that, we can let you go home. We'll let you out first thing in the morning."

Pam picked me up the next day, and I remember going home and sitting on the couch, and Dana comes into the room. She's, let's see, three at the time. She hasn't seen me, this little redheaded, freckle faced little girl.

She comes skipping into the living room there, and I'm sitting on the couch with this big ol' cast on my leg. Her eyes got real big.

"What happened?"

"Well, Sugar, I got hurt."

"How'd you get hurt?"

"I got hurt playin' football."

"Well, who hurt you?"

"The guy's name was Lonnie Sanders."

She shook her head. "Boy, I bet his mother really whipped him good."

I said, "I don't know if his mother did, but I would sure like to get my hands on him."

So, anyway, we go through that season and it was miserable for me. I couldn't travel with the team while I had my cast on, so I went back to the University of South Carolina to watch my younger brother, Butch, play Florida State one weekend. He was a defensive back.

It was my first time back since I had joined the Cowboys, and here

I was with a cast on and all. Ron Sellers was a receiver for Florida State, and he must have caught 13 or 14 passes that afternoon even with double coverage and all.

I had the cast on four or six weeks, something like that. And really and truly, you feel like a bastard at a family reunion. You are just so out of place. Nobody has anything to do with you. The coaches don't even speak to you.

You were the starter, and all of a sudden, you don't mean anything, to anybody. You can't practice, you can't do anything.

Coach Landry started to let me go on the trips, help out, stand on the sidelines and so forth. Heck, I helped the stewardesses on the planes pass out the meals.

In fact, I put on an apron. I could imitate Geraldine Jones, you know, Flip Wilson's character. So I'd act like Geraldine Jones and go up and down the aisles, passing out meal trays on the trips.

We had a good team, and that's what hurt. You really want your team to win, but boy, you'd really like for them to miss you. You'd like to think you were a bigger part of the team than you really were.

But we continued to win. Our record was 12-2 that year. So, I mean, they weren't missing me at all.

The only games we lost were one to New York, which killed Coach Landry because that was always a big game for him and for us. We played them twice a year, and we liked to think we never lost to New York.

We lost to them 27-21, and we got beat in a rematch with Green Bay 28-17. But it was a great season, and we ended up beating New York in New York 28-10 and went on to the championship game in Cleveland.

We got humiliated. We got beat 31-20, but it was never that close. We changed quarterbacks, with Craig Morton going in late in the ball game, and for another year, we were going to finish by going down to Miami for the Playoff Bowl.

It was a miserable year because I had nothing to do with it after having a pretty good start, and I knew that my career was in jeopardy.

Coming off knee surgery as a running back wasn't the greatest thing, the greatest way to end a season.

I did have something in common with a great running back named Gale Sayers. He got hurt the next week on an almost identical type play. Kermit Alexander came underneath the block and hit him on a leg he had planted and that was taking his full weight. He was going left, and it was his right knee. I was going right, and it was my left knee.

A little later, late in that season, we were playing the Bears in Chicago, and Gale. In those years, both teams had their benches on the same sideline, the one over toward the lake, and we wound up standing together, talking.

He's got his cast on and I've got my cast on. Late in the ball game, a fight breaks out. Everybody runs on the field. Almost everybody. Gale and I are standing there with crutches, casts, coats and ties on. We're just talking to each other while all our teammates are out there fighting, except for two guys—Don Meredith and Ronnie Bull.

Both of them played in the Southwest Conference, Bull for Baylor and Meredith at SMU. I can't remember which one said it, but he yelled at the other one, "Hey! Come on over here. I want to fight you!"

"Yeah? You wanna fight me, you come on over here!"

So they stand there, yellin' back and forth at each other while both teams are fighting out on the field and Gale and I are leaning there on our crutches, watching, and we've both basically got the same thoughts:

Our careers are over.

We talked about it. Both of us had had very extensive knee surgery. We knew it was going to be tough. You always think you are going to be different from everybody else. I knew Dr. Knight had done a good job, but I also knew it was a bad injury, and I knew the odds.

I had torn the anterior medial lateral ligament. The ligament itself wasn't torn, but it was torn away where it attached to the bone. If you have to have something like that, that particular way is the best way to have it. So they stapled that ligament right to the bone, just like you take something and staple it together. The difficult repair was that I had torn the cruciate ligament, as well.

They drilled a hole in the bone, and tried to suture the ligament through the bone. The cruciate is so short that it was difficult to repair.

Anyway, the whole year, the basic thing involved the fact I really felt sorry for myself. I felt, you know, one of those deals, "Why me, Lord?"

But right then, we were just two football players standing there, leaning on crutches, watching a fight, and talking about our knees.

Gale, obviously, came back. They made a great movie, *Brian's Song,* about him, about the way he came back, and his relationship with Brian Piccolo, the guy who beat us at South Carolina when he was playing for Wake Forest.

For me, something happened after the season that put everything back into perspective for me. I was invited to join six other NFL players on a tour to Vietnam.

What I saw, what I heard, made the knee seem less important.

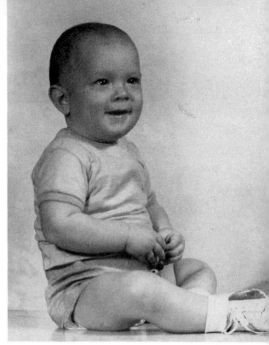

If I ever had a player come up to me with wrists that pudgy, I'd have to recommend a weight program.

I was still chasing baseballs all the way to the country store across from New Era when this was taken in the 1956-57 school year.

I was only five in this picture, and just about to start first grade at New Era.

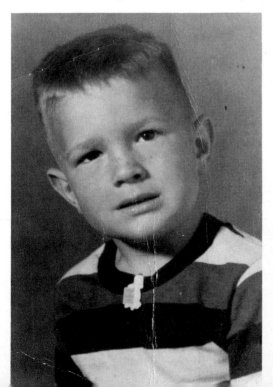

I'll always think a great quarterback was overlooked by the pros. Notice the form even as a 1959 sophomore at Americus High School.

The tri-captains of the 1961 Americus Panthers couldn't find a smile among them, I guess. That's Roy Frost in the middle and Donald Tye on the right.

Coach Jimmy Hightower took us to the 1961 Georgia state Class A championship. I'm next to him, and that's my cousin, Bob Reeves, next to me.

I was a happy senior when I posed for this Americus High School graduation picture.

We had several quarterbacks on the squad as freshmen, but I managed to wind up as the starter on a team where the quarterback also had to run and block.

Some fans came by to commiserate during the 1963 spring game after I tore up a knee in intramural baseball.

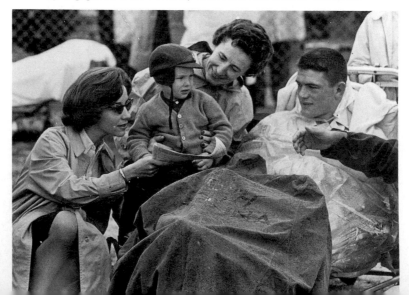

Our senior season was almost done when Coach Bass got his quarterbacks together for this picture. That's Jim Rogers on the left. Coach Bass is on our staff in Denver now.

I'm standing next to Coach Marvin Bass on the far right here, with other South Carolina freshmen in that 1961 class—John Breeden, Ralph Floyd, Marty Rosen, and Larry Gill. Breeden and I were roommates.

Pam and I had known each other since high school, and got married in 1964 before I went back for my senior year at South Carolina.

Lee was a little young to remember his dad scored four touchdowns against Atlanta the day after he was born in 1967.

Maybe Dana's mad because I wasn't able
to get home for her birth nine months
before this was taken in 1966.

I was just starting as a player-coach when
we took this family portrait in Dallas in
September 1970. Pam is holding Laura,
with Dana behind her and Lee not quite
sure he likes the whole idea.

If you want to find one nervous rookie, he's second from the left, second row, No. 30, in this 1965 team picture of the Dallas Cowboys.

Remember this one—it's a rare shot of me at quarterback in 1971 when Coach Landry didn't want to take chances with our starter late in a game.

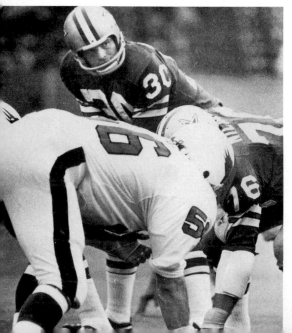

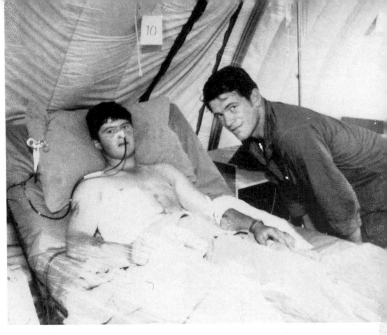

The whole Vietnam trip convinced me my own knee injury really wasn't that important.

Walt Garrison was teaching Lee Roy Jordan how to wrestle up steer on the B.F. Phillips Ranch in 1967. I was assigned to hold the horses while Don Meredith has trouble taking the whole thing seriously.

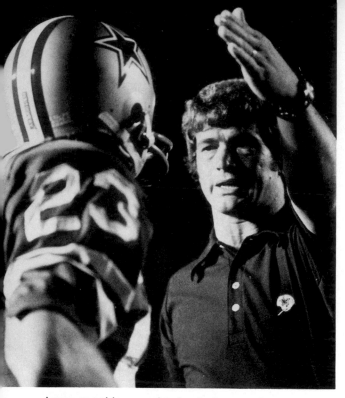

I was coaching running backs here, trying
to show Mike Montgomery how I wanted
him to run a pass route for the Cowboys.

The Cowboys were becoming America's team here in the
mid-1970s. That's me, third from the left and still years
from having my own team.

You never get too comfortable in this game. I'm the rookie in this AFC West coaches show in 1981—and I'm the only one left now. That's Marv Levy to my right, then Don Coryell, Tom Flores and Jack Patera.

That's Roger Staubach on my left, and Duane Thomas over there on the far right at training camp in Thousand Oaks.

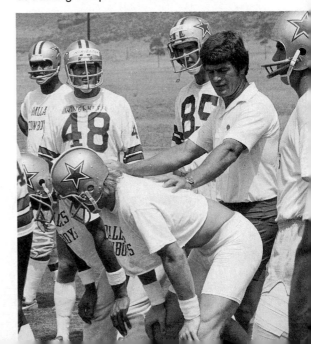

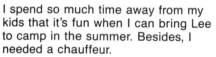

I spend so much time away from my kids that it's fun when I can bring Lee to camp in the summer. Besides, I needed a chauffeur.

It's gonna break three inches to the left, John. The two of us beat Mike Ditka and Jim McMahon in a charity match a couple of years ago.

Two rookies pose arms folded, as Edgar Kaiser and I watch our team warm up in 1981.

Who said coaches never smile? Don Coryell (San Diego), John Mackovic (Kansas City) and Tom Flores (Los Angeles) help me fiddle at the AFC West media gathering.

Hulk Hogan and I met at Billy Graham's Denver Crusade in 1987.

Charles, Butch and Joann help my mom and dad celebrate their 50th wedding anniversary in Americus.

Here's the Reeves family at home in Denver these days, with Lee and me behind Pam, Laura and Dana.

Some players you never forget, and one of those is
Randy Gradishar, our all pro linebacker at Denver, who
helped us win John Elway's opener in Pittsburgh in 1983.

I've taken to wearing suits and ties since this 1981
explosion on the sideline. I'm not sure it has solved my
temper, but maybe it helps.

I look a little worried here, but it's not about my relationship with our owner, Pat Bowlen. I have a good feeling about him and I count myself really fortunate there.

It's hard to tell who is happiest, players or coach, after we captured the AFC West with this 31–14 victory in Seattle in 1984.

# 11

## Vietnam: A New Perspective

THE LORD really does work in mysterious ways. I had come out of 1968 with a bad knee and some terrible misgivings, doubts about my career and my ability to come back. I had come out of South Carolina as a free agent, and built what I felt was a good career, and even tied for the NFL lead in touchdowns in the 1966 season.

I had played in two championship games and felt I contributed to the development of the Cowboys into a really good football team. I was part of it.

And then one play turned all of it around for me, and, like I said, I spent a lot of 1968 feeling pretty sorry for myself.

I was still feeling that way early in 1969 when Coach Landry's secretary called. Pam and I were at home in Georgia. Coach Landry's secretary said Bob Lilly was supposed to go on a USO tour to Vietnam.

But Kitsy, his wife, had gotten sick, and he was not going to be able to make it. So, on short notice, they wanted to know if I would be interested in going. It was late January, and if I made the trip, I would have to get a bunch of shots. I was near Fort Jackson, and could get the shots there.

I told them yeah, I would like to go. And I went up to Columbia, South Carolina, to Fort Jackson, and had about 10 or 12 shots one day, and four or five days later, I am on my way from Atlanta, to Dallas, to San Francisco, where we were supposed to take a 10 o'clock flight to Saigon.

Tommy Nobis flew with me from Atlanta. He was one of the others going. The rest were Dick Westmoreland of Miami; Al Atkinson, of the world champion New York Jets; Billy Ray Smith from the Baltimore Colts, who had just lost to the Jets; Irv Cross, who was with Philadelphia; and Dick Schafrath of Cleveland.

We boarded, and all of us sat in the back of the plane. We take off, and they never turned the seat belt light off the whole flight. It was the roughest flight I've ever had. We stopped in Hawaii, and in Okinawa, and I never closed an eye.

We were in Vietnam for 21 days. We spent most of them flying by helicopter to visit different units all over the country. We would get up at four o'clock or five o'clock every morning and catch a helicopter to some fire base out in the country and visit the wounded and the troops.

We went into some real dangerous areas although I don't think they ever took a chance with us. Whenever we were over an area where they felt like there was some activity they would go up to about 2,000 feet. If we were flying low, you knew there wasn't supposed to be any activity in that area.

But the thing that really hit me was, here I was, feeling so sorry for myself, and I must have seen a thousand soldiers who were missing arms, missing eyes, missing legs, had serious brain injuries, and there was not one single one that wasn't saying, "Boy, I'm glad I'm alive. I'm glad I'm going to get to go home and see my mom and my dad and my girl friend or my wife."

I thought to myself, "This is amazing. Here these guys are thanking the good lord that they are just alive, and I came over here griping about having a knee injury."

It really made a point to me, one that has lasted. There is more to life than just football. I was very fortunate to have even played it. If I never played another down of football, I was very fortunate to have played in 1965, '66, '67 and '68. I had played in two championship games. I had made a good living playing football. Nobody could be more fortunate than I was.

So I kind of went back with a new attitude. In fact, I told Pam, "If you ever see me feeling sorry for myself, I really want you to kick me right in the butt. How can you feel sorry for yourself when you have had the things happen to you in your lifetime that I did?"

One of the first guys I saw was in a Marine hospital in Da Nang. He was sitting there, and he had been a player. How good, I don't know. He was from Michigan. He had lost both legs.

Here was a guy that one time was probably 6-4 or 6-5. Sitting there, he looked like he was four feet. He was just happy that he was alive. "I could have been killed," he said.

But one in particular really hit me. It was a neurological ward. Tommy Nobis and I were the only ones ended up going there. The rest went somewhere else that particular day.

Everybody in there had either a spinal injury or a brain injury. They told us before we went that "You don't have to go. This is really going to be depressing. There are a lot of very serious injuries here, but they really would get a kick out of it if you would."

We went inside, and there was a guy I met. He was from Chicago and he had only been in Vietnam for like nine days. He had stepped on a land mine and got blown up. He had a big scar on his head, and a tube in his throat, and you could barely hear him when he talked.

He was getting all that mucus and stuff in his throat. I had to help him several times while we talked. He was the one that said, "Boy, I'm lucky to be alive. I'm going to get to see my girl friend and my mom and dad."

I remember thinking to myself, "Is his girl friend even going to want to see him?" Here was a guy that probably would never be able to walk. Most of the guys in that ward, actually, lay flat on their back, or flat on their belly. When they turned them over, they put a frame on the bed and the whole deal would just flip over real quick.

They never could move. They were like zombies laying there. It was the most depressing thing, and I couldn't believe the courage of this one kid.

We had a photographer following us around, and he would take pictures and we would autograph them. I remember signing the picture to this kid, and I turned to walk away.

He could barely talk. You had to get up close to hear. And I heard him say, "Dan."

I went back over. "I want to thank you for coming," he said.

I thought to myself, "Here's a kid gave his life up and he's thanking me for taking 20 days out of my life to come here."

It was a great experience. I wouldn't trade it for anything I've ever done in my life. We visited hospitals every day and saw those kinds of people.

They had a prison at Langh Ben, and there was a guy there had coached Nobis' brother in semi-pro football. He was a military police officer. He had the safest job you can have.

About six months later, I am signing autographs at a mobile home in San Antonio, Texas, and this guy comes up. He had lost an eye. They had been overrun in an attack after we left.

There was another occasion we went to a base where some troops were getting ready to go on a reconnaissance mission. They all had their faces blacked up and streaked green and so on. There were three kids in the group, all from right near Dallas. One was from Grand Prairie and another from Arlington, I remember. They were all Cowboys fans.

We brought along NFL highlight films that we would show, and it included the championship game between the Jets and Colts. And Billy Ray Smith would carry Al Atkinson's stuff around because the Jets had won.

So we went to this thing, and sat around and talked to them, including these three kids from my area in Dallas. Well, the next year, I am back in Arlington, signing autographs one day. There is a long line of people, and I knew this one guy looked familiar.

"Do you remember me?"

"Boy, your face looks awful familiar."

"I was at such and such last February when we were getting ready to go on patrol, and you came by."

"What about the other two guys?"

"Well, those two didn't make it back."

I had seen these kids right before they got killed, and they were all laughing and talking about how when they got back they were gonna come out and see the Cowboys again and all that.

It was an unbelievable experience. As far as I know, we were never under fire. We did make a trip up to the DMZ, where we would fly over this defoliated area and all of a sudden see this wall of jungle, and that was it.

We flew up with a Lieutenant Colonel Smith, in this little ol' Marine helicopter. Most of the time, the helicopters we flew in never landed. You jumped down the last five or six feet and landed running. This one landed.

Out where the jungle began, there were men every few yards, about five yards into the jungle where you couldn't even see them. They were the ones who really appreciated us coming up to visit them, but I kept thinking what it must be like to be in one of those holes at night.

It was a sobering experience.

There was one funny incident. After the tour, you get to go back to Saigon for a few days of R&R before heading back to the States. We were back in Saigon, and our escort officer is going to take us to one of these Turkish bath places.

You can get a sauna and a rubdown and all, but nobody speaks any English. I am laying there, and this girl is massaging my leg, and all of a sudden she rammed my heel up against my butt.

It was the leg they had operated on, and the adhesions still hadn't fully broken down. I was still kind of stiff-legged when I went to Vietnam, in fact. And here she was, jamming that thing back and I screamed bloody murder.

I couldn't bend my knee that far.

She didn't know that. I screamed, and it wasn't five seconds before two MPs came running into the room and I mean I'm holding my knee because it's hurting like crazy.

It tore some of those adhesions that would probably have taken another month otherwise. But they thought I'd been shot or something. The girl was scared to death. She couldn't speak English, and didn't know what she had done.

Coming back was another experience. We were flying to Japan, and the plane was full of guys who had been over there for 12 months or so. It was a bad time, 1969. When we lifted off, it was the biggest cheer you've ever heard.

And a few minutes later, we're flying along, and they announced, "We are now leaving Vietnam," those guys cheered, and when we got off in San Francisco, those guys got off and on hands and knees they kissed the ground.

I've wondered since what happened to that kid with the tube in his throat.

# 12

# Calvin Hill:
# Goodbye Starting

I HAD done better than almost anybody expected for three seasons with Dallas. Then came the knee injury, and Calvin Hill. If 1968 was a year of misery, then the 1969 season was a year of change for me.

I began to move toward coaching, although no way would I have thought of myself as a coach in those terms. Not then. Not yet.

In the draft that year, Dallas took Calvin Hill of Yale as their No. 1 choice. There was a lot of controversy over that. Nobody had ever heard of this Ivy League player.

We went to camp. Or, rather, I guess I should say I went to camp. I went early because I wanted to work on my knee. When I got there, the only two veterans in camp were myself and Mike Ditka. They had traded with Philadelphia to get him. Dallas had sent David McDaniels to Philadelphia for Ditka. McDaniels was the receiver they had taken No. 2 the previous year. He was from East Mississippi Valley. He had an unbelievable time in the 40 yard dash. Then, in camp, he ran something like four or five tenths slower. And what they found out was that the field wasn't 40 yards long when they got that real fast time.

Getting Mike Ditka for David McDaniels was a steal.

I had known Mike only a little, when he was with

Philadelphia. In 1967, in Dallas, Tim Brown, a running back from Philadelphia, came across the middle to catch a pass. The ball was kind of thrown behind him. He reached back for it, and he dropped the ball. So he kind of relaxed. When he turned around, Lee Roy Jordan hit him. Of course, from where Lee Roy was, he couldn't see Brown had dropped the ball.

So he hits him and he knocks out all his teeth. He knocked him out cold. Brown had had a whole bunch of bridgework done and gotten his teeth all fixed. He was an actor. And Lee Roy just unloaded on him.

After that ball game, there were several athletes who had been signed to represent Allied Chemicals. Mike Ditka was one. So was Buddy Dial of Dallas. They were paid so much a month to attend banquets or play golf with customers, that sort of thing. After that game, Allied Chemicals had a banquet in Dallas, and Buddy Dial had asked me to attend with him.

Mike Ditka had stayed over, and he got up and talked about the game the day before. "One good thing about playing in the National Football League," he said, "when you play somebody in your division, you get to play them twice.

"When you come to Philadelphia, we'll be looking for Dallas and particularly Lee Roy Jordan."

That was my first experience with Mike Ditka, standing up before a Dallas audience telling them he couldn't wait to get at one of their star players the next time they played.

So when I got to Thousand Oaks that summer to continue rehab on my knee, there is Mike Ditka, who has come in early to try and learn the offense. We play gin rummy. I hate gin rummy. I think it's the worst card game or any kind of gambling game I've ever seen because so much luck is involved.

But Ditka loves it. He'd rather play gin rummy than eat when he's hungry. Every free moment we've got, we're in there, playing gin rummy. I'm not a good gin rummy player and Mike is.

But the cards are running all over. I mean, I am getting cards like you wouldn't believe. I'm knockin', ginnin', just killin' him.

I don't know. After blitzin' him on a Hollywood or something like that, he just explodes. He took a half a deck of cards and ripped them in two, and then took the other half and ripped them, and threw them all over the room.

Then he picked his chair up and threw it up against the wall. And all four legs stuck into the wall.

I just sit there in amazement. "My God! This guy is really...different."

But that's how competitive he was. He couldn't stand to lose at anything.

And he really and truly was exactly what we needed. We didn't have a mean guy on offense. We had good players, but we didn't have an enforcer. We didn't have any tough guys, and that's what Mike brought to us.

We became good friends, immediately, in spite of the gin rummy.

Before the veterans came in, I went out one day to watch the rookies scrimmage, and you could tell Calvin Hill had talent. He could make a run and you would think it was a two yard loss and it was a three yard gain. He was so big and so tall he could actually fall forward for two or three yards.

He also had some great moves.

I was having problems with my knee. When the veterans reported, we were running pass routes one morning, working against the linebackers, and I was working against Chuck Howley. I told Craig Morton, "I'm gonna run a shoot and go comeback."

When I planted my foot to comeback, my knee just gave. Immediately, I figured, "This is it. I'm not going to make it."

Dr. Knight asked them to send me back to Dallas, and he examined my knee.

"What you have is a problem with the staple that holds the ligament to the bone," he said. "I think it's going to be all right. It's just inflamed a little bit right now."

He told me just to take it easy for a couple of days and it would be okay. Well, I am getting less and less playing time and Calvin Hill is getting more and more. It's terrible. I have never sat on the bench in my life.

It's really kind of seeing the writing on the wall and you don't like what you read there.

You can kid yourself, but if you are honest, you knew that basically your career was over. But I still felt like it was going to come around and I was going to end up playing, end up starting.

The key thing was, in that 1969 season we were going to open up with St. Louis, the team we had been playing when I hurt my knee the year before. That's what I am looking for. I want to play this team that had basically messed up my career.

So we go to Houston to play the Oilers in the Astrodome in one of the few preseason games we have left. My younger brother, Butch, has been drafted by the Oilers as a defensive back.

We talked about it before the game. I'm fighting for my career and he's fighting to make the Oilers. He gets in and plays a little bit, and I get in. I remember running a quick pitch, and I went to cut back, and my leg gave way again.

It was frustrating. It seemed like every time you started to get confidence in your knee, something would happen to it and set you back.

On the flight back to Dallas, I talked about it to Dr. Knight.

"I think you have a problem with the bursa pad," he said. "I think it has built up over that staple. It's almost like stepping on a hot cigarette. I think if we take that staple out of there it will alleviate some of the problem."

He gave me two choices: I could go into the hospital, under sedation, have it removed, and be out three or four days. Or, I could get a local. "You'll probably be ready to practice the following day."

There wasn't any question. "Shoot. I want to do it locally so I don't miss any practice. There's only two preseason games left."

So Dr. Knight said he wanted to talk to Coach Landry and see what he felt and blah blah blah. We decided to do it locally.

Well, I had had about four or five local operations, and after each one I swore I'd never have another one. I had that collarbone pin removed in high school, and in college I had a calcium deposit removed from my chest.

In that one, I went over after final exams, and he deadened it, and started cutting and there was all this blood running down my chest.

"Wait a minute. I'm gonna have to lay down." So I did, and he walked over and came back with a hammer and chisel and I started laughing. I thought he was kidding.

He wasn't. He puts that chisel up against my chest and takes the hammer back and knocks the calcium off my chest. So I swore that was the last local I'd ever endure.

But I knew this was the only chance I'd have to be ready to play and hopefully win the starting job or keep the starting job.

I went to Dr. Knight's office. They cut the knee open. They've got the stocking on it and everything, and they pin it back so they can get in there.

Well, both of us thought it would take maybe 10 or 15 minutes. At the most. It ended up taking a little over an hour. I am wringing wet with sweat. I have never been in such pain. That bursa pad was so big he had to cut through it to get underneath it. He took a chisel or something like a chisel to get under the staple and pry it out of the bone.

I was in unbelievable pain. He finally got the thing out, and sewed it back up. We had the next day off, so I've got a little bit of time to recuperate.

I went to practice the following day, and started to put my pads on.

"We don't want you to practice today," the trainer told me.

"I gotta practice today."

"No. Leave your pads. Just jog around the field and so forth."

I did, reluctantly, and the next day I came back and we went through the same thing again. No pads. Just jog.

"I've got to practice. If I don't practice, I don't play, and if I don't play this week, there is no way I'm going to be able to start against St. Louis."

Well, I went out, and I jogged. And on Friday, the day before we are to play, I am coming into the dressing room when Coach Landry comes up.

"I need to talk to you," he said.

I go in, and he says, "I want you to know we have placed you on injured reserve." At that time, people could claim you off injured reserve. He wanted people to know I had not been in pads and I wasn't practicing so that nobody would claim me.

I was really hot. I was so mad. If they were going to do that, all they had to do was put me in the hospital. I could have gone under a regular anesthetic and not had to endure what I did.

That was one time I told myself that if I ever got in that position, I was going to be honest with my players. I'm not going to try to pull the wool over their eyes.

That really made me mad. It's the only time I think I really got mad at Coach Landry.

It also meant I was going to be out four weeks, and that I was not going to play in the opener against the Cardinals.

Sure enough, Calvin Hill starts. I did get to play quite a bit that season because Calvin ended up getting hurt. He had a big toe that got jammed. I knew how painful that could be. I could relate to it. I had that thing the year before.

I played in a lot of games, particularly in passing situations. But it was still a miserable season for me because I wasn't playing as much as I would have liked.

Cleveland beat us 38–14 in the playoffs that year, and we were going to the Playoff Bowl game, and the first day of practice I ran a cut-out route. I ran like seven or eight yards and cut out and caught the ball, and planted my left foot to try and stay in bounds.

I felt the knee give again. They had to send me to the doctor the next day because my knee had swollen very badly. They sent me to the Miami team doctor and drained about 60 cc's of blood from my knee.

I didn't practice all week, and in the game, Calvin got hurt like the first series. I ended up having to play almost the whole game.

Going home, I knew that my career was pretty much over. Lee Roy Jordan and I were going to work in the real estate business with a guy named Glenn Butler.

This is two years in a row we have gotten beat by Cleveland in the playoffs. The two years before that we had lost to Green Bay in the championship game. So there is a lot of talking, a lot of people talking, a lot of dissension on the team, a lot of dissension in the coaching ranks.

Coach Landry had us fill out a questionnaire. What do you think about your coach? What do you think about the head coach? All kinds of things like that.

A few weeks later, I am working in Glenn Butler's office in the same building where the Cowboys have their offices. Ray Renfro was coaching our wide receivers. He called me one day.

"You know, Ermal Allen is going to quit coaching." He was our backfield coach. "You ought to go talk to Coach Landry about possibly being a player coach."

It intrigued me. I knew my career was all but over. But if I could coach and play, maybe I could last a few more years. I really enjoyed professional football, and thought maybe this was a way I could stay around a little bit longer.

I went in and talked to Coach Landry, and he said, "Yeah. Let me think about it."

I spoke at a banquet in West Texas somewhere one day, and came back, and had a message to call Coach Landry. He wasn't in, but his secretary, Marge Kelly, was.

"Coach Landry wants you to go down and talk to the psychiatrist." It's about nine o'clock in the morning. I think it's going to be a short visit.

As I go in his office, he is sitting at his desk. He turns around and stares out the window. It's about the 35th floor of this office building. I am sitting there, staring at the back of his head and the back of his chair, across the desk, with the skyline outside the window.

And the first question he asks me is, "What do you think of your mother?"

I'm thinking wha...? That was the kind of questions: What do you think of your dad? What kind of life did you have? I'm there like three hours. I'm starving to death. I haven't had any breakfast.

In Dallas to this day, every coach has to talk to a psychiatrist. Coach Landry wants to see if the evaluation of you is the same as that of someone who is a professional. I've done it here, and I've done it with most of the coaches I've hired.

It's good. You get someone else's input. I made a mistake hiring a coach here. I don't ever want to do that again. What I felt about him, I didn't listen to. Now, I want somebody else to give me some feedback. So it's good.

It's kind of a psychological profile to see if you and he can work together, what kind of work habits he has. The thing I like is it is either going to verify what you feel or tell you there are going to be some problems.

So, anyway, I go through this thing. How did I do? How do you know when you go through one of those? But in a couple of weeks Coach Landry called me in.

"I would like for you to be a player coach," he said. Of course I took the job. I would make $30,000, and get an additional $4,000 for being a player coach.

The first meeting I go to is a meeting going over these questionnaires. They weren't signed. I would read one and think, "Gosh. I know who that is."

And that's what the coaches were doing. "I know who that son of a gun is," they'd say. "Thats got to be so and so. He'd gripe about anything."

I do think it gave Coach Landry some insight into what the players were thinking. One of the things was that Ermal would be out teaching us one way, and Coach Landry would come up and say, "No, that's not the way I want it."

That would make Ermal look bad. It was little things like that that came out of the questionnaire. I think it got the staff closer together. It gave us a more central focus. We talked about questions regarding the offseason.

We implemented an offseason conditioning program. I spent some time with Alvin Roy, the strength and conditioning coach of the Kansas City Chiefs. Coach Landry put me in charge of our program.

I wanted to get people motivated, and recommended we have an offseason team party, bring in all the wives and get together. We had never done that. Coach Landry and Tex Schramm thought it was a good idea. So we did it. I planned it. I had a band to dance to and I brought in a magician and it really was nice.

We had a great offseason. We had some awards for the guys that improved the most, were the strongest and so forth. Plus, it was the first time we had a weight program.

We went into the 1970 season with good team spirit because of the things Coach Landry had done. The things he had the insight to do—send the questionnaires out, take the players' views into consideration. That had never been done in Dallas.

We took some of the players' recommendations and ended up having a great year.

We went to our first Super Bowl. And I discovered I liked coaching.

# 13

## A (Dallas) Super Bowl:
## Super V

THERE WERE some major adjustments for me in 1970 as a player coach.

I had roomed with Walt Garrison for five years. All of a sudden, I was coaching Walt Garrison. And I was still playing.

You go over the assignments, and you get in the game, and the worst thing you can do is make a mistake. If you miss an assignment, as a player coach, boy, the players are really going to give you a hard time.

It was an unusual year in other ways. That year, 1970, was the year we went to training camp and there was a strike. I was a player coach for the first time, and it looked like we were not going to have any players.

We held rookie camp, and it was obvious right at the start we had some great rookies. Dallas had a tremendous draft that year. We got Duane Thomas, Charlie Waters, Cliff Harris (a free agent), Mark Washington, John Fitzgerald, Steve Kiner.

The veterans didn't report, of course, so we had these rookies in camp for a long time. We scrimmaged the San Diego Chargers rookies two or three times and the Rams rookies two or three times, and what it amounted to was our rookies got tremendous exposure and experience and coaching. They had a chance to impress.

Duane Thomas was definitely an unusual talent. He was extremely bright, had great size and great speed. He could really run the football and catch it, and he could block. He could do all the things you want, and he did them well.

We had some great talents, and we worked them hard. We worked them so hard that summer, in fact, we worried about them quitting. We were in pads every day, hitting, and we would go in meetings and worry about who might leave on us.

We kind of pampered them.

"Look, we'll have a curfew, but don't turn them in. Don't fine them. But we need to know they are in the dorms and so forth." So I am the one designated to go over and check, run the bed check every night.

We had a U-shaped building. The players stayed on one leg of the U, the coaches on the other, and our offices were on the base of the U. We would get through with our meetings at 12:30 or one o'clock, something like that, and I would go over to the players' side and I could hear a pin drop.

I was staying in the players' dorm, I wasn't staying in the coaches' dorm. And I was the only guy over there. I was rooming by myself for the first time, not with Garrison.

I used to go up on the roof and talk to them. Of course, they were scared to death, some of them. I was trying to give them some insight into what was happening, going to happen, tell them this was a great opportunity because the veterans weren't in camp yet.

Because of the great rookie crop, we went into the season with a tremendous amount of enthusiasm and a tremendous amount of excitement among the coaching staff.

We got off to a quick start, and Craig Morton was hitting like 70 percent of his passes when we beat Philadelphia and the Giants, two teams in our division, to start the season. But he got hurt in the Atlanta game on a freak play, and wasn't ready to play in our fifth game at Minnesota.

We were 3-1 at that point, and now Roger Staubach was going to start. But he had an infected elbow, and hadn't practiced all week. They drained the elbow, and got some black stuff out of it that was the ugliest I had ever seen.

But he was the only quarterback we had, and so he started against Minneosta, and then, just before the half, he got knocked out. It was right in front of our bench.

Now, the quarterback that has to go in to play is me. Minnesota is just killing us, and winds up winning 54–13, and things are bad enough without that. I haven't played quarterback since college.

I'm the disaster quarterback, and I'm standing there, looking, and saying to myself, "Holy mackerel, get up. Get up off the ground, Roger."

It was fourth down, and we got out of the half because there were only a few seconds left. Roger recuperated enough during the half-time break that he came back out and played the second half.

But now, we've got to go play the World Champions, the Chiefs, in Kansas City. You have to remember, the Chiefs had started out as the old Dallas Texans in 1960, the year we started, and there had been a real rivalry to get the fans in Dallas until they moved in 1962.

Now here they were, world champions, and they had beaten Minnesota in the Super Bowl and Minnesota had just clobbered us the week before. Here comes the team that chased them out of Dallas. And Calvin Hill gets hurt early in the ball game.

Now, I am in the backfield with Duane Thomas. And in that ball game, I remember Craig audibled against a blitz and hit Hayes for about a 90 yard touchdown, but the game was still real close in the fourth quarter. Craig called a trap play, right up the middle. I'm supposed to carry the ball.

As we're coming out of the huddle, I said, "Duane, you move to the halfback position and carry the ball. I'll play fullback and I'll block for you."

He went 50 some yards for the touchdown.

I came off the field, and I told Coach Landry that was the smartest move I ever made because he ran for a touchdown and I probably would have turned it into a four yard gain.

We ended up beating Kansas City 27–16, and it gave us the feeling that, "Hey, we got a chance. This was the defending world champion and we beat them on their home field."

Craig played that whole season hurt. He had that bad shoulder, and the last game of the season, we played Houston, and he threw about five touchdown passes. We had some confidence going into the playoffs.

But let me back up a minute. Not long after Kansas City, we played St. Louis in a Monday night game, and we lost 38–0. It was in Dallas. Don Meredith had retired, and he was broadcasting the game. They were blitzing Larry Wilson on every play, coming from everywhere.

St. Louis was leading our division at the time, and we had just lost to the Giants the week before, and this was probably the most embarrassing loss we had ever had.

When Meredith was playing, they had chanted, "We want Morton. We want Staubach." Now, at the end of this game, they were chanting, "We want Meredith."

It was a humiliating loss. The players met. Nobody liked us. We were 5–4, and we were going to miss the playoffs for the first time in a long time. Our wives didn't like us. They were missing all that playoff money and everything. We were three games down, with five games to go.

The chances of overtaking St. Louis were almost nothing. But all of a sudden, they go on a terrible losing streak, and our defense gets hot, and we don't lose again.

Defense wins championships, and we had the feeling now, especially after the way Craig threw in our final game against Houston, that we had the pieces all in place. Finally.

There had been all that taunting about "Next Year's Champions."

Our luck was turning, but we would learn it hadn't turned enough. Not yet, anyway.

Our first playoff game, the divisional one under the new realigned setup, we beat Detroit in Dallas 5–0 on a field goal and a safety. For the third time in my career, we were one game away from the Super Bowl.

It meant we had to go out to San Francisco and play the 49ers for the NFC championship and the right to go on to Miami and Super Bowl V, as it was being called by then.

The thing I remember about that game—well, two things—Duane Thomas had a great game, and Walt Garrison played the gutsiest game I think I have ever seen. Duane just did everything. He had rushed 30 times the week before against Detroit, and this time, three days after New Year's Day, he had 167 total yards, 143 of them rushing.

It was a great game for a rookie in his first championship.

Walt hurt his ankle early in that game. They took him inside and taped it and shot him up and he came back and played the rest of the game. He was also playing with two cracked ribs.

We won, 17–10, with Walt catching the winning touchdown pass, and we're going to the Super Bowl against Baltimore.

You have a week at home before you go to the game site, and we used it to put in our game plan for Baltimore. It was all set, and we worked on it that week at home. Then came the weekend.

Coach Landry looked at some more film, and we flew into Miami on Sunday and had a staff meeting at the hotel that night.

We were going to change basically our entire game plan. He had seen some things watching film. Another thing was we didn't think Walt Garrison was going to be able to play, so we were going to put Duane Thomas at fullback and Calvin Hill at tailback.

That week, Walt insisted, "I am going to play. I'm going to be ready by Sunday." So now we switch Duane back to tailback and put Walt at fullback.

As it turned out, if it hadn't been for Garrison, we wouldn't have had any rushing yardage at all in the game. It was a game we had all waited and worked for for years, and when it came, it is still the game most people remember for the weird things that happened.

Between us, Baltimore and Dallas, we had six fumbles, six interceptions, and 14 penalties, and the game was decided on Jim O'Brien's field goal at the finish.

Baltimore fumbled five times, and we recovered four of them. But our fumble came on their 1 yard line at the start of the second half. We had recovered a fumble on the kickoff, and drove to the 1, first and goal, and Duane Thomas fumbled.

Dave Manders recovered, but the officials yelled, "Baltimore!" Billy Ray Smith had jumped up and started motioning, but Dave was standing there with the football. There was no question about it, but they gave the ball to Baltimore.

Of course, they had one where they fumbled it through the end zone and we got possession, and John Mackey got a tipped ball and went 75 yards on a pass from Johnny Unitas. So there were some crazy, crazy plays all day long, and when it was over and they had won 16-13, Bob Lilly must have thrown his helmet 40 yards in disgust.

For me, the hard part to remember is the last couple of minutes when it was tied 13-13 and we got the ball back. On the first play, we got caught holding.

Now it was first and 25. Hindsight is wonderful. Now you wish you had run out the clock and gone into overtime. But we came out throwing, and Craig rolled out to his right and I ran a hook pattern over the middle.

He threw, and it's high but it's a catchable ball. It goes through my hands. Mike Curtis gets it for Baltimore, and it's that interception that sets up the winning field goal at the finish.

It's not how you want to remember your first Super Bowl.

After all those years, we had had chances to take control, had come within one last kick—and lost again.

It really hurt. After all those years of losing to Green Bay twice, losing to Cleveland twice, coming close, we finally get to the Super Bowl, and then lose. In my opinion, we were the best team. To show the way the game went, it was the first time a losing player was the MVP.

Chuck Howley won it.

It was my first year as a coach, and I thought, "Boy, this is an easy business." It was a fun first year. It just ended on a bad note.

# 14

# Duane Thomas: Double Standard

OF ALL the losses up to then, Super Bowl V was the worst.

The two Green Bay games for the championship had been close. The losses to Cleveland had been embarrassing. But the loss to Baltimore had to be the one that hurt the most.

We felt like we had dominated the football game and yet wound up losing on a last second field goal. So I think there was kind of a dedication or a rededication, whatever you want to call it, between the 1970 and 1971 seasons. I saw something similar happen years later here in Denver between our back to back Super Bowls.

We really wanted to get that opportunity again.

By that year, 1971, I was involved a lot less as far as playing was concerned. I was becoming more involved as a coach. The transition was taking place.

We opened the season up in Buffalo, in the old War Memorial Stadium. The thing I remember most about that game was it was a high scoring game, and they had a young running back named O.J. Simpson.

There was one 10 yard run he made, when it seemed like everybody on our defense had a shot at him, that we all knew we were looking at something special.

The other thing that I remember is that one of

our wide receivers got thrown out of the game, and I ended up playing wide receiver. I also played fullback and halfback at times in that game.

That was the season we dedicated Texas Stadium with a game against the New England Patriots. We won 44–21 on October 24. Duane Thomas had a tremendous game. He ran 56 yards early in the game to score the first touchdown in that stadium.

He had been rookie of the year in 1970. It was in that offseason that we started having problems, having trouble with him.

I had brought him in to talk. I had gotten a report from an FBI friend that he was messing around with some people who were smoking marijuana. I had basically just told him he had almost unlimited opportunities in Dallas, and he had said, "I understand. Don't worry about me. I can handle it."

Then, he goes out to Los Angeles, and the next time I see him, he's like somebody different.

He wants to renegotiate his contract, and he isn't talking to anybody. He won't answer the roll. You would call his name and he wouldn't even answer it. So we ended up not calling the roll. The coaches just checked their own people.

I'd be in meetings with him, and I'd ask him a question, and he wouldn't say a word. It was a very uncomfortable situation for me. I'm treating the other five or six running backs I've got completely different from the way I'm treating him.

We won our last seven games that year and won the Eastern Division with an 11–3 record. Then we beat Minnesota and San Francisco again, and finally got that monkey off our back.

We beat Miami in Super Bowl VI in New Orleans. We finally had done it, finally had won that last game, and Roger Staubach was the MVP.

It was kind of a watershed year for us. It was the year our problems with Duane began, and it was the year Roger Staubach finally took over as the Dallas starter, and the year we won our first Super Bowl.

Craig Morton and Roger had been kind of swapping back and forth up through Chicago, which was the seventh game of the season. We lost it 23–19, and in that game, Coach Landry had alternated Craig and Roger every play.

Then, at the end, when we're behind and trying to win the ball game, Craig is in the ball game heading our two minute attack. So everybody assumed, and I did, too, that Craig was going to be our starting quarterback, that Coach Landry had made a decision between the two of them.

But Coach Landry surprised everybody. We had a staff meeting and we had more assistant coaches who felt like Craig should be the starter over Roger because of his experience and so forth.

But Coach Landry felt like Roger was more of a leader, more of a rally-the-troops type of a quarterback. So he named Roger, and we won the last seven games of the season, the two playoffs, and then the Super Bowl. We won 10 straight after that decision was made.

Really and truly, and this is my feeling, we would have won regardless of which was starting because our defense started playing so well.

Getting ready for Miami in the week before the Super Bowl, I played Nick Buoniconti, Miami's linebacker. I knew after that week of practice, with me knowing where the play was going and everything and them beating the heck out of me anyway, I knew that our offense was ready to play a good game.

I was trying to show them how Miami's defense was going to play, and I was playing Buoniconti and I knew our plays and they were still containing me. Miami was a very aggressive team, but they were also very young. This was just the start of their run of three straight Super Bowls, remember. So we planned to take advantage of that aggressiveness and cut back inside their pursuit, and that's what we wound up doing in the game

I was so sore from that week. I can remember I only held for field goals and extra points in the ball game. Near the end of the game, we were ahead like 24–3 or something, and we were getting ready to kick a field goal.

By then, about the only way Miami was going to get back in the game was if they blocked a field goal or got an interception.

"Fake a field goal, but don't throw it," Coach Landry said.

So sure enough I went in and called a fake field goal, and stood up to run, and our tight end was open for a touchdown. But I didn't throw it. I didn't want to take a chance on an interception.

I ended up running for a first down. I remember Shula was so mad. He thought we were trying to run the score up on him. Actually, we ended up not scoring. Calvin Hill ended up fumbling.

That was such a great feeling afterward—winning. After all those years, going from 1966 to 1971, beating on the door and always being turned away.

We went in the dressing room, and everybody was having such a great time, smoking big cigars and laughing and hugging and throwing Clint Murchison in the showers, and the only one not having a good time was Duane Thomas.

He had had a great game, but he's not speaking to anybody.

Let me go back a minute. We arrived in New Orleans on Sunday, and Monday night we all went down to Bourbon Street. We had a young receiver, Margene Adkins, and he was wearing like a jumpsuit. Walt Garrison was fooling around and somehow ripped his jumpsuit.

They wound up screaming at each other. Tuesday is Picture Day. And we're in the dressing room and everybody's going up to get their uniforms and all of a sudden a fight breaks out.

It's Garrison and Adkins. We break it up and I think, "Holy mackerel. We're getting ready to play the Super Bowl and we're fighting each other."

So Coach Landry in his way gets each of them aside and talks to them. We go out for Picture Day, and everybody's standing there and being interviewed and Duane Thomas comes out and goes over and sits by himself on the end of the bleachers.

All the press went over, and he just sat there. He never said a word. Well, he said one sentence. He said, "What time is it?"

So after the game we're in the dressing room, and Tom Brookshire is doing interviews, and somehow he gets Duane Thomas up on the platform and says something like, "Duane this is fantastic. You've finally won the championship. Is this the ultimate game?"

And Duane Thomas looked at him and said, "No. If it was, we wouldn't be playing it again next year."

We were able to overcome a lot of things that year, doing something I never thought you could do and still be successful—basically the situation with Duane.

We actually treated him totally different from everybody else on the team. He had reported late, and been reinstated. He had been traded to New England that summer, but he and John Mazur were wrong from the start.

The story we got in Dallas was that Duane refused to line up in a three-point stance, and Mazur kicked him off the practice field. Eventually the deal was called off and Duane came back. But he had refused to report, and we didn't get him active until before our fourth game, against the Giants.

I always gave a test the night before a game. I wrote out the test, "What do you do on Toss 49, fullback lead?" things like that. I handed the thing out to all the players, and Duane must have handed his in in five minutes.

I said, "Gosh, you hand it in that quick and you're just back in camp."

Then I looked at it, and after every question, his answer was, "It's in the book."

"What do you do on Toss 49, fullback lead?"

"It's in the book."

"Where are you on Slant 34?"

"It's in the book."

So that's another example.

We check into the hotel the night before the game, and he hasn't said one single word to me. About one o'clock in the morning I get a call. It's Duane.

He says, "Could you come down to my room and I'll go over some assignments with you?"

I said sure, I'd be right down. So I hung up the phone and I got to thinking, "This guy's really different. He's weird. Maybe he's going to get me in his room and beat me up or we're gonna have a fight or something."

I went down, and he was just like he had been the year before. Everything was normal. He asked unbelievable questions: He wanted to know where everybody was, "Where's my help coming from?" Intelligent, great stuff. We went over it for like an hour.

He's got these plays down. So then, the next day, Calvin Hill and Walt Garrison are playing. We are planning on playing Duane the second half at fullback.

Early in the second half, the second or third play, Calvin gets hurt. So now I am in the backfield, with Duane. He would never say anything. If he didn't say anything, he knew what to do.

If he wasn't sure, he would kind of look over at me, and I'd tell him. "You're carrying the ball. It's a wide play, underneath handoff," or "Lead for me into the 4 hole."

We went through that year. I had to quit calling the roll because of him. He played well. He did have unbelievable talent. We would have staff meetings, and Coach Landry would say, "We just have to have patience."

It was miserable for me. I was having the worst time of my career. I've got to coach a guy who won't answer roll, who won't say anything.

I remember one day we got out of the meeting, and we walked back and all of the lockers were on this aisle, and Calvin Hill looked up at Duane and said, "Whaddyasay, Brother?"

And Duane looked at him and said, "Hey, I'm not your bleeping brother."

He played well, but it was really just a bad situation. He was a great guy in running to daylight. As long as there was yardage there, he was going to go. But if he didn't see daylight he would almost just kind of collapse. It was like, "I'm gonna get you next time, but you're not gonna get me this play."

But against Miami in the Super Bowl he and Walt both ended up making some outstanding runs and we won the world championship.

As happy as we were, there was an ache inside me, because I really didn't enjoy it. Here I was, player coach, and I really didn't enjoy that year because of that situation. It was totally against everything that I believed in.

I believed it was a team game, and you didn't treat anybody different. Everybody had to be on the same page.

By the 1972 season, I was going to strictly be a coach. I didn't even work out that much in the offseason. I had retired as a player. I went from like 205 to 215 or 220. On top of that, I had quit smoking. I had never enjoyed it.

We had a good preseason until we were out in Los Angeles, playing the Rams, and Roger Staubach started to run and met Marlin McKeever. Roger didn't get up. He had torn his shoulder up.

Now we only have Craig as our quarterback, and we end up making a deal for Jack Concannon from the Chicago Bears. After a couple of weeks, Coach Landry called me in and said, "Look. We need for you to be our backup quarterback. You need to start working out. Who do you think should be our backfield coach?"

We had Ermal Allen, who had become a special assistant, and we had just that year hired Sid Gillman. We talked about it.

I said, "Well, coach, I don't think Ermal wants to be on the field any more. Coach Gillman would probably be the best." So that starts to be a bad situation.

We tried to trade Duane Thomas at this time. They had voided the trade with New England the year before. Duane wasn't talking to anyone. He wouldn't eat with them, nothing. He wouldn't eat meat. He would eat nothing but fruit. He'd go over and bring back a handful of apples and oranges, nectarines, grapes.

We stayed in a dormitory, and he stayed in a room, by himself. He was on the ground floor, and he wouldn't go over to lunch with the other guys. About an hour after lunch he would step out his window. He didn't use the door. He climbed out his window and went over to the dining hall and back that way.

Then he'd come out on the field, and he wouldn't say a word to anyone.

That whole summer with him was bizarre, right from the start.

He had gotten his ticket to training camp, and everybody was excited. "Hey, Duane Thomas is going to report. He's going to report on time." He had been saying all these things in the offseason, of course. Things like "I'm not going to play for them," and "Landry's a plastic man," and "Tex Schramm is a liar and a cheat."

And Tex had laughed and said, "Well, two out of three ain't bad." Stuff like that. Then we thought he had decided to come in on time, so everybody was excited about that.

So we go into a meeting while somebody goes to the plane to pick him up. And the guy calls and says Duane isn't on the flight. "But some friend of his is here. He gave him his ticket. He wants to try out and said Duane said he could play for us."

The guy practiced with us about two days. He's a terrible player. And nobody knows where Duane Thomas is.

So Duane finally comes in, and he's really got his face down. He comes in late one afternoon, and he wants to know where Coach Landry is. I tell him it's the last door on the right.

He's in there for like an hour. I actually went down to the door to listen in, make sure everything was all right. I didn't hear anything. I began to worry.

What's happening? Has he gone in there and killed Coach Landry? Is he just sitting there? What's going on? So I go outside. And I go around and look in the window, and there's a bed on each side of the room.

Coach Landry is sitting on the far bed, and Duane is sitting on the near one, and neither one of them is saying anything. They're just sitting, kind of looking at the floor. It had been at least an hour, and I'll bet you neither one of them said two words.

So, finally, we ended up trading him to San Diego. Somebody had to tell him. So Ray Renfro and I flipped a coin, and Ray lost. He had to go tell Duane that Coach Landry wanted to see him. Ray Renfro called everybody "Partner."

In 1970, when I took over the conditioning program, I had to call Blaine Nye one time about a workout, and he wasn't home. His wife answered, and I had to ask her, "Mrs. Nye, would you have your husband call me?" I didn't know her name.

So I suggested to Coach Landry that when we put out our player list, we include the first names of their wives. He thought that was a great idea.

So did Ray. "Yeah," he said in the meeting. "I come out of those games sometimes and see somebody's wife, and I don't know her name."

"What do you do, Ray? Call her 'Mrs. Partner'?" Coach Landry asked.

So, anyway, Ray had to tell Duane. He knocks on the door. We know Duane is in his room. But Duane won't come to the door.

So Ray is hollerin' at the door. "Partner. Partner. Coach Landry wants to see you, Partner. Bring your playbook."

We finally had to get Roger Staubach to go through the adjoining door from his room to get Duane Thomas to go over and see Coach Landry.

The trade is unconditional. It ends up San Diego can't find the guy. It turned out he never did play for them.

So, that was the way 1972 started out for me, and it was one of the reasons that by the end of that season, I quit football.

# 15

# 1972: A Season Too Many

IF DUANE Thomas helped push me toward civilian life, I have to admit that Sid Gillman did, too.

It had been a crazy preseason as it was, with all that stuff around the Duane Thomas trade, and Roger Staubach being hurt, and me becoming the backup quarterback.

Now, we've got Sid Gillman coaching the running backs. He had just joined us that year, and now I am the quarterback in ball handling drills during camp, during practice.

I hand the ball off, and Coach Gillman is telling them this is what you do on this particular play. And it would be wrong. The read would be wrong, or whatever.

I would say, "Coach, no. We have to take a cross-over step and he cuts off the tackle's block."

And he'd say, "No, that's not the way I want it. I want him to do this."

So, we had several confrontations, Coach Gillman and myself.

Finally, Coach Landry called me into his office. "Look," he said. "I know you know how this play is run. But if we don't have Coach Gillman coaching the running backs, then you have to. And you are now a quarterback, and you won't always be able to be with them."

It was frustrating to be in a meeting with Coach

Landry and Sid Gillman. And there'd be Ray Renfro, Jim Myers, myself. We could make a suggestion about the passing game, and Coach Landry would argue, "Well, I don't think that's a good idea."

But Sid Gillman could come up with any idea, and Coach Landry would say, "Boy, that's great."

I mean, to us, it wouldn't even make any sense. But Coach Landry had this thing about Sid Gillman. Gillman was supposedly a genius as far as the passing game was concerned. So, it was a frustrating season for me.

All of it started closing in. I had gone through all that Duane Thomas stuff, then I was playing quarterback and still sitting in on these meetings, and there was this stuff with Sid Gillman. I had had to go from like 225 to 215 in a two week period of time.

Coach Landry called me in. "Okay. You're making (I don't remember exactly, but it was somewhere like $25,000). If you are also going to be a player coach, we'll pay you another $7,000." Well, I went through about five games, and I'm still being paid on the basis of $25,000.

I finally went in and said, "Coach, am I going to get paid for playing quarterback, too?"

They did catch me up on it. Except for one game in 1971, that was the only year I actually got to play quarterback as a pro. That 1971 game came early, against Philadelphia. Roger threw an interception and got knocked out, and Craig Morton went in, and we got way ahead, like 35-7.

There are about 10 minutes left. Coach Landry called me over.

"You know," he said, "it's ridiculous for us to take a chance on Craig getting hurt. He's the only quarterback we've got now. Why don't you go in and finish up."

Well, that makes you feel good. He doesn't care if I get hurt. We made a couple first downs. I was calling my own plays, we were moving the ball, I know my limitations and I'm just throwing little short passes and handing the ball off.

All of a sudden, here comes a messenger in. He called a screen pass. So I went back on the screen pass, and the guy reads the screen pass, so now I have to roll out and we end up having linemen down field. We get penalized and end up not making the first down.

I had to stick the needle into Coach Landry a little bit. I went over and told him, "I was in great shape until you started sending in plays. I was in great shape."

So that was the first time I played quarterback in the National Football League. Now, in 1972, with Roger hurt, I did get to play quite a bit.

There was one incident I've got to tell about. It was a game in Dallas, the 10th week. We're way ahead again, so I go in the game in the fourth quarter. And I remember as I came out from center and turned to hand it off to Calvin Hill—it was a sweep around the right end—something popped in my left knee.

I barely make it, but I do hand it off to Calvin. And I'm walking to the sideline, and it is really hurting. Something is locked in my left knee. I'm thinking, "Holy mackerel. Here I am, playing backup quarterback because we don't have anybody else, and Roger won't be back for a while yet. What are we gonna do now?"

Just as I got to the sideline, it clicked out. It was okay again. It doesn't hurt any more. I can bend my knee. So I made it through the game, and that night, Pam and I went to a restaurant.

It's a very nice Italian place in Dallas, kind of fancy. And Pam and I are sitting there, and I'm thinking, "What was wrong with my knee? Why did something catch in there?"

While I'm thinking, I'm reaching under the tablecloth and feeling around on my knee. "There's got to be something in there," I think.

And I feel around—and I feel a little thing floating around.

It was like a bone chip, and I've got it. It's outside the joint and I've got it pinched between my fingers.

I told Pam, "I've got it! Let's go to the hospital right now. We've gotta get this thing out of here."

So I go limping out of this fancy restaurant, all bent over because I don't want to lose that thing, holding my hand outside my left knee, people looking up from their dinners, wondering what this is all about.

Pam drove me to Baylor hospital, and we called the trainer, but he was at a party at Clint Murchison's house. So were the doctors. So I called there, and told them I had found that bone chip, and had my fingers right on it, and to come over and get it out.

So they left the party and came down and ended up taking this thing out of my knee. When they showed it to me, it was about the size of a wisdom tooth. It was just a piece of calcium deposit.

I was ready to play the next week.

So I ended up playing the whole season as a backup quarterback, and we opened up the playoffs against San Francisco. I was on kickoff coverage, and holding for field goals and extra points, and playing backup quarterback.

I had been in the league eight years, and there I was on kickoff coverage.

"Reeves," the guys on the other team would say. "What're you doing on kickoff coverage?"

"Aw, you come into this league on kick coverage and you go out on kick coverage."

Then, right before the San Francisco game, Coach Landry told me he had deactivated me and activated another player. I have to admit it upset me. I had gone through the whole season, done all those things, whatever they asked, and now I wasn't going to get to play in the playoffs.

But they activated Roger, and the logical guy to be taken off was me.

The way it turned out, it was the right thing to do. San Francisco ran the opening kickoff back for a touchdown, and at the end they had us beat. Their coaches had already come down from the press box onto the field. We were down by 12 points with only a couple minutes to go.

We had put Roger in for Craig, and Roger threw a touchdown, and then we tried an onside kick, they got it and we knocked it loose, and Roger threw another.

It was an unbelievable finish, and we ended up winning 30–28. It was the same day Franco Harris made the Immaculate Reception in Pittsburgh's game against Oakland. That game had been on just before ours.

But we went up to Washington to play in the championship, and it wasn't even a contest. They beat us 26–3.

When that season ended, that's when I decided I wanted to get out of coaching.

We coached in the Pro Bowl, and all that week I kind of struggled. Was that what I really wanted to do? I had had the bad experience with Duane Thomas, and I had had the bad experience working with Sid Gillman, and I told myself I had to be happier doing something else.

There was another factor, too. Being a coach means a lot of time away from the family. The kids were growing up and I was never around when the water heater went out or they had something they needed me for, and Pam wanted a more settled life, too.

So I told Coach Landry during that week that I was going to go into the real estate business with some friends and was going to give up coaching.

Looking back, I guess I had to go through it to learn that coaching was what I really wanted to do.

# 16

# 1973: The Unhappy Civilian

I GUESS we all have to go through periods when we look at other things, and it's only when we look back we decide what we had is what we wanted in the first place.

For me, that period was 1973.

There was a moment, a little before Christmas 1973, when I came as close as I'll ever come to never going back to coaching.

It was a period when I almost completed a land deal.

If I had, I think I'd probably still be in the real estate business. But I didn't, and, since it was the *only* deal I would have completed in my 18 months as a civilian, you can imagine how I finally felt when I got back with the Cowboys for 1974.

I had ended 1972 struggling, struggling in my mind whether or not football was really what I wanted to do.

My kids were of an age when I wondered if I shouldn't be spending more time with them. At that point, I had been in training camp for seven straight years, six weeks at a time each year out in Thousand Oaks, California. So that was 42 weeks, almost a year of my life, I had spent away from my wife and kids in training camp.

I felt it was important as a father to have a normal type job where I could spend quality time with them. And I thought I could be happy doing something else.

I had some people who had talked to me in Dallas about going into the real estate business. Of course, about that time, everybody was making all kinds of money in that field.

They were syndicating this and that, selling farm land 40 miles outside Dallas and telling folks that five years from now it's going to be just like Los Angeles. You'll have freeways going through this land.

I went into the business with a guy named Butch Wheeler. He had just started his company. He was new, too, so he couldn't give me a lot of guidelines or a lot of help. So I struggled right off the bat. I studied and took the real estate exam and passed it.

Then, I'd only been out of football three or four weeks when I got a call at home one night from Coach Landry. He said, "Under any circumstances, would you be interested in coaching?"

"Well, sure. Under certain situations I'd have to say I'd be interested."

"Would you be willing to talk to me?"

So I met him at the Hilton Inn one morning for breakfast. He told me that Sid Gillman had just accepted the head coaching job of the Houston Oilers. He wanted me to come back and head up the passing game.

He said he would give me more responsibility than I had had before. That was really intriguing, really interesting. I would have more say in the offense, and he offered me a lot more money. He also at that time—and it was the first time it had been said—told me, "Well, you know, I'm only going to coach a few more years. I have part ownership in this club, and when I do decide to retire, Tex and I'll have some say in who is going to succeed me. Certainly, you would have to be a candidate."

There was nothing said other than that—that I would be "considered."

I remember calling my older brother, Charles, and talking to him. And Pam and I sat down and talked about it. And I think if it had not come so quickly after I had just made the decision to get out of football I would have taken it.

We debated it and Coach Landry would call me every night. "I need to have an answer."

Charles told me, "You need to think about it, sit down with Pam and talk about it, and pray about it." And he said, "You're not going to know. There's no answer going to come like a bell goes off and indicates this is the right answer and that's the wrong answer."

I just decided finally that I needed to give life outside of football a chance. So I ended up turning it down, and going into the real estate business, and I struggled from the start.

It ended up costing me thousands of dollars. I had a friend from another real estate company that helped me, and eventually I left Butch because we just weren't making any deals.

My savings were going pretty fast. So I went with a guy named Bill McPartland. Bill was building 100 townhomes. He wanted me to be a public relations kind of guy—look over things and handle all the problems and he wouldn't have to worry about it.

It seemed like we would always be a month behind. We would give them a date in January and here we are in March and they haven't moved in yet. You'd have to get the subcontractors, and they'd be late, or you'd have to get a wallpaper guy to come back and do it again, and the people are mad because their townhouse is not ready yet.

So we've got all these problems, and whenever we did it seemed Bill would have a tendency to go out the back door and there you'd be left. You'd have a situation where a guy delivered a couple truckloads of brick and he was supposed to be paid on Friday and here it was Tuesday of the next week and you're holding it back because just a day or two interest with all these millions of dollars is worth a lot of money

So I'm caught in all these situations, and now I've got all these townhomes people are unhappy with, and I'm thinking to myself, "All of a sudden, I've got a hundred Duane Thomases."

It taught me a great lesson. It makes no difference what you are in, you are going to have problems. It's your ability to deal with those problems and handle them that determines whether you are going to be successful.

Right before Christmas that year, 1973, I had put together a farm deal and we were offering one of these interest only for five years and then pay it out over another five years deals. It was going to close right before Christmas, and that deal was going to make me more money than I had made in like three years coaching.

Five guys put up like $200,000 some in earnest money—and then interest rates went sky high. And all of a sudden, the five guys who were going to be partners in this syndication decided to forfeit the $200,000 rather than close the deal.

So I'm sitting there with a commission I was really counting on, one that would really let me stay in the real estate business, and all of a sudden that thing went out the window.

It was a sad, sad Christmas. I had a friend, Dan Christie, who was from a little town, Plano, Texas. He had pretty much put together this deal of syndicating another smaller deal, and they had let me in on the deal and we closed that smaller one right before Christmas.

So I made a couple thousand dollars commission. It was my first commission, so I had a little bit of money right before Christmas.

At that same time, right after Christmas, my dad and my two brothers gave me a loan for like $18,000. It helped me pay back a loan another friend had made me, and I've never forgotten that.

My dad and my brothers could be hurting, and as long as I've got some money, whatever it takes, they don't have to worry about anything.

The good part was that I was getting to spend more time with my kids. This guy that I worked for, Bill McPartland, had a bunch of ranches, and we'd go up there on weekends and I'd ride dirt bikes, motorcycles, with the kids and we'd have a great time.

I was spending more time with them, and that was good, but I wasn't happy. I could go to real estate functions, a party or something, and they'd start talking real estate and I felt like a redheaded stepchild. Totally out of place. And yet, somebody could start talking about football and I felt comfortable. I felt like I could add something to the conversation.

I talked to Pam. "This is not for me," I told her. "I'm not getting any better at this. I'm not learning anything in the real estate business and I'm really struggling. We're either going to have to go back to Georgia, or I'm going to have to get back in coaching."

It had been over a year. It was the summer of 1974 by that point, and the Cowboys were getting ready to start camp out in Thousand Oaks. So I said, "I'm going to go by and talk to Coach Landry. I'm going to let him know I want to get back into coaching so that if somebody contacts him for a recommendation, he can let them know."

I had had some opportunities that previous year when I was out. One was with Tommy Prothro in San Diego. I'll get to that in another chapter.

So I went out and talked to Coach Landry, and told him I was interested in getting back in and if he heard of anybody looking I'd appreciate it if he would mention my name. He said he would.

I went home, and it had to be the following day or the one after that. My timing had to be absolutely perfect. He called me.

"Dan, Jim Garrett has just been hired to coach at Houston in the World Football league." Garrett had just been hired to coach the Cowboys special teams. "Would you be interested in coaching the special teams?"

"Yes, sir. I would."

"We're getting ready to go to camp. How soon do you think you could be there?"

I told him I needed to give Bill McPartland at least a couple week's notice. We left on good terms, but it wasn't a good time for him. We were winding down that project, and it wasn't an ideal situation for a man who had really helped me out.

But this was a chance I couldn't pass up. I wanted to get back in coaching. The funny thing was, that time when I quit, and Coach Landry had offered me the expanded responsibilities, he had also offered me $39,000.

Now, he offered me $20,000 to coach the special teams.

By the time I got back to Thousand Oaks, they had been in camp two weeks. But when I walked in, I felt like a big weight was off my back. I was comfortable. I was coaching again.

# 17

## America's Team:
## Super Bowls and Interviews

THAT SEASON, 1974, wasn't a great one from a team standpoint. We didn't make the playoffs for the first time since I had been a Cowboy, but I was back coaching, and now there was no question:

I was a football coach, no longer a football player. My whole attention was on coaching, on teaching.

Gene Stallings helped me a lot at that stage. I was two weeks late getting out to Thousand Oaks. Mike Ditka had become a coach in the year I was out, so now we were both young assistants together.

Even though that particular year wasn't a good one, from a Dallas standpoint, the ones that followed put Dallas up as one of the glamour teams, I guess you'd have to say. I can't remember when I first heard that phrase, "America's Team," but in the next four years we went to three Super Bowls.

Anyway, when I got to Thousand Oaks in the summer of 1974, I had never coached special teams. I had coached the backs, and had played some backup quarterback, but I discovered I liked having special teams. Coach Landry didn't have time to give a lot of attention to them, so I could come up with different ways of using people. If they worked, I felt as if I had accomplished something.

But I had never had to get up in front of a whole team at the blackboard and explain something, and this is where Gene Stallings helped.

He would get up every morning with me at 5:30, before breakfast, and we'd go into a classroom and he'd make me explain that day's assignments, what I was going to say, and he'd critique them.

"No, that's not the way you want to explain that. You want to get them involved, and this is the way you do that. You don't say, 'This is what the fullback does.' You say, 'Okay, if you are the fullback, what do you do?' "

The next year, 1975, was the year of the Dirty Dozen, and the Shotgun, and the Hail Mary Pass, and the start of that run of Super Bowls. Our biggest problem then was we were going to Super Bowls at the same time Pittsburgh was.

By 1975, I was back coaching running backs. I was making more money because Monte Clark had tried to hire me at San Francisco, and Coach Landry had told me, "Go out and talk to them. But give us a chance to talk to you and see if we can't keep you here."

So I got a good raise from the $20,000, but not back to the $39,000 I would have made if I hadn't quit in 1973.

I was excited. The previous year, I had drawn up all our third down plays off film. In the off season, I recommended we cut out third downs and make a special reel. Coach Landry agreed.

We had started searching, researching ourselves during that offseason, and one of the areas where we had been weak was in third down situations. In a staff meeting, we were talking about the reasons why.

At that time, everybody was playing double coverage on outside receivers. They were playing man on tight ends and backs, or playing zone by doubling the outside people, with twin safeties.

So, the backs could only be effective up to about seven yards deep coming out of the backfield. Your tight end could be effective, but he was really your only receiver. So they could really double cover your outside and have two linebackers or a safety and a linebacker double cover your tight end.

That left man for man on the backs, but they didn't have to worry about them past that certain depth.

Mike Ditka was the one that mentioned it. "Well, if we go to a shotgun," he said, "we can put those backs up on the line of scrimmage. Now, we've got five receivers. That can create some problems for the defense."

Coach Landry thought about it. "Well, if we do that, one of the problems we're going to have is protection." So we spent like the next two or three weeks just talking about protection. When you get in the Shotgun, get up in a triple wing, with nobody left in the backfield, the first thing you're going to do on defense is see if they can protect the quarterback.

We would meet on that from early in the morning until we went home. We spent more time on that, on finding protection for the quarterback in the shotgun, than on any other single thing while I was at Dallas. We changed our whole protection scheme.

Still, we felt like we had an idea that would work. We could free one of the backs. He wouldn't have to worry about checking to block before he went out. He could really get down into that 12 to 15 yard area and be a factor in the passing game.

I remember when we started out in the preseason, everybody kind of laughed when we shifted into the shotgun. Other teams thought it was funny. But we noticed we were running the same plays that we had in our regular attack.

We had to spend a lot of time on the snap to the quarterback from the center. We also had to teach the quarterback to slow himself down in his drop.

If he starts already five yards back, he could get back to 10 yards too quick, our pocket wasn't deep enough. Plus he would be ready to throw when our receivers hadn't completed their routes. So we worked on the blind snap from the center, and then getting Roger to discipline himself to go back slowly. This way when he hit 10 yards, his receivers were ready.

Other than those two areas, we didn't have to spend a lot of extra time. But the other teams were. Nobody else used it. It was taking up a lot of their practice time. It really helped us. We became a more effective offensive football team.

That was the year a dozen rookies made our football team. Mike Ditka really did an outstanding job with the tight ends and special teams. He had that blood and guts mentality of getting downfield and hitting people. That's what special teams are all about.

I need to mention something here, going back to the draft that year. We really had an outstanding one, but I remember that was the year Walter Payton came out. At that point, we really didn't have a running game at Dallas. And so, the night before the draft, they asked the coaches to write their choices on the board. We really weren't involved as much there in the draft as our coaches are here in

Denver. We had looked at some films of players at our positions, as we normally did, 10 or 12. And all the assistants wrote on the board we wanted Walter Payton.

The next day, we ended up drafting Randy White. We were disappointed because we thought Walter Payton was the way to go. But it turned out Randy White was a great choice, too. In that draft, we got White, Thomas Henderson, Burt Lawless, Bob Breunig, Pat Donovan, Randy Hughes, Mike Hegman, Mitch Hoopes, Scott Laidlaw and Herb Scott. We turned it around in one year.

We ended up being a wild card, and had to go to Minnesota for the playoff, and that was the game where Roger hit Drew Pearson for the winning touchdown with the Hail Mary Pass, and where a fan threw a bottle out of the stands and hit one of the officials, Armen Terzian, on the head.

On that winning drive, Roger also hit Drew on a fourth and 21 on a play where Drew went up to make the catch and came down with one foot in and one foot out, but officials ruled he had been pushed out. I don't know how that would have come out with today's instant replay, but it gave us a first down.

The whole thing was an impossible situation, because you don't score in that kind of deal. Yet we scored.

And then when Minnesota got the ball back, the first play, I can remember the bottle hitting Terzian's head. He went down like somebody shot him.

The other thing I remember, and it has stuck with me, is that several defensive players, Alan Page and Carl Eller and Jim Marshall started running off the field toward the dressing room while the game was still in its final stages. I thought that was kind of strange.

That win sent us to Los Angeles, and I think the Rams were so elated they didn't have to go up to Minnesota to play that they forgot they still had another game to play. We won 37–7. Roger threw four touchdown passes. Preston Pearson caught three of those touchdown passes and had one of the greatest playoff games I've ever seen.

The shotgun was perfect for him. Nobody could cover him one on one coming out of the backfield. We really hurt people with him coming out of the spread in the shotgun.

I remember one other moment in that Los Angeles game: We had a pretty good lead by the half, and we were down near their 15, and we didn't want to take a chance on an interception or something. So Coach Landry sent in a shovel pass.

And as the messenger was running on, you could hear their coaches on the sideline yelling, "Watch for the shovel pass!" And you could hear their players say, "Watch for the shovel pass!"

And Coach Landry on our sideline says, "Oh, my God. He's gonna get killed."

Well, Hacksaw Reynolds was covering the other back and we ran the shovel to Preston. He went all the way in for a touchdown and he wasn't even touched. It was our day.

Pittsburgh beat us in the Super Bowl that year down in Miami. We played a good game, but Lynn Swann made a big catch on the blitz, and we had a punt blocked and missed a chance to win.

We were young, it was a great season, and it was a fun year. It was my second year back, but my first coaching the running backs, and at that time, I knew I wanted to do everything I could to prepare myself to be a head coach.

I knew this was what I wanted to do.

We went 11–3 but lost to the Rams in the first playoff game in 1976, and the thing I remember is a play we didn't call. In fact, it's a play we never did get to work until we got to Denver years later.

Right at the end of the game, we are getting ready to get the ball. We are down 14–12, and Coach Landry and I are talking on the sideline. We had a play in the game plan out of the shotgun, where Roger hands the ball off, and then we throw it back to him downfield as a receiver. The quarterback is eligible out of the shotgun.

We thought it was going to be a great play. "Coach, what about the throw back to the quarterback?'

"Well, it won't be any good. We'll be in the two minute drill and they'll probably be in a zone, laying off, and it won't be any good."

Well, about then, Charlie Waters blocked a punt, and we've got the ball on the Rams 21 yard line. So now, we're not in the two minutes, we're in plus territory, and that would have been a great play there.

But we throw four passes, and don't score, and lose.

The thing that hit me when the game was over was that we had forgotten about that play. The whole offseason I am thinking about that play. Why didn't we throw it? It would have been perfect.

The next year, 1977, we used that play the first time. Staubach is so wide open I can't believe it. We called it, with Ron Springs, a left-hander, getting the handoff. He is going to his left. I am watching Staubach. He hands off, lets people chase Springs, and takes off for the end zone.

I can't believe how open he is—and Ron throws to a wide receiver instead and it was incomplete.

So I'm up in the press box. Boy, I'm screaming: "Get Springs on the phone! Get Springs on the phone!" They can't get him for like five minutes. Finally they do.

"Coach, I know. I know."

It was so long before we finally got that play to work. We completed a pass to Gary Kubiak up in Buffalo one year, and then in 1986 we threw a touchdown to John Elway in the opening game against the Raiders. But it took all those years before it finally worked.

Well, of course, in 1977 we were 12-2 and had a good team. We went to the Super Bowl and beat Denver. That year I had taken over coaching quarterbacks and running backs.

The thing I remember about 1977, and not because I ended up in Denver, is that we ended up playing them the final game of the regular season in Dallas. They were 11-1 at that point, and we had already lost two.

Craig didn't play in that game. We watched film before that game, and I worked on their defense. I'm looking at these defenses and I can't even call everything they are doing. Our terminology didn't even cover it.

They were doing things with linebackers I had to write in. Finally about 1:30 or two in the morning I said, "The heck with this. I've got to get some sleep." I hadn't even finished. They caused us all kinds of problems.

We had looked at maybe five games, and nobody had converted a third down and short yardage against them. They were stopping everybody. We ended up beating them 14-6. But neither of us was thinking Super Bowl at that point.

Really, the Super Bowl turned on some big plays. It could have turned the other way. The game could really have been turned early if they had recovered a fumble.

We got some breaks early that could have gone the other way. Then our defense just completely dominated. There's no question our defense won that game.

We had planned to use two tight ends in that game because we felt Tom Jackson was good on the weak side but not as good on the strong, and Bob Swenson was good on the strong side but not as good on the weak.

Then we discovered that Jay Saldi couldn't play at tight end. He hadn't recovered enough from an injury, and we had to put Butch Johnson into his place and that didn't have the same effect.

I learned something from that, though: Never put all your hopes on one formation or one guy.

The next year, we went to the Super Bowl and lost to Pittsburgh again in one of the most exciting games the Super Bowl has had.

Dallas was an exciting place to be in those years. My name was beginning to come up after almost every season as a candidate for openings with other teams.

I interviewed in Atlanta after the 1976 season, but to be honest, I didn't feel I was ready to be a head coach right then. I also flew to Atlanta when Patriots owner Billy Sullivan was trying to replace Chuck Fairbanks after the 1978 season. We spent a whole evening at a hotel there, talking.

But the Patriots weren't sure how Commissioner Rozelle was going to rule, and they eventually picked Ron Erhardt from their staff that April. That was a good move for them.

I also interviewed with the New York Giants, and with the Los Angeles Rams during those years. And Auburn came out to Dallas and talked to me before they hired Pat Dye.

I have to admit I had the head coaching bug, even though I also felt I had a great job on the Cowboys' staff in Dallas. But, after all these interviews and still not getting a head coaching job, I'm thinking to myself, "I'm never going to get a job. This is the way it's always going to be."

They were great years, and I was still young, and we had been to three Super Bowls and Dallas was a great place to work and to live. We had had a couple losses in the playoffs in 1979 and 1980 that kept us from going to four straight Super Bowls.

After the 1980 season, we were disappointed, but we still had a good football team with a lot of good players. All of the jobs had gone by. None were open. We had already got a good start on 1981. We had done our research, analyzed our 1980 season, and started working on our playbook.

That's when Edgar Kaiser called that Friday, and my career in Dallas was over.

# DENVER YEARS

Part IV

# 18

# 1981: A Denver Beginning

WHEN I was in Dallas as an assistant coach, I used to think about the times we were on the practice field and it was raining like crazy.

I used to think, "Boy. When I become a head coach, we aren't going to practice in weather like this. We'll go in. We'll make it up some other time."

That first year in Denver, nobody knew the offense. Joe Collier, the assistant head coach of defense, and I met, and tried to get the offensive and defensive terminology as close together as we could. The whole process was late because I didn't get hired until March, and we didn't have a minicamp until real late.

We brought everybody in. I had changed the entire system, terminology, everything. The first vivid memory I have as head coach in Denver is the first practice. We go out on the field, and it's the worst weather you have ever seen. It is in May, but the weather is December. It is raining, it is sleeting. There's snow mixed in—wind.

And I'm standing there, watching, and thinking, "Now. I've got the whistle around my neck. Now I can blow the whistle any time I want to."

I couldn't blow it. "We've gotta stay out here as long as we can because we are so far behind now."

I know, to non-football people, some of it wouldn't sound like much, but it was a total change-over. The numbering system was totally different.

In the Denver system before me, their numbers to the right—the numbers on the spaces between linemen, out from the center—were even. At Dallas, the holes on the right side were all odd numbers. In other words, for me, the right hip of the center was the one-hole. For the staff here before me, it was the zero hole.

Outside right guard for them was the two. For me it was the three. Right tackle was four to them, five to me. So it was the exact opposite. If I called "49," to them it was a quick pitch to the left. To me, it was the left half sweeping to the right. You'd have linemen crashing together because the numbers were exactly the opposite.

Most teams, it is even to the right, odd to the left. Dallas, and now Denver, are the other way.

The reason is that when Coach Landry went to Dallas, he went from being a defensive coach with the New York Giants. He always looked at the play from the defensive side—reversed. And so he numbered things that way on defense.

But he also ran the offense, and because Dallas was starting from scratch in 1960, he installed the numbering system he was comfortable with, odd numbers to the right.

The numbering system was just one example. We didn't change everything. A lot stayed the same. We just wanted to make certain that when Joe or I said something, we were talking about the same thing.

If I had been able to come here and bring in a whole new staff, we would have started completely different and been basically on the same page. But Joe was here, his defense was established and used to doing things, and I didn't want him to have to change something that was working.

But I wanted to change the offense, and I was the only one that knew it. I didn't know if the old Denver terminology covered all of what I wanted to do, so when I arrived, I put in the offense I knew— the one I was comfortable with—including the numbering system.

We made the changes we had to, and left the other things. When Joe wants us to do things, run things to give his defense pictures, he'll still use the old terminology: full, halves, splits, where we'll use reds, greens, browns.

Those were some of the things we had to work out in those cram sessions that spring and summer. When I came here, that first day, I interviewed each of the coaches individually.

I told them at that time I didn't know what I was going to do as far as staff was concerned. I retained all of them except for Paul Roach and Whitey Dovell, and don't ask me why I didn't keep them. It was just one of those things. I felt it was right to make a change there. When you interview somebody, you get a first impression. For some reason, I just didn't feel comfortable with Paul and Whitey.

I never got to know Whitey. When I did finally get to know Paul, I realized I made a mistake. But at the time you just go on your gut feeling.

I kept the defense intact and let them work on their own. As I told Rod Dowhower and Fran Polsfoot and the coaches I worked with on offense, "Whether we have an offensive coordinator or not, I know the offense and I'd like to work with you guys first and then make some decisions."

They were all very easy to work with, and we aren't talking about a bad coaching staff. They had won. They had been in the Super Bowl. I knew they were good coaches. The main thing was, could we work well together?

I kept the defense together, so I wouldn't have to worry as much about it. The more I worked with Joe, the more I was convinced that this may have been the greatest thing that ever happened to me. He was so easy to work with. He was so even tempered. He was so organized. He was so positive.

And if he disagreed with something I was doing, he'd tell me. So I didn't have to worry about the defense. My strength was working with the offense, anyway.

My No. 1 priority when I got a job was going to be hiring a defensive coordinator, and I ended up inheriting a great one. We have some shouting matches on the sideline at times, but they have only lasted a few seconds in the heat of a game.

Then, one or both of us will apologize to the other. That's coaching. My hollerin' at him has been out of frustration more than anything else, and we have never had a disagreement that lasted more than two minutes that I can remember.

We've never even come close to a split. It hasn't even entered into our minds. My mind, anyway. I guess you'd have to ask Joe for his view, but if it has, he's never mentioned it to me.

We've never even had a really bad disagreement. All of them have been us not stopping them, and me saying, "Joe, we gotta blitz." Or me saying, "Joe, what the hell's going on?" And he'll say, "I'm trying every damn thing I know to stop them." Something like that.

I call the offense, so I realize how frustrating that is. I know how

I'd feel if Joe said, "What the hell is going on?" every time the offense didn't work.

I think I've become better. When I go up to him I try to make it more of a suggestion: "Have you thought about doing this?" We talk about it, and he'll either convince me it isn't the thing to do, or he'll say, "Yeah, we might try that."

I've never given him a directive, except in the sense of saying, "Joe, I'm going to take responsibility. We're behind and we've got to blitz them." He'll say, "Every play?" And I'll say, "Every play."

I think all coaches do those types of things. Our philosophies, though, are exactly the same. When I was offered the Atlanta job years ago, I would not have gotten the same results Leeman Bennett did with his all-out blitzing because I just didn't believe in that.

Joe and I in so many ways judge talent exactly the same. You have to play with the talents you have. I don't know we have ever been on exactly the opposite side on personnel.

Now, every assistant coach is loyal to his people, and I wouldn't want it any other way. But, as a head coach, my responsibility is to make a judgement as to who will be better two or three years from now.

A great example last year was Darren Comeaux and Mark Munford. If a guy has been around three or four years, like Comeaux, and he's not starting, and there's not a tremendous amount of improvement, then you take the young guy and see where he's going to be in four or five years. Yet a group coach, the majority of the time, is going to have a feeling and a closeness for a player and is not going to want to make that change. He'll take the veteran because he knows what he can do.

So there's a case where, as head coach, you just have to make the call. Another, maybe better example, is Barney Chavous and Andre Townsend. If somebody has been with you 12 years, it's not easy to let him go.

But, if you are going to be a better football team with Andre, then you have to make that decision. It is never going to be easy, and it is going to hurt somebody. It is unusual to have a Randy Gradishar or Bill Thompson or Louie Wright step in and make a retirement decision.

Most guys are not going to say, "Hey, it's near the end and it's time." That just doesn't happen.

When Barney came in to sign his last contract, he wanted a three year contract, and he wanted it guaranteed. There was no way I could say to Barney, "Three years from now you are going to be the starter."

I could say, "Next year, my feeling is you are going to be the starter." What we came up with was, "Okay, when the season is over, come in and we'll talk. If I invite you back, it's with the idea you will make our football team.

"If I don't invite you back, then you need to consider retiring or being waived." Well, after his first year on that contract, after the 1985 season, we felt like Andre was coming on. I said, "Barney, I'm going to invite you back to training camp."

I could not look at the situation and see that Barney Chavous would not make our football team. I could look at it and say, "Barney, you're getting close now as to whether you are going to start. Andre is coming on and we've got some young players. So, as long as you want to pay the price and get ready and understand there's a chance in preseason you might not be starting. At that time, you have got to make the decision whether you want to be a backup. And we have got to make the decision do we keep a guy like Barney Chavous as a backup or do we keep somebody else?

So we go into the training camp in 1986, and Joe and Stan both felt like Andre needs to move in there. Andre is ready. Barney will still make our team because he gives us some depth and experience and so forth.

But, we feel like we need to make a change as far as the starter is concerned. I say, "All right, but we need to call Barney in and let him know that, and then let him make a decision."

So I called Barney in, with Joe and Stan in the room. It was in training camp. "Barney, we're going to move Andre into the starting lineup," I told him. "You are going to be a backup. I can't tell you right now if you are going to make our team or not. You do realize we are going to have to make a decision. If we do have somebody, I would prefer to keep somebody young as a backup. But, we don't have anybody like that right now. I can't make that decision right now. It will be made three or four weeks down the road.

"You need to make a decision now as to whether you want to go ahead and compete on those conditions, or do you want to retire?"

His immediate reaction was, "I want to be waived."

I said, "Certainly, Barney, if that's what you want, we'll do it. But in my opinion, nobody's going to claim a veteran who has been in the league as long as you have with the salary you have."

Every player thinks he is going to be claimed. That's the way we left it. I talked to Stan. I said, "Stan, you need to talk to him." Stan realized it. Joe realized it. We all did. The chances of him being picked up don't happen.

Stan talked to him, and Barney talked to his wife, and then as it turned out, the news broke that day or the next day, I can't remember. We were waiting for Barney to make his decision, and he made it to retire, which was a big relief to me.

I had gone through that with Riley Odoms, who wanted to be waived, and nobody claimed him.

Andre ended up playing well. He played like we thought he could, and Freddie Gilbert came in later and gave us some depth. It worked out okay, but there is just no easy way, no painless way, to go through something like that. I had a similar situation with Tom Jackson, and it had been very painful not to put Rubin Carter back on the roster at the end of the 1986 season.

Give some credit to Pat Bowlen. A lot of owners would have dropped him, but we kept him on at full salary. That was a big money decision—one based on heart and the fact he had been such a vital part of our team for so long. It was not a good business decision. It was the most human thing, and Pat never blinked an eye. I would love to have brought Rubin back on if there had been a way to do it that didn't hurt us as a team.

You don't make decisions based on whether somebody's gonna say, "Yay, yay." You make them based on what is best for the team and for Rubin Carter. It hurt Rubin when I couldn't find a place for him. It hurt me. I would love for Barney Chavous to have come on our team and gone to the Super Bowl with us that year. But would it have been fair to cut a Freddie Gilbert or a Tony Colorito to make room for those guys? No.

Those are the decisions you have to live with. You don't like them, but you have to live with them. And they happen every year.

But those things were all in the future that first summer. We went to camp up in Fort Collins, and there is always a question in your mind. You think you are ready, but this is the first time that you have really been in charge. And I think the biggest thing that helped was I had so many guys with experience on the staff.

We had a good working relationship, and that's the thing that got me through the first training camp.

I'll never forget the first preseason game. We had worked a lot on assignments and on defense. That was different for me. In Dallas, the defense had always worn arm pads, and they would hit, but they would give. It would be like Moses parting the sea. Holes would open up and our offense would look great and we would move the football.

Not here. Joe felt like, for the defense to play the way they were capable of playing, it had to be live blocking but no tackling. Well, I mean we couldn't get through the line of scrimmage. The defense was jamming everything up at the line.

It was really frustrating. But we were working on assignments and we were getting better. Guys were starting to understand terminology. The holes were numbered different, and they were starting to grasp all this. We were making progress.

And then we get ready for that first preseason game, against the Jets. And the Jets are not a 3-4 team. They have a four man line. We have not practiced one single day against a four man line. Now we have to start looking at the Jets.

We get killed. It's in Denver. It is my first game as a head coach, and it is not even a contest. It is 33–7.

I'm standing there, watching this, saying to myself, "Am I really ready to be a head coach?" I really felt like it was a coaching mistake. We hadn't worked on the four man front. We hadn't given our guys a chance.

So, the next week, we are down in Miami against the Dolphins. We lost 24–14. The thing that was so amazing was that in the second half, we only had the ball three times. We played better, though, and then came back to Denver against the Green Bay Packers.

It was my first win. When Bart Starr won his first game as a head coach, against Dallas, I wrote a letter congratulating him. When I won my first—against him—I got a real nice letter from Bart.

We closed out with a win at Cincinnati, with our rookie quarterback, Mark Herrmann, bringing us a victory in the two minute drill. I didn't have a chance to overcoach him.

Anyway, we went into the season with a 2–2 record and some confidence.

We open up against the Raiders, the defending world champions. It is my first real game as a head coach. We ended up beating them 9–7 and Fred Steinfort missed five field goals for us. A lot were real long ones.

It made our players realize we could play with the best. It was an interesting season. Steve Watson and Craig Morton had an unbelievable year. Steve caught a 95 yard pass, a 93 yard pass. We jump out ahead of San Diego 35-0 and I think I'm dreaming. Craig has a couple games where he throws four touchdowns back to back.

We ended up 10-5 and going into Chicago for the final game. Chicago is struggling. If we win the game, chances are we will win the division. If we lose, San Diego is going to win it.

To make matters worse, Craig got the flu that week and couldn't practice. They had nothing to lose. They faked a field goal, did all kinds of things, we threw two interceptions for touchdown returns, and ended up 10-6 and out of the playoffs.

San Diego was playing Oakland on Monday night. I watched, and before the game, they announced Jim Plunkett was not going to play. I kind of sank back. There was no way the Raiders were going to win.

San Diego won, and went to the playoffs with a 10-6 mark, same as ours, but they had a better division record.

I wasn't disappointed in the way the team played, but I was disappointed we were sitting at home and not in the playoffs.

We went through an undefeated preseason in 1982, and then had five turnovers against San Diego and got beat 23-3 in the opener. Then we played the world champion 49ers and beat them on a field goal the next week. Then the strike hit.

That was really frustrating. You couldn't talk to your players, you didn't have any control over them, they lost their conditioning and we lost any continuity we had. It became a 2-7 year—the first losing season I had ever experienced as a professional.

We just weren't a good football team when we came back.

I have heard it said many times that you learn more from losing than you do from winning. It's very true about yourself, about your players.

It's easy for people to get along, to have companionship, and as you hear said so many times in sports, love for one another, when they are winning. The true test is when you are losing. How do people react to those situations?

I learned a lot about myself. I learned I could handle those situations. I didn't like them, but I could handle them. I could be the same person going through adversity as when I was on the top of the world.

And it brought a lot of humility. I'm not so sure I didn't think I was probably God's gift to the coaching profession before that 2-7 year.

You are patting yourself on the back after a 10–6 season instead of thanking the ones around you.

It was almost as if the Lord was getting my attention. "Hey, I got control. If you don't believe it, I'll show you."

I certainly didn't look at it as some kind of blessing then, though. It was tough to be the same person. There were a lot of things you wanted to do. But when you thought about them, you knew they would be bad.

They were things you wanted to do on instinct, quick reactions. You are frustrated. You are mad. Your pride is hurt.

And then the self-doubts creep in. "Am I really a head coach in this league? Can I do the job, or am I kidding myself?" The thing I learned about myself was that I could stay basically the same person. I wasn't a raving maniac. I still screamed, and hollered, but I do that when I'm winning.

But if you can go 2–7, and not have self-doubts, I think something is wrong. I had a lot of them after that second season in Denver. But I also began to realize I was not totally in control of everything. So it kind of brought my feet back down to the ground.

And I hope I never get up where I think I'm better than everybody else. I realized I was lucky to be where I was, and then I just had to work hard and hope that things worked out.

But that season did get my attention. You go 17 years, always winning, and you say to yourself, "Well, I'm the reason." You get pretty cocky. A 2–7 season makes you realize how many people are really responsible for any success. You have to have good people around you.

So I got that in perspective that winter, but the doubt was there, and I'm certain it would come rushing back if we were to go through another bad season. Coach Landry used to say every year is a teaching and learning experience.

"If you win a football game, you teach. If you lose, you learn."

That second year had been a learning year. I had done a self-evaluation and then when Louis Wright came up to me later that year, and I discovered that one self image I had was wrong, I had to take another look. But that's for later.

So I learned, and I learned humility, which I think is good for anybody. It also made me rededicate myself to getting it turned around.

Coach Landry used to say the difficulty in this business was handling success. It's easy to do something when you are not successful.

The first step was getting ready for the draft. We're going to pick fourth. It's exciting, because you know you are going to get a good football player.

We had excellent scouts, and I would start reading the reports, but really it wasn't organized as far as grouping players to where you could weigh them against each other. I felt that one of the areas we needed to standardize was how we evaluated people.

The scouts would put a grade on a player, but you might have a hundred '5s' on your list. Which '5' was the best? Who could best fit into our team?

I made them change the whole rating system. We spent a month in 1981 working on the draft, trying to get them in some kind of order. We weren't involved in the draft as coaches in Dallas. You didn't know how they put them up on the board or anything.

I came up with some categories. "This is a super player. He is going to star his first year." And the next one would be "This is a good player, but he will probably take two years before he's a starter." There were others.

We worked together, with the scouts. I was 37 that first spring, the youngest head coach in the league. Most of the scouts were much older guys. The thing that was neat was we had a good time and laughed and worked and got some things done. We got some good players out of that 1981 draft—Kenny Lanier, Dennis Smith, Steve Busick.

But after that season, I realized that was where I needed some help. I wanted somebody to give them direction. After the 1981 season I had hired Reed Johnson from Dallas to coach our special teams. But then I told him I needed him to direct our scouting.

Without question, it's one of the best moves I made. Working with the scouts, he came up with a system. When somebody said, "He's a 5," we all knew what a '5' was. When they said "He's a 6," we knew what a '6' was.

It gave them some guidelines because of specifics, height, weight, speed and so forth. If he didn't have those, he couldn't be say a 6. You'd have to drop him a grade. Immediately, without looking at the film, I could look at a grade and know what type player he was.

We became a good organization scouting. We put our own players into categories, so we could compare college players to ones we already had.

So all that went into 1983, when we were going to have the fourth choice in the whole draft.

We spent a little time talking about quarterbacks, but not a lot. I had made the decision that our football team had more pressing needs than a quarterback. We knew, picking where we were, we had no chance at John Elway.

He was the only quarterback we felt could come in and have an impact on us because of his scrambling ability. But to bring in another of those quarterbacks we just felt—and this was the staff talking—that we had more pressing needs. We had other positions where we could get a guy who could come in and contribute, help us quicker.

If we couldn't get Elway, we weren't going to spend a lot of time looking and talking, rating the quarterbacks and so forth. We knew there were a lot of great ones in that class.

We also knew there was a lot of talking going on between Baltimore and other teams, reports that John wasn't going to sign with them and so forth. So we made some preliminary contacts with Baltimore, and for what they were asking for him, we knew there was no way.

It would devastate us as a football team. We had Steve DeBerg, and we had a young quarterback in Mark Herrmann who wasn't going to be, say, an impact player. But we felt he had a future.

Baltimore at that stage was talking about two or three No. 1s, plus players, and there were some teams talking to them in those terms.

Denver had gone through a period before I got here where there were a lot of deals made, a lot of No. 1s and so forth given up. We were kind of paying the price for those deals right then.

So I just felt there were more pressing needs. Some good offensive linemen were coming out. We thought we had a chance to get a real good one.

I guess the first time I really thought there might be a possibility was that morning of the draft. The draft started at six o'clock here, and we were all in the office early. At 5:30, the phone rang. It was Frank Kush, Baltimore's coach.

He said, "Who are you taking?"

I said, "Well, if everybody takes who they said they were going to take (Elway, Curt Warner and Eric Dickerson, in that order), we would take Chris Hinton.

"Would you be interested in trading if we had the pick right behind you?" he asked.

That was San Diego's choice. I thought to myself, "They've made a trade. The Chargers are going to wind up with Elway." I wasn't too happy with that thought. Then, I was trying to figure out what they wanted, and I decided they wanted the guy we wanted, Hinton.

Why would they move from fifth to fourth if it wasn't Hinton they were interested in?

So I said, "Well, if it comes to that, give us a call. We'll make a decision at that time."

I went back and we started talking about it. "If they do make that move, what is it worth to us to move one place, to give up Chris Hinton? Who would we take?"

We were still talking when the draft opened, and right away, ESPN announced Baltimore was taking Elway. It stunned me. I thought maybe they are going to take him and then turn around and trade him to San Diego.

So we went along and everything went like we thought it would and we took Hinton. Then San Diego took Billy Ray Smith, and by then I didn't know what the deal was. Then they came on ESPN again and said no way Elway was going to sign with Baltimore.

The second round came and we took another lineman, Mark Cooper. At the end of that round, Edgar Kaiser and I were talking.

"I wonder if there is any way we can get to Elway?" he said.

"I don't know. But Kush called me this morning. I know they were interested in Chris Hinton. They wanted to swap places with us because they wanted Hinton."

He thought for a moment.

"I've got a good relationship with Irsay," he said. "I almost bought the Colts when I was looking for a team and wound up buying Denver instead. I'm going to make some preliminary calls."

I didn't think any more about it, but when the draft ended, Edgar came back to me.

"Look, I've made some talks with Irsay. We're not out of this thing yet," he said. "Give me a list of what you would be willing to give up—players, draft choices or whatever."

I did that.

Over the weekend, Edgar called again. He said they were really interested in Hinton and Herrmann. It didn't make any sense to keep Herrmann and trade Steve DeBerg, the veteran guy. There were some other players listed. None of them were starters.

They were interested in Herrmann because he had played at Purdue and was from the Indianapolis area. In retrospect, that was interesting. I guess Irsay was already thinking of that move.

Anyway, the next Monday, we were playing in the Quarterback

Club Golf tournament. Edgar said, "Look, this thing is going, and it could possibly be today."

Well, that wasn't my best day of golf. I played like nine holes in a trance, and I rushed into the clubhouse. All the way around, I kept thinking, "Edgar was really excited. And he told me they really liked the players we offered. Also, Irsay had had some kind of a run-in with both San Diego and the Raiders. He thought he had a deal and the deal didn't work out and he thought they were the reason it didn't go through.

So I called Edgar at the turn. He had talked to Irsay again.

"You got a pencil?" he asked.

"Yeah."

"Okay. Write this down. Chris Hinton."

I wrote down his name.

"Mark Herrmann."

I wrote that down.

"And a No. 1."

I wrote that down.

And then he didn't say any more. I waited.

"What else?" I asked.

"That's it."

"Shoot! I'd make that deal in a second," I said. I felt like that was a great deal for us, because really what we were doing was getting John Elway for a No. 1 and Herrmann. We would have taken Elway if we had the No. 1 pick, and they would have taken Hinton.

And if you had John Elway, you didn't need Mark Herrmann.

"That's it," Edgar said.

"The only thing is, it is contingent on us signing him. If we don't, the deal is off. So we are going to fly in there tomorrow night, and hopefully we'll have it done. Marvin Demoff is his agent, and we'll have Marvin fly in on my private plane.

"We need for you to meet us at the airport, the private area over by Ports of Call on the south side of the field."

For once, nobody in town knew about it. There weren't any rumors, nobody had heard about it. The Nuggets were playing the Phoenix Suns that night in a playoff game, so I went to the game.

All of a sudden, I had to leave at halftime, and now all the media knew something was up.

What Edgar had also done, he had flown John in on a private

plane. Demoff had come in on an earlier one, and Marvin and I were talking when John's plane landed. Marvin walked out and got on the plane with John.

They basically worked out the contract, okay'd it, and we took John and brought him over to our offices for a late night press conference.

The one hurdle we had was whether we could sign him. The credit goes to Edgar. He had the line of communication with Irsay. I'm sure Kush and I would never have made the deal. Kush took him because he wanted him, just like everybody else did. He wasn't going to make a deal for him.

As a coach, you just fantasize about getting a John Elway.

And we had him. It was a great result from an awful 2–7 year.

# 19

# A Long Lunch

I DON'T know who was the more uncomfortable—
Louie Wright, or me.

I had always viewed myself as a players' coach. At
Dallas, I was closer to the players than to the staff
because I had been a player, then a player coach,
and had always stayed close.

And I thought it had carried over as a head
coach.

Now, on a July noon, here was my team captain
telling me if I wasn't careful I was going to lose
them.

He said they felt I was unapproachable. My out-
bursts on the sidelines during a game were hurting
us, I was insensitive, and our practice schedules were
too demanding.

"Nobody's happy," Louie told me. "You just say,
'That's the way it's going to be,' and that's it."

The whole thing had come early in training camp
in 1984. We had moved up to Greeley by then. It's a
nice practice site only about an hour northeast of
Denver, good facilities, and still close enough to the
city.

Charlie Lee, the coach I had hired from Texas my
first year, who had gone into our public relations de-
partment, came up during a morning workout and
said Louie wanted to talk to me. I said fine, I'll see
him at the dining hall.

I had no idea what Louie wanted to talk about. I just figured probably he was going to say things were going good, something like that.

Well, we got our trays, and went over to a table, and I could tell Louie was nervous, really nervous. That puzzled me a little. After it was over, I had to admit I would have been, too. In fact, I can't imagine going up to Coach Landry when I was a player and telling him what Louie told me. I had to admire his guts.

Louie had done what he was supposed to do as our captain, as our player rep. He had let me know I had a problem, and obviously not a small one.

Some of the things he talked about, the practices, running conditioning laps after practice, we had already begun to change as a staff. We had met that winter and spring and decided we could get the same things done other ways, so that was going to be changed, anyway.

The other things, my temper for example, were things I had to take back to the room with me and think about. I guess the one that bothered me the most was the one about the players not feeling comfortable about being able to talk to me.

I thought it was just the opposite. I had always thought of myself as a players' coach, but saying it, and having guys feel it were different. I wasn't getting my point across.

I wasn't being the coach I thought I was. It was hard for me. It hurt. It's like somebody criticizing you. Sometimes it's hard to take. I know Louie indicated during our last Super Bowl he feels I still carry a grudge. Really and truly, I don't. I'll talk about that in a minute.

So I told Louie at lunch that day, "I appreciate what you've done, how hard it was. I'll look into these things because I must not be getting across and that hurts all of us."

Then Joe Collier came up. It was a little later, after we had started playing games and had gone through a bad one. He told me that, "Some of the players have mentioned to me that you were hollering at them during the game. It really bothers them that you aren't supportive and so forth."

I said, "Wait a minute." I sat down, and I tried to explain how I am. There were a lot of things I saw about myself that I didn't like. I didn't like the fact that when I played games, people didn't want to be my partner.

I didn't like going along fine on the golf course, then all of a sudden after three or four bad holes turning into a different person. Pam had told me once she wouldn't play tennis with me any more because of my temper when I'd hit a bad shot.

It's me. I cannot be comfortable that way. I cannot joke around when I feel I am performing poorly. I have to concentrate, and to concentrate, I can't laugh and joke. When people see that, a lot of the time they think I'm mad at them.

I can understand that. If a guy is your partner, and you don't speak to him for three or four holes, what's he going to think? But I'm not mad at him. I'm mad at myself for not getting the job done.

Ever since I've played sports, my way of getting myself into something, of getting out of one of those bad ruts, is to yell at myself. And somehow, that carries over into coaching, and it was hurting the team.

I looked back at the way I had always done things. All through grammar school, high school, South Carolina, the pros, I was an average athlete. The only way I could ever get myself to be successful and win was to really get on myself, really get mad at myself.

When I did, I always seemed to respond. I could always seem to concentrate better. So from my viewpoint, that's what I was doing. I was screaming and hollering at them because that was the way I got myself up. I felt it would lift them, too.

When you try to explain that to the team, a lot of things you were as a kid come to mind. They were things I had never tried to explain to myself.

When I used to play tennis, Pam would tell me, "Nobody wants to play with you. Nobody wants to be your partner. You get too mad. You are just too competitive."

I had never noticed it until those things started coming up. I really wasn't a lot of fun as a partner. I couldn't do things just for fun. If you kept score, I had to win. That was the most important thing, and that hurts you in a lot of ways.

The players didn't understand that, didn't understand me, what the shouting was all about. I had to sit down with them and ask them to try and understand that side of me.

I don't like to see that streak in my kids, and yet I do. They've got some of the same traits bred in them that were bred in me. I'd love for them not to have the temper I have, not to get mad at everything.

We can be playing a little game at home and they are just as bad, just as competitive, as I am. I used to bump my daughter Laura out of the way just playing basketball in our driveway.

So I did a self-evaluation, and I could see things Pam had been telling me about all my life. And I didn't like those things.

I don't say I made a drastic change, but at least I did make the effort. I called a meeting and I got up in front of the players, the whole squad.

"Look," I told them. "I am that way. I can't be something I am not. You have just got to take it for what it is worth. I am not really hollering at you, I am hollering at your performance. I want your performance to move up. I move mine up by hollering at myself, and I try to get yours up the same way. It's just the way I am.

"What I am saying is I can't change that. But I am going to try to control it better. I will promise you that. I am also going to try and control another thing:

"Some people you can holler at and they respond, and some you holler at and they shrivel, get driven down. I've got to do a better job of knowing which type each of you is and not holler at those it hurts."

So that meeting with Louie helped in that respect. It brought it into focus, at least. I'm still not perfect, and never will be. I finally started wearing a suit and tie on the sideline to remind myself to control my temper.

I also had to reconcile myself to the fact you cannot be as close to the players as a head coach. Your assistants really should be, that's part of their jobs. They have to be sensitive to all those little nuances—know how the players are feeling—moods, those things.

But as a head coach, you can never be as close as you would like. For one thing, as the years go on, there is an age difference. You also have to make decisions that affect their lives. If you get too close, I'm not certain you can make those decisions as well—the ones that are for the good of the organization but are tough on the player.

I knew I had to build more patience. It was one of the strengths of Coach Landry, and I really have worked hard at it.

Patience was one of the reasons Dallas won its first Super Bowl. He had such patience with Duane Thomas when a lot of us coaches just wanted to get rid of him.

He also had patience with us. From that standpoint, he was good to work for. I would hate to think where I'd be if I had not worked for Coach Landry.

It hurt me in some of those job interviews, though. "I wish you had wider experience," people would tell me. "I wish you had worked a little under Don Shula, or Chuck Knox," or so on. I'd only coached under Coach Landry.

It would have been nice to get that added exposure, input, from men like Shula and Knox and the others. But to do that would have meant you probably got fired somewhere else, and that was one of the strengths of Dallas, that continuity and stability.

Besides, in the 1970s, the National Football League had gotten into a trend of hiring a lot of college coaches—John Ralston, Dick Vermiel, Tommy Prothro. Pro assistants weren't getting the top jobs. It took Red Miller to reverse that trend.

One of the things I thought about after that lunch with Louie Wright was the start of the 1970 season, when I officially became a player coach with Dallas. Calvin Hill had come in the year before, and I knew my playing days were essentially kind of numbered.

For two years in a row, we had lost to Cleveland in the playoffs. The two years before that, it was Green Bay. There was a lot of talking, a lot of dissension on the team, a lot of dissension among the coaches.

That was when Coach Landry had each of us fill out a questionnaire. "What do you think about your coach?" "What do you think about the head coach?" All kinds of things like that. And he took some of the suggestions to heart. I knew I had to do the same thing with what Louie told me.

The key thing about Coach Landry was the fact he is such a great teacher.

He stressed the fundamentals. The people on our staff who I think are excellent coaches are those who deal in the basics. They are good technical teachers. That's the way I was brought up. Coach Landry made you teach.

He didn't want you to assume that anyone knew anything. Here I coached Roger Staubach for five years, and he won championships for us and went to the pro bowl and all. And yet every summer I did the same drills with him, just as if he didn't know a single thing.

We started from ground zero every camp.

Coach Landry was easy to work for. You hear so much about coaches who work late hours, maybe sleep on a couch in the office three or four nights a week. We were never that way. He thought it was important to spend time with your family, and I've carried that over here.

We would always leave the office around seven or eight o'clock. We might get in there at four o'clock or 4:30 in the morning to work, but

I came home and had dinner with Pam and the kids. After we had dinner and spent time with the kids, then I would look at some more film or whatever.

So he was easy to work for from that standpoint. He was also a great guy to learn from. He was especially well organized. He was a person who, when you presented something to him, you better know what you were talking about.

You couldn't come and in and say, "I think we ought to run Power 47 near 0 pinch." He had to know why. In detail.

You had to be able to say it was a good play because the film showed the other linebacker came across in a certain way and you could block him. The fullback could handle that block. It's one of the better plays that our running back runs. The defense has a certain number of defenses that they play, and Near 0 pinch will adjust to handle all of them. He challenged you that way. You better know what you talked about. He never went into any situation that he wasn't extremely prepared.

Another thing he has is great vision. He could look at a situation or a person and say, "Two years from now, this is where he'll be as a player." He could look at a situation and say, "If we don't replace this guy, we're really going to be hurting."

He was willing to wait for a guy to develop, and could anticipate. That is probably the basis of his great patience, and that's something I've tried to cultivate. But when a Louie Wright comes up, you have to wonder how good a job you are doing at it.

One thing that bothered me was a story that came out at the last Super Bowl. It said Louie felt I still carried a grudge, that I resented what he'd told me.

I don't, but I'm not sure I ever can convince Louie of that. I think he still feels I hold it against him. It goes back to our first Super Bowl, the one in Pasadena. The story about that lunch was getting a lot of play that week, and it seemed like that incident came up every time they talked to me and every time they talked to Louie.

So we were walking out to practice one day, and I turned to Louie and said, "Aren't you getting sick of that thing? I know I am." I thought he understood I was just kidding, but I guess he didn't.

Saying something, and having people understand what you mean, obviously aren't always the same thing.

# 20

# The Drive: A 98 Yard Classic

I HAVE been around a lot of big ball games, but our game in Cleveland on Jan. 11, 1987, is without question the most exciting I have ever been part of.

We had another great game with the Browns at our place in Mile High Stadium a year later, but in that one, we had to hold off the Browns. At Cleveland, we had to do the impossible, and we did. I will never forget it because of what we did, the way we did it, with so little time and so much at stake.

It showed what a great athlete can do. With everything resting on his shoulders, John Elway came up with some key, key plays, and so did a lot of others.

I get goose bumps just thinking about it again.

We started inside our own 2, but from where I was, it looked like about the 6 inch line. Everybody talks about the drive, about the total length, and they should. It was one of the great drives in league history, the best I was ever part of either as a player or a coach. But to me, there is no question the toughest single play on that whole march was the first third down we faced. We needed two yards and we got two yards and an inch.

It was third and two, at our own 10. I called a time out. We had to decide: run the ball, or throw? But that was just half the decision.

I also had to decide, with that much time on the clock, a little more than four minutes, "Do we go for it on fourth down if we come up short?"

If you go for it and don't make it, the ball game's over. You have left them at your own 10 or 11, easy field goal range, and that would put them out of reach. They led 20-13. A field goal was all they needed, and if we came up short, I would be giving them one almost free.

We had worked the whole season, the whole year, to get to this point. For that matter, we had worked six years to get there, to that decision. We had gone 13-3 two years earlier and lost our first playoff game. We had gone 11-5 the year before and hadn't even gotten into the playoffs. Now here we were, third down, the wind blowing in our faces, and Cleveland has one of the best defenses in the league.

Up in the stands across from our bench, I could see Cleveland fans already starting to celebrate.

We ended up running Sammy Winder over left guard and he made it. By inches. I remember, I could hardly watch when they came out to measure it. It gave us a first down at our 12. Then John was flushed and made a good run himself up to the 26 on what was supposed to be a pass play.

On the next play, the same play but to the right, he hit Steve Sewell up the middle at our 48.

That was when I thought, "We can win this thing!"

When I saw Steve get it, I knew we had a chance, particularly with John's arm. We had been in that position so often we were pretty battle experienced from the past couple of years.

Until that play, it was survival, a down at a time. Now we had a chance, especially when John threw another completion, this one to Steve Watson for 12 more yards down to Cleveland's 40.

It was getting quiet in the stadium by then—and John gets sacked. Dave Puzzuoli trapped him for a loss of eight after an incomplete pass, and all of a sudden, it is third and 18.

We are worried about getting the pass off, but by now I don't worry about the next decision. Now, we definitely have to go for it on fourth. We took a time out after the sack, and I told John, "Just make sure that if they give you the short yardage, take it and we'll try to get the rest on fourth down. You don't want to get trapped and wind up having fourth and 20 something."

Well, for some reason, and I think it's because somebody blew a coverage, they covered our short guys and left Mark Jackson wide open coming in behind them. That was another key, key play.

It gave us a first down at their 28, and it was definitely getting interesting. We had an incomplete pass, but then got 14 and another first down on a screen to Sewell for a first down at the Browns' 14. Then John missed a throw to Watson. There were 42 seconds left and he lined up and ran right, all the way down to the Cleveland 5 and out of bounds.

That's where John made a great throw to Mark. He actually threw it off his back foot while backing up, and he just drilled it and Mark made a great diving catch.

We had come 98 plus yards in 15 plays, in just under four minutes—but it wasn't settled yet.

You have to worry about the extra point. Everybody regards that as automatic. Well, it isn't, as Chicago proved against us last year on Monday night when we beat them in Denver 31–29 and the difference was two missed extra points.

Besides, we were down on the open end of the Cleveland Stadium, the lake end, where the wind comes in and the fans were doing their Cleveland barking and dog bones littered the ground. People were throwing things out of the stands. I worried, "What if Rich Karlis slips on a dog bone like somebody would slip on a banana peel in a comedy? What if we lose because of a dog bone?"

Well, of course, he didn't. He made the extra point and we went into overtime tied at 20.

Then our defense did a great job because we got a very poor kickoff and they got great field position. But our defense just stuffed them.

We got the ball for the first time in overtime, and the big play on that drive, no question, was hitting Steve Watson to set Rich up for the field goal. Elway hit Orson Mobley first for 18 yards. Orson made a great catch on the play, right in front of our bench.

But the key was when Elway scrambled to his left and started to run and then hit Steve down at the Cleveland 22. It was third and 12 at midfield, and we would have had to give the ball back. You never want to do that in overtime, especially on the other guy's field.

Sammy Winder got us five yards and two and then one, and it was fourth and three at the Cleveland 15 when I sent Rich in with the field goal unit.

It was just an unbelievable feeling to see those officials put their hands up when Karlis kicked that field goal.

It's funny. As soon as he kicked, I didn't watch the ball. I watched the officials underneath the goal post. I knew the first guy that was going to signal would be the guy underneath the post. I shouldn't say I didn't watch at all. I watched the ball at the start, and from where I was, it looked like it was going left. That's when I switched to look at the guy underneath.

I knew he'd signal first.

I actually thought he had missed it, and then all of a sudden that guy threw his hands up. It was over.

I don't remember what happened then. I have no idea. I've seen it on film since, but I can't remember anything I did at that point. I just remember jumping up and down, being happy, and wanting to get in on the celebration with all the players out on the field.

That feeling, coming back the way we did, and knowing we were going to the Super Bowl, is indescribable, and I have been there now seven times.

Cleveland is a tough place. Thinking about it that week, getting ready to go there and play, I kept remembering back to my playing days in Dallas. Cleveland was our big rival, a power—I had played in so many big games against the Browns in that same stadium.

When the merger came in 1970, Cleveland moved to the American Football Conference and that rivalry died, but the Browns have always had that great tradition.

Cleveland and the Broncos were both young as far as playoff experience was concerned. Cleveland had been out of it for a while and we both had young quarterbacks. And then somebody reminded me that back during the war between the AFL and NFL, Cleveland owner Art Modell had once said he would never want the Denver Broncos playing in his stadium.

With all that, I was excited about going up there again, getting back into that atmosphere.

It lived up to my memory. When we got off our bus at the hotel, a bunch of Cleveland fans on the sidewalk formed a kind of corridor to the hotel door, and they barked at us. All night, they drove past the hotel and barked. We could hear them, even on some of the upper floors.

It was the same hotel we had stayed at when I was with Dallas. It's close to the stadium, and when we pulled up, I recognized it right away even though they had changed the name.

Then we pull up, and all those fans are there, barking, and I'll tell you, those people took over the personality of a dog. I mean, they put on those faces and they actually looked like dogs.

And they barked exactly like them, and everywhere you went that weekend, that's all you heard. I read later that the Cleveland Symphony on Saturday night ended its performance by starting to bark at the audience, and the audience laughed and started barking back, and pretty soon the whole symphony hall was filled with musicians and audience barking at each other.

I think it's great when a city can respond like that, and that's what we went into that weekend, that kind of charged up atmosphere.

We had to be there a day early because it was a championship game and the league requires it. We flew in on Friday. Because we got there pretty late, we put on a great dinner up in one of the ball rooms, just for the team and the traveling party, so they wouldn't have to go out in all that barking.

The team even got a woman to play the harp, and I mean she was great. Whatever music you wanted to request, classical, country, any music you wanted, she could play it. I think she was with the symphony, and I've wondered since if she played for us that night and the next night was one of the musicians who were barking at the audience.

So we had a great meal that first night. It was cold, and nobody had to go out, and it was relaxing. In that championship atmosphere, you really didn't want to go out of the hotel. But then, trying to sleep was almost impossible with the horns blowing all night long and the people barking.

The next morning, Saturday, we went down to the stadium just to take a look at it and see the dressing room, get settled a little bit. It had been raining and the field was so wet we didn't work out. We just walked along the sideline. The rest was covered.

Standing there that morning, I reflected that when I was at Dallas, we had won a game on that field one year 9-7. I had to hold for field goals, and we had kicked three to win it, and I had to hold for each of them. And on each, I had to brush the water out of the way, and kind of build up some mud to kind of put the ball on so it would be up above the water. And the wind is always swirling there, and it's always cold coming off that lake.

That's the way it was that Saturday.

Before we get back to the game, I want to tell you about something that happened the week before, in our team meeting before the Patriot game. It was something I think helped us to win the playoffs. It was something Mike Ditka used with the Bears the night before their Super Bowl.

I had every guy get up and talk about what the next day meant to him.

It was great. Everyone said something so unique it got everybody excited about the game. But also it helped each one focus on his own role. "This is important to me. This is what I've got to do to help us be successful."

It had been so successful that we did it before the Cleveland game, too. And the one that still stands out in my mind from that second session was Darren Comeaux, one of our linebackers.

"I figured it out," he said. "There have been 20 Super Bowls up to now, and somewhere between 45 and 49 guys on each of those teams. That's some 1800 players. That's all that have ever played in that game. This is a unique experience: If we can win this thing tomorrow, we will become one of that little group from among all the guys who have ever played football at any level."

I was really moved. It hit me. I played or coached on five Super Bowl teams up to that point, and I had never thought of it that way. Each of them in his own way said something I thought was really good, but Darren's was special.

Anyway, game day, you could feel the excitement in our team, and I really felt there was confidence there, too. When we walked out for pregame warmups, it was cold, but it was dry. The field was in pretty good shape for that time of year.

It was going to be a chance for two good teams to play without the weather being a factor.

When we started warming up, we were in the end zone on the open end, and we got bombarded by dog bones. They threw them at us all through warmups and after a while they got so thick you could hear them crunch underfoot when you walked around down there.

It was really dangerous and I was upset. I told the NFL people I thought it was ridiculous. "Somebody could lose an eye. Somebody could be seriously hurt." But nothing was done to stop it.

Our team had been through enough tough games to be ready. I felt good about it. Early, probably the toughest decision I had to make was going for it on fourth down at Cleveland's 1 in the second quarter. We trailed 7–3 at the time, and going for it was totally against my beliefs, my philosophy.

But I just felt we had to score. We were down there in a game where nobody gave us much of a chance to win, and I thought we needed to take every opportunity to run with it. Thank goodness Gerald Willhite got in there and it got us started.

We were in the game and tied at 13 in the fourth quarter, and then all of a sudden Dennis Smith slipped down and they were ahead with five minutes left, and we've got our backs to the wall.

You just feel numb. You are going against a very good defense and you have to score seven points. Even against a normal football team that is difficult to do. So much is on the line, but all you can do is think about one play at a time.

You at least assume you are going to get it around the 20, so while the Browns were kicking off, John and I were talking about what we wanted to do, how we wanted to start. It's something we normally do under those circumstances.

"These are the plays I'm thinking about," I told him. "Are you comfortable with them?" You don't want to call something the quarterback doesn't want to use.

We had a flea flicker we hadn't used in the game to that point, and I thought it had a chance. I didn't think it was great because they would probably be in a prevent defense, but there was still enough time that they might look at a reverse as a possibility and we might get one of their guys out of place or something.

We had an outlet in case. John kind of frowned when I mentioned it, so I knew he didn't like it. And about that time I was thinking about some other play, and watching the kickoff—and we fumbled it.

My heart was in my throat. "We have the ball," Mike Shanahan hollered over the phone from upstairs. But it looked like it was on the 6 inch line.

The first play I thought about was a play action pass to get us out of there. I figured they would be expecting us to run it and so we were able to hit Sammy out in the flat and he got us out to the 5 or 6.

Then we ran Sammy, and that's when we came up to that third down play I was talking about earlier, the one I still think was the most important single play in the whole drive.

My thinking at that point was all or nothing. I didn't think we had time to get the ball back again. I was pretty much decided to go for it on fourth down, but I was debating, too. Regardless of what I did, I was going to be second guessed if I didn't make it.

If you were stopped on fourth down, the game's over. You have conceded. If you punt, and they run the clock out, people are going to say, "Well, why didn't you go for it?"

I still wonder whether I would have ordered us to go for it on fourth down. I don't know to this day. I'm just glad it never came to a decision. Knowing me, I would probably have decided to punt, use up our time outs and try to get the ball back.

If we had gone for it on fourth down, I don't think there is any question my staff would have let me call anything but a fullback lead up the middle. If it had been inches to go, I would probably have run a quarterback sneak.

Would I have thrown? No. I don't have that much guts.

It was the biggest relief you can imagine when we made it.

Somebody said later I took over all the play calling on the drive, and I don't know. Mike and I had talked to each other so much and learned to work together, I'm not certain who called what. See, I had never done that until Mike came here. I didn't want anybody talking to me, so I had somebody else on the headset and I would call all the plays in a series and then talk to them on the headset afterward.

Otherwise, it could ruin your concentration.

When Mike came, he started calling some of the plays in preseason, some of the games. I would get on the headset with him, he would tell me what he wanted to run and I would send it in. But I felt I wasn't involved in it as much as I wanted to be. I had more experience in calling the plays and didn't want to completely sever myself from that.

I was the one that had to go up there and say this is what we did and I am the one who needs to be responsible.

But we learned to work together so well I can listen to Mike and it doesn't take away from my concentration. And he has some great ideas, great thoughts.

Usually, I do take over the whole thing in the two minute period because you don't have enough time to worry about a lot of things. But I'm sure that on that drive Mike was always making suggestions.

I think the play we ran to Mark Jackson was a suggestion from him. The pass to Steve Sewell. I'm sure we were still talking, suggesting plays to each other. You had to work at least a play ahead.

Let me talk about how my thinking went during that sequence. Even when we were back against the goal, before that first third down, I was thinking that if we got out a little, the way they were playing a twin safety we would try to get a pass to Steve Sewell.

We ran it twice in a row, but the first time John took off and ran, instead, out to the 26. The next time, we hit Steve up at the 48. It was the same play.

On the long one down to Mark, I knew that, on film, in that area they liked to run a zone. So if we got there, and we did on Mark's catch, I wanted to run a screen pass. So I was thinking, "If we get this first down, the screen is what I want to run next."

We got into plus territory, where I knew their man defense took over, so I wanted to run John on a quarterback draw. Down there, we wanted to run the shoot route, shoot the back straight into the flat.

So we had Gerald going out into the flat as the primary receiver. Mark was just an outlet, but Clay Matthews was covering Gerald like a blanket. When John saw that, he switched back to Mark.

Mark had beaten this guy underneath and John hit him. He was backing up and everything and he still drilled it in there.

I never really got exhilarated until I saw us score, saw Mark roll over and bounce up and hold the ball up. Really and truly, when you are calling plays you are so involved, concentrating so hard, you just don't have time.

People say, "98 yards, five minutes left." Well, you just don't think of it that way. You think this play, then this play, what defenses do they like to play here . . . or here . . . what plays can we use . . . what formations . . . who do I have to have in the game to make this play work?

After, when it was overtime, and we were kicking off, I was on the sideline, and that's when I thought, "It's a shame anybody has to lose this game. What we have just accomplished is unbelievable."

I remember immediately thinking back to when I started watching football, back in the 1950s, the New York Giants and Baltimore game. How exciting that game was. That's what I thought about there on the sideline in Cleveland.

I remember thinking, "These things don't happen very often, and they are happening to us."

That's when it hit me. And then to win it—unbelievable.

The dressing room was jubilation, and that dressing room has not changed since I was a player. Anybody who ever played football, it's a shame they couldn't experience what we felt when we went into that cramped old place out of the cold that night.

That is what football is all about, that moment. Like Darren Comeaux said, you don't realize how special that is.

We had a tremendous repeat with the Browns the next year, at our place, in some ways an even better game. But for me, there will always be something special about Cleveland, and what we managed to do there that day.

# 21

# Pasadena: A Yard Shy

THERE WAS just an empty feeling, the morning after Super Bowl XXI. It's like you've gone through a season, and it's been a disaster. You have done almost everything you set out to do. But the "almost" just kills you.

You have accomplished a bunch, but then at the end, when you have lost, you feel like you haven't accomplished anything. All you really do is start thinking about "Why?"

Why did you not win the game? Why didn't this work? Why didn't that work? What if we had done this?

For us in 1987 in Pasadena, of course, it all basically boiled down to the first half. I was disappointed for our football team, and I really felt for Rich Karlis. More than anybody else, Rich probably felt like the loss was on his shoulders. But the fact was, we would not have been there—we would not have come close to being there—if it wasn't for Rich Karlis.

Then, the thing I thought about the most that next morning was being first and goal to go on the 1 yard line at a time we could have taken a 17–7 lead. I kept going over and over that in my mind. I wanted to know what happened on that. I felt like we had some good plays, but they hadn't worked.

Why?

The first play, for example, was one where we were running John on the rollout—a Rollout 'A' Corner. We had a tight end to that side, the right side. We were going to block just like we do a running play. As far as the line and everybody is concerned, they blocked just like they would for Toss 39 Halfback Lead.

But on Rollout 'A' Corner, instead of the halfback blocking the force guy—the cornerback who comes up—on this one the halfback goes to the corner as a receiver.

So either the corner has to cover him, or if the corner comes up, the halfback is going to be open and John can hit him. And instead of letting the fullback run the ball, we let John run it so we would have one extra blocker. And with John's speed and an extra blocker, it's a good play.

I felt good about the play because we had option run or pass. So we ran the play.

When Sammy Winder ran to the corner, the defensive corner went with him as well as the inside linebacker. So he eliminated two people from the running play. But what happened on the play was their linebacker, Carl Banks, penetrated, got penetration on Dave Studdard. We had Studdard lined up at tight end on that play, right end. And so our guard, Mark Cooper, was pulling around for the inside linebacker, who was going to be Harry Carson.

But Carson had turned and gone to the corner. So now all Cooper has got to do is pick up the off linebacker. We also had our off tackle pulling to block that same guy. But because Banks penetrates, when Cooper pulls to go around, he gets knocked down. And our off tackle, Dan Remsberg, gets knocked off, also.

So the fullback coming around ended up picking up Banks. So instead of having two extra blockers, it turns out we lose two guys because Banks penetrates into our backfield and John lost a yard.

Then, the next play, we went to a Pitch 31 Trap. Now, on second down and long yardage, three or four yards, they had been blitzing up the middle. It's second and two. This was a chance for us to catch the blitz, and if they don't blitz, it's a good chance of trapping, getting what we call a passover block.

We were trying to get Carson, but he filled so quickly we didn't get to him and he stuffed it right at the line of scrimmage. No gain. Two good plays, and we're a yard farther back than where we started.

Both of those plays, in my opinion, were good plays. I wouldn't change either one of those plays. But now we've got third down and two yards to go.

I should have gone to four wides, four receivers. I should have gone to a play where we spread the defense out and give John some room to either find a receiver or run. I wouldn't second guess myself on the first two plays down there, but I would on this one.

But I called a goal line play again. And in goal line situations they had shown against Washington, they had brought in an extra linebacker, Pepper Johnson, a big guy, about 240 or 250. We didn't think Steve Sewell could block him. Steve had been running our goal line stuff.

So we had Bobby Micho in there at our rover position. We brought him across and shifted him over. And when we went to run the play they had two guys there. The guy that came across with him when Micho was in motion lined up on him. The other defensive back lined up outside of him.

We had told Bobby to block the guy that was over him. But when he did, the outside safety forced real quick and forced us to cut back. The pursuit just wiped us out. When Bobby shifted over and that guy came with him, you know he's not going to force. He's going to cover you, man for man. But Bobby hadn't had that much experience in that situation. We should have had him block the outside guy.

We were trying to go wide and hit a crease to the left. It was a play we had used and scored on when we played them in New York earlier in the season. This time, Banks caught Sammy Winder going left and it was a four yard loss. They just stuffed us on three plays.

And then we attempted a field goal and missed it.

But that sequence is what stuck with me the most that night and the next morning. We had been moving the ball on them. They really had not stopped us up to that point.

I would have taken my chances if we had gone in at the half leading 16-7 or even 16-9. We had a chance to score, minimum, six. Realistically, we had a chance to score 10 and could have gone in up 20-7 or 20-9. Instead, we don't get at least six, and we give up two that never should have happened. I saw—I saw!—Clarence Kay catch that ball. But they ruled he didn't, and they couldn't find the replay that proved he did until too late. So we got backed up and they got a safety. Even then, we drove down and missed another field goal at the end of the half.

We had the team thing afterward. I guess I won't call it a party, but it was nice enough under the circumstances. My family was so upset I was trying to cheer them up. Pam and Dana and Laura were crying and knew that I felt very badly.

I was trying to be upbeat, and I didn't say anything at the party. I didn't think I should be moping around. The organization had a lot to be proud of. We had a lot of friends there and we ended up having a great party.

I didn't sleep very well. It was late getting to bed and then we had to get up early in the morning to get ready to leave. So I ended up thinking about all the things we could have done, should have done, the things you always think about after a loss.

That one just ended up being bigger than other ones, to come that close and end up losing 39–20. I would have bet my house that they wouldn't have beaten us bad. So I was really disappointed in the outcome.

We just couldn't stop them the second half. They gambled on fourth down on a punt, and made it. They just played a great second half and we didn't play as well as I thought we could on either side of the ball.

They stopped us the first three times and scored all three times. They scored 21 points and we didn't even make a first down. That was really the ball game.

I thought the whole week leading up to the game was good. First of all, we had decided we wanted to keep the players from any type of distractions. So we had the charter with the wives come out later in the week.

I think all the wives were upset because they weren't supposed to come out until Thursday or Friday. I remember Pam was upset— after 20 some years of marriage and what we have been through—all the pain and suffering she has gone through with me being a coach, the hours I've been away and all of a sudden it is the greatest moment that I have had as a coach and she can't share in it.

She didn't come out until Friday. She had a right to be upset.

So that was one thing. The constant calls you get from people wanting tickets is another. You hear from people you haven't heard from since high school.

But the game itself, one of the things that sticks in my craw and really upset me, is trivial, but it is the type of thing that makes a football team.

They came up to us in the dressing room before the game and said "We only want the players on the field who we are going to introduce. We want everybody else to be on the sideline."

Now, that's the league that's telling you. Well, the whole season our whole team had always gone out to the middle of the field, on the road or at home. Then when whatever unit it is is introduced, offense or defense, the whole team comes over to the side.

So, I said, "Okay. If that's the way the league wants it, we'll do it." So we go out and we do that. And it is completely different. Our guys go out and everybody is on the sideline.

And all of a sudden, you look, and the Giants are being introduced and the whole damn team is on the field. So that really irritated me. I mean that made me mad.

Here we were, doing what the league says. Why could New York be out there and we couldn't? It's kind of a superstitious thing that players have. A lot of them do things a certain way, including going out in the middle of the field. And all of a sudden you don't.

Halftime always is tough. You are so accustomed to a short halftime, and then they have such a big halftime pageant and you have so much time. And the dressing rooms in Pasadena are so poor.

It's amazing. You think of the Rose Bowl as the epitome of college and professional football—this huge, famous stadium—but the dressing rooms are archaic. There is no room. You have offense and defense in the same room and it gets hectic during halftime.

Of course we had the lead, but we had not scored there on the goal line. It should have been a lot worse, and you always worry as a coach about missing opportunities.

So halftime seemed to take forever, and we had a long time to think about it. I think we would have been better off just to go back out there on a normal rhythm. Then, when we do go back out, they are playing "New York, New York."

Here we are playing in the Super Bowl, which is supposed to be a neutral site, and they are playing that song and all the Giants fans are singing and the place is rocking. It's like we're playing New York at home. And that surprised me.

It was unbelievable. I don't think it had anything to do with the game. I don't think it affected our players. But it was really strange that a league halftime show—a league production—would wind up playing "New York, New York" when the teams were coming out for the second half.

And then you have to face the press at the end of the game. That's the tough thing. I know there are going to be questions:

"Why did you run those plays, first and goal on the 1?"

But, to me, the thing I wanted to get across was the fact that the best football team won. I've been to so many Super Bowls, seen so many where nobody gets credit for winning, just blame for losing. Well, there wasn't any question that New York was the best team that day. They deserved to win.

I wanted to make sure they got the credit, and I could do that in the press thing.

But it was a tough time. The other side is extremely happy and you are extremely sad.

Then, the next thing I remember is finally getting dressed and going outside, and I had made up my mind that I wasn't going to make the people around me feel bad even though I felt terrible inside.

Then I go outside and Pam and Dana and Laura are crying. So I ended up trying to cheer up my own family. Then there is that long ride back down to Newport Beach on the bus.

We hadn't eaten since the pregame meal, about two o'clock. And we've got no food on the bus. I said if this ever happens again, I'm going to make sure we've got something because I'm starving to death.

I know our players were.

On the plane the next day I was still thinking about the game. I felt like our players were going to be dedicated for the next year, for 1987. We had to wait a long time for our plane. It was fogged in in San Francisco or something, and we all had to stand around out on the tarmac at the airport.

So I got to visit with the players, and then I heard about the parade they were planning back in Denver, and I thought that was a terrible idea.

It was like celebrating losing an election. But it turned out to be the greatest thing that could happen for all of us. The fans. I couldn't believe the fans.

We got there and had to bus everybody from the airport downtown for the parade. Guys didn't want to go. Their wives were there and the guys just wanted to go ahead and take their cars and just go home, but we insisted that, "Look, they went through this. Let's at least go."

And it touched everybody. They would really have missed something if they hadn't gone. It really did make everybody feel better. Not that you could feel better after losing a Super Bowl. I don't know how many it was but it looked like a million people out there that night.

It looked like one of those parades you see in New York City with people hanging out of buildings and crowded up next to the buses and all, and then packed around the Civic Center. The players couldn't believe it.

There was one funny incident. There had been several death threats on Rich Karlis after the game, and when we got on the bus and were riding along, somebody yelled out to Gary Kubiak:

"Hey, Rich. Sorry about the game." And Gary thought, "Oh, my God! They think I'm Rich Karlis and he's the one that's got the death threats."

I wish I could tell you why I've been lucky enough to go to seven Super Bowls as a player and an assistant and now as a head coach, and why some other players and coaches have never been able to go.

I just know that the thing that had bothered me before that 1986 season was that we had been knocking on the door, and we didn't have a thing to show for it. Not even a playoff victory.

We had been 13-3 in 1984 and we got beat the first playoff game. We're 11-5 in 1985 and we didn't even make the playoffs. So you worry about those things. I mean, we're 10-6 my first year and we don't even make the playoffs. We're 9-7 one year and get beat in the wild card playoff game. Recordwise, we are one of the better teams, but yet we didn't even have a playoff win.

Then all of a sudden I felt like we had a chance. I didn't think anybody was dominating in the American Football Conference. There were good teams, a lot of balance. But to me there was no team dominating like the Bears had dominated.

Winning against New England in our first playoff game gave us a lot of confidence, and it gave John a tremendous amount of confidence. He has been playing well for two or three years. But it was a matter of getting over the hump, winning those games that you have gotta win.

By the time we defeated New England and then Cleveland, there was so much difference in him in the Super Bowl. He just had all the confidence in the world by the time we got to the Super Bowl. That has to give anybody confidence, to do it under those circumstances.

He played great in the Super Bowl. He was super in a losing cause. I just thought it was a great year.

Ours is a tough, tough division, and you are going to have peaks and valleys. I was irritated when we lost so badly to Seattle up there the last regular season game before the playoffs. Even though we had won the division and it didn't mean anything, I think you should always play like champions, and in that game we didn't, and it made me mad.

But this team has played hard ever since I have been here. Our defense has always kept us in the game. Our offense has pulled some out. We have played together as a team. Oh, the first year there were a lot of feelings, offense and defense. But I think we have come together as a team.

We know we don't have to rely strictly on the defense to win. The defense doesn't have to worry about holding people.

The season was good, and was topped off by two great playoff games. And I really thought we would win the Super Bowl. There wasn't any question in my mind we would win it.

I guess that's why it was so disappointing that we didn't. That and the fact there ain't nothing that says you are going to get back. There are too many good football teams.

Too many things can happen.

# 22

# It's a Family Job

YOU KIND of grow into head coaching as a family, I think. I believe the experience you had as player, the experiences you had as an assistant coach, really helps your family deal with your being a head coach.

The rhythm, understanding the wins and losses, the aches and pains, the tremendous highs and the tremendous lows. Pam and I grew up together, dated each other in high school, and then got married while I was a player at South Carolina. We have spent our whole married lives in that atmosphere.

And the kids also have spent their entire lives in it. Dana was born in Georgia, and because of football, I wasn't there. That's part of football—the part that is very difficult.

That's a hurt that Pam has had. She knew I couldn't do anything about it, but that still is a void. Since I became a head coach, I have really gone out of my way with players when their wives were having a baby. I've let them leave practice, let them go home. It just happened this year with one of our players.

I know how difficult it is not to be there. Dana was born on a Tuesday and I didn't get to see her until the following Monday. I do think that you have to be a special kind of woman to be a wife of a professional football coach.

Lee was born and we were at home that weekend. Yet the team doctor told me, "She better have that baby Friday. If not, I'm going to induce labor because I'm not going to miss the game Sunday." And he did induce labor.

Again, a football game gets in the way of family life. The next day, I scored four touchdowns. Lee isn't aware of the other part, but all his life he has been aware of the fact that the next day his dad scored four touchdowns. It was written up in the paper, and we've kept those stories in the scrapbook. He delights in that.

Dana and Laura wonder why I didn't score touchdowns for them when they were born.

There is a toughness to being a coach's wife. You know that football is a big part of your life and your husband may not be there at times to help you deal with situations.

Our kids learned that very early in their lives. They would go to games when they were finally old enough. I can remember going to Texas Stadium and being up in the press box, and Lee would go around the whole stadium. Everybody knew who he was. He'd come into the press box and he wasn't watching the football game; he was eating all the barbecue sandwiches and the hot dogs and drinking the cokes. That was part of being a coach's son.

But the kids also felt it when you lost a game. They'd go to school the next day and hear kids tell them how bad the Cowboys were or how bad a coach their dad was. They had to develop some tough skin.

I can remember my first year here in Denver, our opening game against the Raiders. I had gotten Dana tickets, four tickets, and she invites a friend, and they both had dates. They sat in the stands.

We ended up winning the game, and she came home in tears.

"Daddy," she said, "I'll never sit in the stands again. They called you every name you could think of." I can remember that game, the first time we made a mistake, I heard people screaming behind me, "Go back to Dallas, Dan. We don't need you here."

You have to listen, but you have to let it be water off a duck's back. That's the way people are. In college, we were playing North Carolina State. I threw three interceptions. I remember coming off the field, and a drunk walking up to me, and slurring, "Reeves, you're the worsh quarterback I've ever seen."

And the very next week we played Clemson. I threw like three touchdown passes. I came off the field, almost in the identical spot, and the same identical drunk says, "Reeves, you're the greates' quarterback I've ever seen."

So that's the nature of our business and your kids have to have the same kind of thick skin that you have.

When they are little, they don't understand. It's when they get older and do understand that it really means something to them. When they were little, I don't ever remember a problem with them.

When I was an assistant coach, fans were more apt to criticize the Cowboys than to criticize me, so it didn't affect them as much.

I can remember one particular game, though, when we were playing the Redskins, and whoever won the game was going to go on to the playoffs and the loser was out. We're down by 13 points with a little over two minutes to go.

John Riggins, who I don't think had fumbled all year long, fumbled. We recovered, Roger Staubach took us down, we scored, and pulled within six. The defense held them, we got the ball again, and with just a second or two, Roger hit Tony Hill in the end zone and we won.

It was one of the greatest finishes I've ever seen. We hadn't played very well, we were completely out of the game, and we had come back and won.

After, I got in the car, and we started driving home. I said, "Boy, I heard something today I never thought I'd hear. I heard Dallas fans booing Roger Staubach."

Pam looked across the seat at me. "Well, if you heard the Dallas fans boo then you should have seen your son."

"Lee! You booed Roger Staubach?"

"Well, Daddy, everybody else was," he said.

"Do you understand that when you boo Roger Staubach you are also booing me, because I coach him?" He didn't understand that. He just understood everybody was booing Roger so he did, too.

I knew then, when I heard Dallas fans booing Roger, that anybody was susceptible to being booed. Here's a guy had led us to all kinds of Super Bowls and comeback thrills and everything, and yet when he's playing bad, they boo him. That's just part of the game.

When I became head coach here, the kids were old enough to understand. Dana was really hurt at what she heard that first game, so since that time, my family has never sat in the stands at Mile High Stadium. They sit in the box with the owner, and I think that's good.

You've got 95 percent of the fans behind you through thick and thin. But some don't agree with every play you call or they get angry when mistakes are made or when you lose. We don't do that often at Mile High, but we hear it when we do.

But it really hurts your family. When I became head coach, my children learned to handle it. They learned to pick and choose their friends. It was very difficult for them when they came here. They didn't know if kids were their friends because they liked them or because of who their daddy was.

I know a lot of people have to deal with more adversity than this while they are growing up, but I think our kids have done a great job, and I think they are better kids because of it. They know that life is not always roses. There are losses, too. And they hurt.

I try not to take it home, but Pam and the kids help me a lot there. When we lose, I'm not the nicest guy to be around, but I try not to make them miserable. I try to forget about it.

If I'm going to preach to my football team to forget about the last play, even if it's an interception or a fumble, then I have to try and practice that as well.

Usually we go out to eat as a family after a game. We have several places in town that are quiet and nobody messes with us. A lot of times we just go home, and since the kids have school the next day, we'll spend time with them, and then just Pam and I will go out. We don't have a set routine.

But we really don't go out with people. We like to be together as a family. And if I'm hurtin', bleedin', they do a great job of picking me up. And if we have won, they do an even better job of keeping my head from getting too big.

One great example was our first Denver Super Bowl in Pasadena. Lee was down on the sideline with me. He wasn't doing anything but he was there. After all the times we had gone through together, I wanted him to be a part of that.

Pam and the girls were up in the stands, and they could look down and see me on the field. They knew I was hurtin'. Afterward, I reflected on what we had accomplished. I wasn't excited about losing, but I wanted to kind of set the tempo. I had made up my mind I would be positive and not spoil the party. I came out of the dressing room, and there were Pam and Dana and Laura, and they were just sobbing.

I ended up cheering them up, instead.

That was the first thing Pam had mentioned after we came back from that great win in Cleveland that year, all the heartaches and pain and suffering we had endured as a family, and now we had finally made it to the Super Bowl.

If there was one thing I regretted about that first Super Bowl trip, it was that I didn't bring Pam out that week until Friday. She had gone through all this, for all these years, and she should have been able to share in that week.

So last year, in San Diego, I brought her out early in the week. I had made up my mind the year before that if we ever got back to that game, she would share the week with me.

She's been by me all those years. She was the first to say, "If that's what you want, that's what we'll do."

Well, almost always. There was the time in 1973 when Tommy Prothro took over the San Diego Chargers. He offered me the job of offensive coordinator. He flew me out to San Diego to talk about it.

It was freezing in Dallas when I left, and it was like 78 and sunny in San Diego. And I was interested. But Pam had this feeling about California. I had spent all those summers away at Thousand Oaks—been gone all those months—and all that sort of associated with California in her mind. She didn't want to raise children there.

She wouldn't even go out to visit. Tommy Prothro was doing everything possible to get her out there while I was there. It was like a recruiting trip in college. He wanted me to sign right then and there, but I wouldn't.

I went back to Dallas, and of course we eventually decided to stay there.

As for what a move can do, there was an incident with Laura that I'll never forget. It was the afternoon I flew back to Dallas from my first meeting with Edgar Kaiser. I had accepted the job, and I was getting ready to head back up to Denver for the press conference.

Pam has gone to pick up two of the kids from school, and Laura comes in. She's our youngest, and she was nine at that point.

She was making a sandwich in the kitchen. I was sitting at the kitchen table, and I thought that would be a good time to tell her about the move to Denver.

She was spreading peanut butter and jelly on the bread.

"Laura," I started. "How would you like to live in Denver?"

"Wouldn't." She didn't even look up.

"Well, you know, I'm going to be a head coach in Denver. We're gonna move to Denver."

Now she turned around. She put her hands on her hips.

"You did that without even asking me?"

# 23

# A Christian Coach

I WAS very fortunate to have been raised in a Christian home.

I can remember being involved in the church from the time I was very little. But I don't think it ever registered with me how fortunate I was, how lucky I was, until my rookie year at Dallas.

I took all the things my parents gave me—the things I was so fortunate to have—for granted. Then, because I was a Christian, I was asked to speak at an Easter sunrise service in Gatesville, Texas—at the state reform school for boys.

I went down. It was kind of a cold, dreary, rainy type morning, not the sunshiny day you normally associate with Easter Sunday morning. The weather broke just about the time the sun started coming up, just about time for the service.

I was sitting up on a little platform, and they marched 870 some kids in front of me. They were between eight and fifteen years old. They all had on these little blue jean and denim jackets.

I sat there and wondered, "What in the world can a kid eight years old do wrong and be in a reform school?" When the service was over, the pastor of the reform school church told me that over 80 percent of those kids came from a broken home. They didn't have a mom or a dad or anybody who cared enough about them or loved them. Nobody saw they had a chance to go to Sunday school as I had. Nobody cared if they learned the difference between right and wrong.

Some of them had done things that were very minor. Because they came from a poor family, nobody hired a lawyer to keep them from going to a reform school. A lot of these eight-year-old kids were really thrown into a tough situation.

That's the first time it really registered with me that I was fortunate. I made a pledge to myself I was going to give my kids the same kind of opportunity my parents had given me. I was going to see to it that whether they liked it or not, they were going to Sunday school and church. I wasn't going to make them join the church. But they were going to be there and listen and make up their own minds.

Through the years, that's what Pam and I have done. The church was very important in both our lives, and I think it has really helped our children to be around that kind of atmosphere.

At Dallas, I could see what being a Christian really meant to a guy like Coach Landry. He had gone through some tough years when everybody said we couldn't win the big games and so forth. But he seemed to be the same all the time. I admired that in him. He was a very strong-willed person, and I knew that was because he was a Christian.

It made an impression on me because I was trying to mature and become a father and become a parent and raise children. When I entered into coaching, and became even closer to him, I saw there really was something different in him than there was in a lot of people.

I don't think there was any question it was because he was a Christian. He had a faith and a belief that regardless of how the world perceived him, he had somebody strong to rely on.

I got involved in a Bible study toward the latter years I was in Dallas. We were very fortunate our group was guided by Dr. Howard Hendricks, who is one of the better writers of Christian books.

We had this study club every Thursday night. It involved a lot of players and some of our assistant coaches and so forth. We went with our wives. It was almost like a history class. It really helped me.

A lot of things bothered me as far as the Bible was concerned. For example, you read the Bible, and Christ was assembling his apostles. He went up to Peter and said, "Lay down what you are doing and follow me." And Peter did. Well, that puzzled me—relating it to real life. How could someone just drop what they were doing and follow a man across the country?

Then you find out the world was so small—that wasn't a huge area.

It wasn't thousands, or even hundreds, of miles. It made it more understandable. There were a lot of similar examples.

Mike Ditka was another one involved in that study club. We had a lot of real fine Christians. Roger Staubach was probably the most noted. He was very strong. We had a good group.

That was one of the things that really concerned me when I became head coach at Denver. Was I going to have a Christian group of players? I really do think, in my time as an assistant coach and now as a head coach, that players who have a foundation of being a Christian are the easiest to coach. This is a team sport. You can't put yourself before the team. People who are Christians have an easier chance of that happening because they are used to putting God first and family and friends second before themselves.

They don't seem to be selfish—don't seem to have some of the little problems some players have regarding the team concept. I'm not making a general statement. It's not always true.

When I came here, I was astounded at how many Christians we had on the team, and what a strong group they were. It included Barney Chavous and Rubin Carter and Randy Gradishar and Steve Foley and others. It made a big impression on me. I was really excited. I knew that with a nucleus like that, we would have a team that definitely was not going to be a selfish football team.

At the same time, I would never ostracize somebody who was not a Christian. If you look at it properly, it is an opportunity for you to try to influence that person.

The only time I have ever had a problem is the fact it irritates me to no end when someone takes the Lord's name in vain. I can't abide that. For some reason, it really gets underneath my skin. I've only had to call one player in and ask him to stop doing that—Glen Hyde.

"I would appreciate it if you would do it just for me," I told him.

He said, "No problem. I don't even realize I'm doing it sometimes."

And I think he really did make the attempt. I use "damn" and "hell." Sometimes I'm trying to be emphatic and trying to think of something to say and I do it for lack of a better vocabulary. But to put "God" in front of "damn," I can't stand that.

Swearing has not been a basic part of my experience in football. It may be true in some cases, but not for me. Not in high school, or college, or Dallas or here. Some of it has to do with what you allow. If you allow your players to fight, there are going to be fights.

Mike Ditka has changed in that respect. I saw him grow as a Christian. Now, Mike is more like me in his attitude toward swearing. I get so mad sometimes I lose sight of this and I slip and swear. That's because we are all sinners.

To me, the biggest fallacy is in people's perception of Christianity and their belief that you can't be a Christian and still be competitive. Mike and I are intensely competitive. When you read the Bible, you'll find many places where it definitely says you don't have to live your life without being competitive. It says for instance in Paul that "the race is to the swift." You are supposed to run the race and win the race.

That's true. Some of the most competitive people I have ever played against are strong Christians. Nobody I have ever competed with or against is a stronger competitor than Roger Staubach. Nobody.

Yet Roger is also the strongest Christian I have ever been around.

But some people think that's a contradiction. It came up in Super Bowl XXII. How was the National Football League going to condone Joe Gibbs and me going to a devotional service together on the eve of the game, bringing players with us?

Joe and I didn't all of a sudden win the championship games and then become Christians. I was a Christian all my life. I was a Christian when I took the job in 1981, and I was as competitive in 1981 as I am right now. Same for Joe. He became a Christian later in his life, when he was at the University of Arkansas, because of Raymond Berry.

We weren't all of a sudden going to be in the Super Bowl and not be competitive because we were Christians, because we prayed together the night before the game. It didn't make any sense to me that anyone would resent the fact we were going to have a devotional.

Why make an issue of something like that? It turned out to be one of the highlights for us, for sure, of the week. We heard a great speaker in Dr. Robert Schuller of Los Angeles. I didn't know how strong a Christian our Larry Lee was until I heard him that night. Joe talked. I got up and talked, and the Redskins' Darrell Green got up and he was so inspirational he got a standing ovation at the finish.

We all have an opportunity to touch people's lives. I'm glad that I have it in a positive way. There is no question in my mind that I am where I am right now because this is where the Lord wants me.

We don't always understand it. I have lost two coaches here, Fran Polsfoot and Richie McCabe, and it was tough to see them die of cancer. But I know that I became stronger in my faith because of those two situations, and I was able to handle it because I was a Christian. And I saw people's lives change because of Richie and Fran.

The Lord uses a lot of situations to mold people. Adversity molds people's lives more than success. I became a coach in 1970 because I had that knee injury in 1968. One led to the other, although at the time I wondered, "Why me, Lord?"

I don't know. I'm sure a lot of people would argue the point and say the last two Super Bowls might have been different if I was different. All I know is they happened the way they did, and they weren't easy situations. But I was able to handle it and handle the people around me because I do have the faith you have to have to be a Christian.

The faith part worries a lot of people. But there is nothing if you don't have faith. I feel God closest to me during the tough times. I think everybody has their moments, their periods of doubts, but they have grown less for me. There is no doubt in my mind about my faith now. But questioning things, asking why did this happen, you always do that. You really have a tendency to feel God's presence, have him close to you, during the tough times.

I just know I would have had a tough time these past two years if I wasn't a Christian. The neat thing about my relationship is that I talk to God every morning. You have to know it is real for you to be able to do that. To pray to somebody you don't think is real, you couldn't do that. I pray every morning when I take my shower. That's how I start the day.

What amazes me is what he does with the small amount of time you invest. I just wonder sometimes if I really worked at it hard, what kind of relationship I could have.

I have seen people's lives change because they began to believe and began to study. Jim Ryan, one of our linebackers, is a great example. He has gone from being a non-believer to being without question the leader on our football team now. That's Randy Gradishar's influence on him when Jim first came here.

It's great to see those type of things happen. Unfortunately, in the world we live in, it's the other changes in people's lives that are publicized.

# 24

# Drugs

WHEN I started playing, the only drugs I ever saw being used were amphetamines. Older players used those things like they were candy. They would take their wives' diet pills. The first time I ever took one, I was in college and we were playing Virginia.

It was halftime, and it was a hot day. The basketball coach who eventually got fired at South Carolina, probably because he had the whole basketball team on amphetamines, gave me one at halftime.

"Take this," he told me. "It will give you some energy."

I took it. About the middle of the third quarter I thought I was having a heart attack. My heart was beating that fast. I said, "Man, these things aren't for me." It scared me to death. I didn't know what to do.

I took them that time and one other time. We were in San Francisco for a preseason game. I took one then. That was my last time. It did the same thing.

Walt Garrison had started taking them in college when he was going to rodeos. They would drive all night. He would use them to keep him awake. He and I were rooming together, and I finally got him off them.

We would come out of a game and start drinking a beer or something without eating, and he would get mad, mean. He'd want to fight. Finally, it was either his marriage or the pills, so he got off of them.

But all that stuff in the book, *North Dallas Forty,* that was a crock. It was fiction, but there were things that people would remember. And they'd say, "Well, that was true because I remember it." And then they'd think the rest of it was true, and it wasn't.

For example, Mel Renfro was trying to buy a house in north Dallas. And because he was black, he couldn't buy it. So there was something about a black player couldn't buy a house in north Dallas.

Then all the garbage about the drugs and the parties and stuff gained credence. Not that they didn't have parties. A bunch of those guys—Pete Gent, Dave Edwards, Craig Morton—all lived in an apartment complex in Dallas. It was where all the stewardesses lived. Women probably outnumbered the guys three to one.

They had some great parties. But as far as the drugs are concerned, I never saw any. I did not see marijuana.

The first time I saw marijuana period, saw it with my eyes, was already after I was coaching. It had to be like the latter part of the 1974 season when I came back as a coach. One of the players showed it to me in a pouch.

I said, "What in the world are you doing with that?"

"Aw, I bought it. I just wanted to see what it was like." Until then I didn't even have any idea what it looked like. It looked like grass seeds we used to get when we'd get alfalfa.

But nobody I knew smoked it. And looking back on it, there's no question I can see now what I couldn't see then. I know it sounds odd to admit that in this day and age. But you can't apply 1988 awareness to the early 1970s. A lot of us were naive about drugs in those years. I knew Thomas Henderson would fall asleep in meetings, for instance. Now, that would immediately be a warning signal. But not then. I thought Duane Thomas had a problem. I had gotten a call about him after his first year. He had been rookie of the year, and after the season he went to California. He came back to Dallas, and an agent friend of mine, an FBI agent, said he had picked up some rumors that Duane had messed with marijuana.

I was coaching Duane then, so I called him in and talked to him.

"You can own this town," I told him. He was from Dallas, he had been rookie of the year, had that great first season, and everything was going his way. He had gone to West Texas State.

"You just got to watch what you're doing. You don't want to do anything that would jeopardize what you can accomplish in this city. You're sitting on top of the world right now. And being a good looking black person you could really own this city."

He agreed and everything, and went back out to California.

He came back in about a month or so. I remember sitting in my office and I heard this loud music. We had these little cubicles, two coaches to a cubicle. He came walking down the hallway with one of those ghetto blasters in his hand, sunglasses on, and that's when he said he wanted to renegotiate his contract.

He said the Cowboys were taking advantage of him, he wasn't making the kind of money that he should make, and that's when he went into the thing about Landry being a "plastic man."

Looking back on it, I can see Thomas Henderson was sleeping in meetings. I just thought he was staying out too late. I knew nothing.

My whole education with drugs started when I came to Denver.

It started when I had to begin dealing with players as a head coach. I am sure Coach Landry had some problems with players and drugs in Dallas, but I wasn't aware of them. We never knew about it as a staff.

When I came here, they had had an investigation because of an undercover guy. Three players were supposed to be implicated—Tom Jackson, Billy Thompson and Rick Upchurch. It was like the second day on the job when I get hit with that from the league office.

Of course I know who the three players are, but I don't know them personally. B. T. and Tom were cleared, and so was Rick. They were implicated because the Drug Enforcement Agency had arrested a guy, and he implicated them by saying he had sold drugs to them.

They were all cleared. But I had to go through all that mess, and then later had the problems of dealing with Rick. He was the first one.

Then we started testing every year, and if anybody showed up on anything, regardless of how small it was, I always talked to them. I brought them in before we ever started a league policy.

I only had those two major problems, Rick and Clarence Kay. I mean, I've had some problems with alcohol with players, more so than with drugs.

I don't mean to say it's all right to be an alcoholic either. But alcohol is legal and drugs are not. The addiction process is the same. It is identical. And that's the reason something has to be done.

Clarence is a tight end, and we had to send him off to a California clinic in December of 1986 for a month's rehabilitation. It had started with alcohol and progressed to cocaine and he needed help.

He has been on a regular testing program ever since he got back and remained clean ever since.

Drinking is the macho thing to do, and that's an image that has betrayed people from the time they are in high school. My kids, going through high school, knew parents who thought that was great. They let their kids drink beer and everything. I never let our kids have what they call a keg party or anything like that.

Everybody always asks, "Why does an athlete get involved in drugs?"

I'm not sure there is a good answer. But the thing people don't realize is that all athletes, including myself, want to be liked. Not because you are a football player or a basketball player or a baseball player— you want to be liked because you are you.

So, if others are drinking beer, you want to fit in. If they are sitting around smoking a joint, you want to fit in. Athletes are susceptible that way.

Plus, the one thing we know about cocaine is that it is not a drug that is done by yourself. It is a drug that you do with people. And if you've got money, then those people are definitely going to want to be around you because you are the one that is going to supply the cocaine.

Some of those I have dealt with have said, "Hey, you really learn whether those people who have been around you are your friends or not when you quit." They drift away from you. And they drift away because you aren't buying the coke any more.

As a player, I used to see the people hanging around the hotel lobbies on the road. I don't see it as much now that I am a coach. I usually go straight up to my room and we go out to eat and I don't pay as much attention to it.

One of the reasons I don't is that we have super security guys who travel with us now.

It helps, but I don't know that any of us realistically can say we don't have a problem. I wasn't aware of Clarence's problem, for instance, until it happened.

I mean I had suspicions. But until they give you the ability to spot-check, I don't know of anybody who can say their team is without problems.

I know the players association has fought that concept. They cite freedom and individual rights. But I think all players have a right—the right to know that that guy out there next to them at least has his head screwed on straight. You would like to think that when they go out on the field they are giving you their best.

Every guy I have ever talked to, that's one of the things I've told them. Guys that have tested positive for marijuana say marijuana isn't bad.

It's bad, and it's getting worse. Where it used to be 1 or 2 percent pure, it's up as high as 13 percent pure now. That's not a 13 or 14 percent increase in the things that go to your brain. It's like a 900 to 1000 percent increase in the things that go into your brain. It can really affect you.

That's one of the things that I've told them. I tell them, "If you drop a pass, or you miss a coverage, or you blow an assignment, I'd like to think it's because it was an honest mistake and you got fooled on the play or something." I don't want to have to worry, "Is this guy messing with drugs?"

And you have no way of knowing.

Plus I could see what has happened to Clarence Kay.

I remember one of the first real clues we had that Clarence had a problem was when we would look at film, and he was getting off almost a full count behind the snap.

I would like to think if we have somebody on our football team who is drifting toward a problem that we could head it off before it becomes serious.

Steroids are another big problem. And yet we tested for steroids this year, and I have yet to hear from the league office (by March of 1988, months after my team appeared in its second straight Super Bowl).

Some of the injuries that are happening are because of steroids.

Their bodies just can't handle the type of weight they are carrying. You look at some of these 300 pound linemen and I don't think there is any question that is part of it. I'm not saying all 300 pounders are steroid products. But some are. I don't think we have a big problem here in Denver. But I think we have some players, whether they are still on them I don't know but I think they have messed with them.

We ought to all compete on the same level. Nobody should have an advantage because of something that they take, something pharmaceutical, something not natural.

I never thought during my playing days that taking amphetamines made you play better, but some thought they did. I know I never played better. I can definitely say that. The couple times I took them it didn't help me at all.

The players on amphetamines had more missed assignments. In their mind, they could play better because they were pumped up. But I don't think anybody's statistics proved that.

To me, random drug testing is the only thing that is going to solve the problems we are talking about. The players are protected because their teammate isn't on drugs, and they aren't going to get hurt because some guy is on drugs and nobody can do anything about it.

I don't think it's only a protection for the ownership. I think it's a protection for the fans, and for the players themselves. Testing is a great deterrent. If a person has a problem, testing will help that person keep clean.

I've always felt that way from the time I first had a problem with a player as a coach. I had a year when a couple showed up on marijuana. I put them on a testing program, and they came in at the end of the season and said it helped. "It helped me say no," they told me.

I think that's true of Clarence. It gives Clarence a reason to say no. It helps him with the peer pressure part of it, which is a big part.

And I definitely think there needs to be something done on steroids. There's enough evidence to lead you to believe they do increase injuries. You get more muscle mass, more bulk—but you do not get more strength in the ligaments and the tendons and the joints. And therefore you are more susceptible to those types of injuries.

They know steroids affect the liver. They know that. And they can cause problems in the reproductive process. What long term damage it does we won't know for years. But there is enough evidence to indicate there are going to be problems.

It's also just as important to make sure we all are competing on the same level. Games are won and lost on minute things. They say steroids enhance your performance. If they do, that could be one. Then there is the injury part of it. What are you doing to the people who aren't on steroids? If a guy who is a linebacker is normally a 225 pounder, and all of a sudden now he is a 245 pound linebacker, you are getting hit with 20 pounds more force. You are causing other people to get hurt.

It is another thing that has to be done through collective bargaining. But it has to be done.

I agree, it is a matter of individual rights. But the owners, too, ought to have rights. And the fans ought to have rights.

The sad thing about steroids is sort of like alcohol. It is the macho thing to do. When athletes are in high school they can see steroids as an aid to a scholarship, a college career, and eventually a pro career. Again, like so many things, they are more dangerous to you when you're in the growing stage, the formative stage. The league has got a film out now, a panel of five doctors talking about steroids, that I think is going to be helpful. It will at least get these guys' attention.

I should amend one thing I said earlier. I said the first time I ever actually saw marijuana was when a player showed it to me when I was coaching. The first time was when I was in Vietnam, in the spring of 1969, walking through a village, and an old lady had some rolled up in cigarettes in a plastic bag. She was trying to sell them to us.

But 1974 was the first time I saw it in a football atmosphere. I had seen amphetamines used. A lot. They called them greenies, L.A. turnarounds, yellow jackets, a lot of things. I don't see them now. I'm not saying it doesn't happen. I just don't see it as I did then.

# 25

## Summing Up

THIS GAME is so fleeting. It really is.

Jack Rule says golf is like grabbing smoke. So is coaching. You reach out, and grab it, and think you've got it. And you open your hand—and it's gone.

A few years ago, we played against Chuck Noll's Steelers in Pittsburgh. Now Chuck Noll is a guy who has won four world championships. Nobody else has won four. He had the greatest run in the history of the game in the 1970s. Yet they were booing him. I could not believe that. Fame in this game is as fleeting, as uncatchable as smoke.

A successful team, a star player, a coach, we all have to know it isn't going to last forever. I think the league, too, has to be aware that as popular as we are, it can change.

When I came into the league in 1965, football was extremely popular. You didn't seem to have a lot of the controversies that are part of our game now.

Joe Namath was signed right then. At the time the old American Football League had made the decision they were going to go after the National Football League quarterbacks. It started to escalate salaries, and the next year, it was the merger and Super Bowl I.

So I have seen a tremendous growth in the game's popularity and the number of players in the league.

And I've been through the merger, realignment and expansion.

I also have seen a lot of problems arise in that period. The NFL has done a good job of handling many of them. But not all of them.

A lot of issues and things, to me, are still the same as they were back in my playing days when they first popped up. For instance, I don't think the relationship between the union and management has changed a bit. There are still tremendous problems there.

Being raised as I was in the South, and with my daddy owning a road construction company, I am not a pro-union person. I think at one time there was a big need in the country for unions. The worker needed it for protection and advancement. How much of that we really need now I am not sure. I think we are being hurt in the economy as far as competing with the Japanese and other nations.

But I know professional football, and to me, it is totally different. Nobody makes you come out of college and play professional football. You go to college, get a degree in whatever area interests you, and then you graduate and come out and try to find a job in that area. Or you can go into football if you have that chance. But it is strictly your choice. What role should unions play in that? I don't know.

There is a tremendous lack of trust between management and union, and that has not changed one bit in the last 20 years or so. Management feels like it can't pay this and the union says we are not going to play unless we get this. So we get strikes. We have had two of them, devastating ones, in the seven years I have been a head coach.

Communication between management and the union is probably as bad as it was in the first strike back in 1970, when I was still playing. We have made no progress there. I wish I knew the answer. I just know it is a precarious situation for a coach. On one side, you are working for management, which is paying you. On the other, you are trying to maintain a good relationship with players.

I also know it is a short life. I have had 10 knee operations myself. There are a lot of things players should get for what they are doing.

But should that player come in and play four or five years, and be set for life? I don't think that's the way it should be either.

There has to be a happy medium somewhere.

Another thing that has really escalated, and it is because of the society we live in, is the drug issue. We have made progress in the NFL, but we have a long, long way to go. As I mentioned before, I don't think there is going to be an answer unless we get spot testing, random drug testing.

That is the only thing that will put the problem into perspective and make people feel good about the integrity of the game that is involved.

Another concern is where are we going as far as steroids are concerned? My knowledge is limited, but there are some unbelievable advantages to be gained with their use. Again, the integrity of the game is involved. So is the safety of the player, as I talked about in an earlier chapter.

Where steroids are concerned, I think the NFL is still in the dark ages. Colleges, the Olympics, other pro leagues have made progress. The NFL hasn't done anything.

You can't ask, "Do you have any problems with drugs on your team?" You don't know until you have legitimate, random testing. And you don't know about steroids until there is a central policy and the power to enforce it.

We don't have those in the NFL.

The one thing I have discovered as a head coach is that every time I think, "Nothing new can possibly happen, nothing can come up next year I haven't already dealt with," something does.

Just when I was congratulating myself on a stable coaching staff, I have had to spend a spring and summer completely rebuilding my offensive staff. Now I can't make some other changes I was thinking about. But that is what I mean. Nothing stays the same.

Salaries are escalating. Costs are escalating. How much more can people stand for ticket price increases? It will have a long-range effect on attracting future fans. The safety of our players has got to be one of our major concerns. That has to be a top priority, eliminating critical injuries where they are injured for life.

The approaches pro football takes are going to affect colleges and high schools. We have to be careful.

There is a tremendous turnover in our business. I was looking at a group picture from the coaches' meeting in 1981, my first season. I am now third, behind Don Shula and Chuck Noll, in terms of longevity with the same team in the American Football Conference. Chuck Knox has been coaching longer, but he has been with several teams.

It is sort of like talking about the Super Bowl, whether there should be that much hurt, that much stigma on the team that loses. But that's the way it is when you lose in this business.

Whether an owner likes it or not, there is a tremendous amount of pressure. It takes an extremely strong person to handle that pressure, resist it, and say, "This is what we are going to do."

The easiest thing is to have an owner say, "Yeah, we are going to make changes." It's like me, when we get beat 42–10 in the Super Bowl and everybody is calling for major changes. What if I just say, "What area are they criticizing? Okay. That's the area I'm going to change." That's no answer.

To an owner, people will say the head coach needs to be fired. There have been 57 coaches, head coaches, in the two conferences since I came into the league. Actually, if you count Joe Gibbs and me who came in the same year, that would be 59 coaches on the 28 teams.

It's a quick fix, but has it been fixed? No. I know a coach who has won the Super Bowl, but who asked, "If I go six and ten, what will happen?" If you took the guys who have won the last four Super Bowls, Bill Walsh, Joe Gibbs, Mike Ditka, Bill Parcells, they have the same problems as I do.

That's just the nature of the game. Coach Landry and Coach Noll and Chuck Knox and Don Shula, Bill Walsh, it doesn't change for them. Look at all the criticism of Coach Landry this year.

A lot of it has to do with the people around you who can make it fun. I'm not close to anything like burnout. I don't think Tom Flores would have quit if it was still fun.

But that's not new. Go back to 1965, and there were always five or six coaches every year who were let go.

Why does a guy win and another lose? So many things are involved. It starts with the ownership. Look at the franchises that have been most successful, most stable. They give the coach the chance to win, to be successful, without interference. That's a big factor.

Then, as an owner, you need to hire a guy who has the ability to work with people. Some owners just get guys with the wrong chemistry. To be successful at anything you have to have good ownership and hire people who can get the most out of others around them.

Another key is somebody who is willing to work hard. There are no shortcuts. I don't say you are going to outwork somebody to win. But you have to make certain you don't leave out any little detail.

Now, there is no question some guys just are not cut out to be head coaches. What separates them I really can't say. I guess if you knew that there wouldn't be all those changes I mentioned. Either an owner wasn't tolerant and patient enough, or the coach didn't have authority enough, or he didn't have enough ability.

Good organizations don't blur the authority a coach needs to do the right job. The Super Bowl is a good example. We have lost two. We have learned some lessons we need to apply the next time we go.

That's what I am looking at. We are going to be better because of that experience.

I'm going to handle things better. I'm going to do things better, and our team is going to do things better. The first thing you do when things don't turn out the way you want is a self-evaluation.

I made notes after the first Super Bowl loss. I made a lot more after this last one. You definitely have to do things differently.

How? Well, one example is that both teams that won went out on Sunday. We went out both years on Monday. I think the extra day is important. The next time, we'll go out a day earlier.

Looking at it from the standpoint of the two people most affected by all the crush, the coach and the quarterback, I think John Elway and I have been more cooperative than we have to be. I know it distracted me and I suspect it did John, as well.

We are going to cooperate, but next time the required press conferences are the limit. Too many things happen. I just know that in my entire career, there is a minute difference between winning and losing.

Little bitty things make the big differences. We have got to do a better job, me in particular, of not being so cooperative that it affects what you do or your preparation.

I also definitely would try to put our team up at a different hotel the night before the game. We did in Pasadena. We didn't this last time but Washington did. It was done in Pasadena because we were so far away. This year we didn't.

And I would discourage families coming out and staying with the players until late in the week. I wouldn't have rules against it, but I think I need to take that approach. If you are home, that's one thing. Other family members have a room they sleep in, a bed they sleep in. They have a regular routine.

When you are in a hotel room with kids and wife and everything, that's a distraction. The last two years have shown me it's best if the wives come out as late as they can to be with their husbands.

It has always been a problem, but I have always felt you tried to approach the game as much as you can like a regular season game. What we do in the regular season is you stay at home. For the Super Bowl the league doesn't give you a choice. They make you go to a hotel for an entire week prior to the game.

Anyway, those all are little things, but we are going to explore them.

One of the biggest elements of our job now is dealing with the press. It's imperative that you handle the press properly. If you don't do that correctly, the first time you fail it will be compounded. Handling the press is not brown-nosing. That's probably the worst thing.

I'm talking about dealing with them honestly and candidly on a day-to-day basis. And I think that's all they really ask, that you be honest and not play favorites. A lot of things are involved in dealing with the press, but those two are the most important—honesty and not playing favorites. Nobody likes to be scooped. All the guys work hard, and nobody likes to think you gave someone else information you didn't give me.

Do I like the press? I respect the press. I know they have got a job to do. I wouldn't like their job, and I assume they wouldn't want mine. They can assume they know how to run my job, but they never have been out there when it's third and goal to go with about 20 seconds left. I can always call it better after the game, too.

I respect the press. I don't respect some of the things the press does. I don't think everything has to be investigative. I don't think some things they write are fair. I don't agree with some things, but they don't agree with everything I do, either.

I think I respect people who work hard in their job more than I do some that, to me, just show up and don't really work at it. It happens in my business, as well.

The relationship is much more—I don't know if confrontational is the word but there is so much more investigative stuff going on now. Head coaches can be prepared to deal with some things, but there is no way to be prepared to deal with the press until you have to do it as a head coach.

As for the Super Bowl, even if we had won, we would still have some weaknesses that I would be very, very concerned about. I would not be sitting here patting myself on the back thinking we're there and we don't have anything else left to do.

The fact we lost 42–10 hurts. But getting beat like that maybe makes it easier to look at it and say we have to make some changes here and do some things different there.

Two weeks before the Super Bowl, we were a helluva football team. I kept reading how great we were. We were even favored. I looked at it and I knew we had weaknesses. A lot of things bothered the heck out of me, and a lot had to do with injuries. We were still not the football team that we could have been with the people we had out.

In one game, one loss, it was like we were a team that didn't deserve to be there. We were an embarrassment to the city of Denver. That's baloney. That's the nature of that game.

I've got too much experience and too much maturity to let it affect me and the job I have to do and the way I'm going to go about doing it.

We're going to learn from the losing experience. I do not live in the past. We learn, we adjust, we change. We have an opportunity to do what only one other team in history has ever done.

We can go to three straight Super Bowls. Three in a row is a heck-uva goal. There are 13 teams that think they have a chance to get to the Super Bowl from the AFC. All I know is, to do that, they first have to take it away from us.

We are going to remember we got beat 42–10, but it won't be a bur-den on our shoulders. We won two AFC championships, and we did it because we earned it. It wasn't a fluke. We darn sure earned the vic-tories that got us the Super Bowl trips.

So if we go back, there are things I will do differently. And I think we have an organization and players and a staff that are looking at what they can do differently.

One of these days, we are going to be world champions, but I'll tell you what:

When we are, I'm going to be doing the same things I did the morn-ing after Super Bowl XXII—looking to see how we can get better.

I can only assess my situation, where I came from, where I am. First of all, had Coach Landry had an owner who wasn't patient, he would never have gotten past 1964. Clint Murchison would have fired him when that was what everybody was demanding that year. In-stead, he gave him a new 10 year contract.

He gave him the ability. This is my man, he said. He saw within Coach Landry a man with the potential to work well with people, a man who was well organized, all the things he thought a coach should be. Then he stuck with him, he didn't wilt under pressure.

Dallas has been successful because of that. But Coach Landry went from 1961 to 1966 before he had a winning season. A lot of peo-ple don't last that long these days.

He had an owner that allowed him time to get the job done, and he had the power to get the job done. He didn't have power over every-thing, but he had power over the football part of it.

Then, he surrounded himself with good people. When I came to Denver, I was young enough to be able to demand those powers and I had an owner who was willing to give them to me. Maybe even more important, he was willing to stick by me. My first year, I was 10–6. But the second I was 2–7. In fact, Edgar was much more supportive in 1982 than in 1981. He was that type of owner. "Is there anything I can do? Don't worry about it. Get your job done."

Because of that, I never felt the pressure of having to make decisions based on "Boy, we've got to win right now." I was still making decisions based on what would be good for this football team three years from now, four years from now. He showed me in 1982 that he was that type of owner.

Now, that ownership has been passed on, and I feel Pat Bowlen is that type, too. But Pat has not been tested at 2–7 or 6–10 or something like that. He has owned the team three years, and we have been 13–3, 11–5, and 10–4–1 and gone to the Super Bowl twice. Still, I have a good feeling about my relationship with Pat, so I am really fortunate there.

Plus, if something happens within the organization, I don't have to say it is the defense's fault, the offense's fault, special teams' and so forth. It is my fault because I am in charge of that.

Until you win, you are always going to have that problem of how good you are. Somebody asked once if I ever tried to compare myself to Coach Landry. No. I'm not trying to be humble. I'm not trying to be anything. I have never looked at myself and said, "Boy, you are on the threshold of doing this or doing that."

We haven't had that absolute success yet. So I haven't accomplished what I want to accomplish. As I said at the start, as that motivational speaker told us the morning before Super Bowl XXII:

We've been successful. We haven't achieved excellence. That's the next goal. Some day, I'd like to go back to visit in Americus, maybe even go out to New Era, stand there, and look around, and think of all the years since then.

When I do, I'd like to take a Super Bowl trophy with me.

# Index

921
REEVES      Reeves, Dan

Reeves

1364